SUCCESSFUL MARKETING
for the

Safety Management

SUCCESSFUL MARKETING
for the Small Business

Dave Patten

Kogan Page

To Malcolm Allan of Glasgow
who gave me my first chance
in marketing

First published in 1985 by
Kogan Page Ltd
120 Pentonville Road
London N1 9JN
Reprinted 1986

British Library Cataloguing in Publication Data
Patten, Dave
    Successful marketing for the small business
    1. Marketing — Great Britain
    2. Small Business — Great Britain
    1. Title
    658.8   HF5415.12.G7

    ISBN 0 85038 941 0 Hb
    ISBN 0 85038 942 9 Pb

Printed in Great Britain by
Billing and Sons Limited, Worcester

Contents

Acknowledgements

John Leach of Muchelney for saving me from the worst excesses; Tom Insall, super salesman, for imparting his closing techniques; Keith Holmes of Williton Box for the section on packaging and the Webb family for typing assistance. Finally, thanks to Henry Clark for the encouragement to start.

Introduction

Small firms remain so usually because they lack marketing flair or promotional expertise. They believe that advertising is an expensive indulgence, the results of which are impossible to quantify. 'The newspapers are only interested in flying pickets or royal babies. Selling by post is best left to the *Reader's Digest* and agents only bring debts.'

This is a personal book written from my own experience of close working with several hundred small firms over the last 15 years. In that time I can recall only a handful that were started because the entrepreneur was a marketeer. The rest set up because they had a particular skill in production either forced by redundancy or from development of a hobby. The biggest hindrance to their expansion or indeed survival has been a lack of marketing ability. In far too many cases the owner did not appreciate the problems of marketing his product until committed to a definite line of approach.

This practical book stops short at the 20-man company who are probably employing their own advertising agency and PR firm. Below that are the million or so loners and partnerships struggling to improve sales with limited capital and a nagging bank manager.

A wag has described marketing as 'sales with a college education'. Marketing covers more than just selling. Market research, advertising, sales promotion, public relations (PR), press coverage and packaging are all part of marketing. Almost any fool can make something: the hard part is disposing of it at a profit. Few small firms develop a proper marketing strategy. They are production orientated: selling and promotion are tacked on as an afterthought. Advertising expenditure is often begrudged but should be treated as equally important to the growth of the business as a new machine or employee.

History tells us that the United States markets what Britain invents and Japan exploits. Insular, declining Britain looks around to market what products it already has while the other side of the Atlantic decides what is lacking and then sets about producing the right product. It is an attitude worth copying, but there are limitations.

Stick to your last

Most of us are blessed with few skills and talents. We have to make the best of what we've got. Any new firm would be well advised to start out doing what they know best. Every year the Official Receiver lists the number of liquidations, giving a breakdown of activities and the reasons for failure. Near the top is invariably, 'Going into a field without sufficient knowledge'. I'm often amazed at the people who seem willing to plunge into a fresh activity, mortgage the house and pawn mother-in-law, yet have only the haziest notion of the practicalities.

A nose for marketing

The limits to a firm's growth are rarely premises or capital but profitable markets. No firm can survive without profits. The top 10 per cent of your sales efforts generate those profits that finance growth. If you stand still decline is not far away.

Size has little to do with it, or a fat purse. Success in marketing comes from looking at every problem and turning it into an opportunity. Are you the problem or the solution? Try a fresh approach, look for the new angle.

It is this strong marketing awareness that singles out successful companies. They tend to use punchy ads, bright print without being brash, show a thirst for new products and have an aggressive stance in their market. They combine it all with a total belief in where they're going.

Before you start

In the interest of simplicity I have talked about *products* when products *or* services are implied. The successful product manufacturer will realise that the service element of his business stands in equal importance. Except where indicated in the text please treat them both as interchangeable.

Chapter 1
Principles of Marketing

Marketing is common sense. Many small firms have unconsciously practised the principles for years without ever analysing what they are doing and why. This first chapter explains some logical steps which formalise established patterns of successful trading.

Marketing is a pervasive activity. In the progressive firm it creeps into areas far removed from the eventual market-place. No one buys raw materials without thinking through the production processes to what the finished goods will be like. Bought-in components must reach quality standards that do not impair the final article. Costing is a vital element of the price that will be charged. Detail design can radically improve the appearance and performance bringing increased sales. Poor staff morale can easily be detected in service trades, reflecting badly on the firm's image: few feel comfortable being served by indifferent staff.

All these links in the chain to the consumer have an effect on the marketing success of the small firm.

Make time to plan

The first demand is research and planning. Biographies of the world's leaders invariably highlight how they have deliberately set aside time to think. They take themselves off to plan, something few small businessmen feel able to do. It's difficult with all the pressures of finding sales, doing the VAT return, chasing debtors etc, but unless you can create some quiet time your business will inevitably lurch from week to week. Time spent planning before action is never wasted. I'm not suggesting you draw up a five-year plan but merely some realistic objectives around which your firm's progress is planned. You must know your competition, its strengths and weaknesses, what your customers want (who are they anyway?), any gaps in the market and a welter of other details. Not to be lost in all this is the reason for running a business — profit not turnover.

The benefits come first

Marketing is all about needs and *benefits*. It doesn't matter what you have to offer — it's what the customer wants that is important. All your marketing should be directed towards answering the customer's question, 'What's in it for me?' You must distinguish between features and benefits. The latest tyre may have computer-designed diagonal treads, but the benefit may be greater tyre adhesion in the wet. Modern typewriters feature drop-in cassettes, but the benefit is no messy fingers when changing ribbons. Benefits can satisfy emotional reasons like pride, status, prestige or power or just basic needs like hunger, shelter or sex. It can be as simple as a saving in money or as complex as the fulfilment of a lifetime's dream — buying your first Rolls Royce. A drill salesman is selling holes, not bits: the amount of metal that can be removed and the saving in downtime when changing the tool.

The motor trade is a good example. Few know or care about the complexities of engineering beneath the bonnet. The customer is more interested in miles per gallon, service intervals and the guarantee period. He is not terribly concerned whether the car sills are phosphate treated or electrostatically sprayed — what does worry him is whether they will rust through in three years. One more example: British Gas can rightly be proud of the revolution they have brought about by turning a dirty old-fashioned industry based on coal gas into a technologically advanced distribution network for North Sea fuel. Millions of appliances have been converted while old gasholders have vanished. The image of 'high speed gas' has been created by bright attractive housewives and top chefs portraying the virtues of 'controllability'. The benefits have been stressed time and again.

The public (and industry) buys what it needs. The most expensively promoted item won't create a market if Joe Public doesn't want it. There's a belief that if you promote a product hard enough it will sell and make the supplier a fortune. Some people will try a new item once, but if it's no good they won't buy again. Even today, with all the sophisticated management test programmes available, only one new product in around seven will survive to the second year. New business failures are of the same order.

Look for the gaps

Unique products are rare and there is competition everywhere. Even the Bible has different versions in plenty. It is a question of evaluating the strengths and weaknesses of the existing competition and yourself. Where do you fit in the market-place? What can you offer that is a little bit different? There is one small firm that makes telephone equipment. As they employ only six people it might seem curious that they survive against the muscle of GEC and Plessey. But they specialise and make only shipboard systems, mainly for tankers. The market is small and to the majors not worth troubling about. So long as they do not encroach on the large firms' market they will probably be left alone.

Build a framework

I suggest you sit down and examine what you're about. You need to be aware of your products or services, your potential or existing customers, and how you are going to reach them, and the competition. Put simply, you will need to know:

1. Your products and services — what you can offer.
2. The customers, present or potential.
3. The competition, price levels and performance.
4. Distribution.
5. Area.

How to carry out the detailed research is covered in Chapter 2 but it will involve the following:

1. PRODUCTS AND SERVICES
Existing businesses will probably have a range. Single-product companies are rare and vulnerable to seasonal swings in demand or changes in fashion. Many new firms start off with one idea but prudence soon dictates that they develop and broaden their base. Each product type may sell in differing quantities and, because of variations in materials and manufacture, the profitability varies as well.

It is important, as far as you are able, to know and account for which items are profitable. Remember the 80/20 rule that seems to hold good over a surprising range: 80 per cent of your turnover will come from 20 per cent of your stock. Without that analysis you will not be able to say which lines are to be pushed and which are makeweights.

A year's accounts by themselves are not of much interest. It's what happened last year *in comparison* that counts. The accountant always looks for *trends*. Your own pattern of trading needs checking. What are the trends in your own product line?

2. CUSTOMERS

Adam Smith a long while ago said, 'Production is no use without consumption.' Manufacture by itself is useless without a sale. Your most priceless asset must be your customers, not your products, machinery or plant, but the people you can convince to buy the fruits of your labours. Not once but continuously. Some firms have built up such a loyal following that it almost doesn't matter what they produce — the customer will buy it. You can't stretch that too far but it has been proved.

A firm I know makes costume dolls, collectable items. They mailed a few thousand customers giving the barest details and without stating a price. There was a very good response — some even sent cheques.

Some firms survive very well on one customer — the government. Others need thousands. It depends on your market. You need to know the total number of customers and the average sale per head. What are the trends? Are the customers trade or consumer? Is the mix changing? Which are your key accounts? Do you retain your customers — repeat business — or are you continually having to search for more? What else can you sell your old customers? Where does your future growth lie?

Successful marketing is achieved by discovering all you can about your customers and the end users of your products. After all, they are the ones who keep your business going. What has made them customers in the first place? What attracted them to your particular product and what use do they make of it? Major brand advertisers are always trying to home in on the heavy users — those who are addicted buyers. Buyers (and users) fall into different categories — age, sex, location, light or heavy, first time or regular, industrial, domestic or overseas etc. The categories for your product will vary from many other suppliers, but the common thread is that they have bought from you. The simplest way of picking out the points from the mass of information is to draw a *grid* and list the types of product and customer type you wish to analyse. Let's look at a typical service garage:

The customer	Sales							
	Petrol	Oil	Derv	Tyres	Batteries	Accessories	Repairs	Forecourt
Private								
Commercial								
Contract								

Further analysis can be made on the age and make of cars going through the workshop, the geographical location of account customers, the proportion of cash to credit and so on.

You are building up a customer *profile* and establishing which *market segment* you are in.

Market segments
Most products can be slotted into a quite precise segment of the market. Service trades follow the same pattern. For example, there is a firm of Mayfair dry cleaners who give a door-to-door service with liveried vans and uniformed delivery men. The price charged reflects its up-market image. Contrast that with the wire hanger and plastic bag service of the corner shop bargain cleaners.

The importance of understanding what segment you are in lies in selling other lines to users in the same category. The specialist supplier should capitalise on the know-how gained on initial orders by exploiting sideways in that market. The more work you can gain along similar lines the more proficient you should become. Much of marketing revolves around contacts, knowing the right people to see and influence. The more you can immerse yourself in your market, the more effective your efforts will become. You will then be thinking more about *markets* than *products* and bringing forward features that are needed.

3. THE COMPETITION
Don't be disappointed to find someone else down the road doing exactly the same thing as you. Every product has some competition. The only people in a monopoly situation are our beloved nationalised undertakings — coal, electricity, gas etc, but they seem to compete extensively against each other, at our expense. The great thing about business is that it is run by individuals. Approach and performance differ. Some are energetic and motivated, others more knowledgeable, but it is how this expertise is *applied* that counts.

There are two small village shops near me, one of which has

recently changed hands. This one, instead of competing directly to win trade from the other, has pursued a more individual approach. The wife has gone in for home baking, home-made ice cream, delicatessen produce and a range of speciality cheeses. They are hoping to attract a wealthier clientele than the competition.

Fish and chips would seem to be a pretty commonplace business, but one enterprising shopkeeper has built up, not only a mobile round, but also fish and chip suppers for clubs. He takes the goods to the customer.

There's more on finding out about the competition in Chapter 2.

4. DISTRIBUTION

Your product can be sold in a variety of ways: direct (post, advertisements, at the door, farm gate, shop or van sales, party plan etc) or through a third party (agent, wholesaler). A product, or more usually a service, can also be franchised to others. Each channel of distribution must be examined to see if it is appropriate in terms of patterns of trade and acceptability to your suppliers and customers. For example, it is often tempting to bypass the retailer and sell direct. If you do so your price must remain the same as that in any retailers you retain, or you will lose their custom.

For many sectors there is an established pattern of selling and distribution, from a manufacturer through a wholesaler to the shop. To ignore that means raising and training a sales force, carrying larger stocks, instituting a credit control and collection system. The initial margin may seem tempting but is often illusory.

You should ask yourself:

1. What is my most appropriate method of distribution in terms of convenience, turnover and profit?
2. What are the industry trends?
3. Can I open up another channel?

5. AREA

In the same way that generals need to know where the enemy is and their own troop distribution, you need to know where your customers are to be found. Freight and carriage are expensive items and salesmen's trips are costly. Missed opportunities are more so. Get a large map of your sales area and stick it on the wall. Code some coloured pins by customer type and get to work, one pin for each customer. There could well be large gaps exposed. Is this because your advertising is not reaching the area or has a new competitor opened up? Maybe your salesman prospects only round his home.

Time on the road between calls is dead time and costs you money. Can some of the far-flung clients be better served by phone or should you aim to fill the intervening gaps to make a round trip worth while? Look at the trends of growth. Examine new housing developments and trading estates. *Plan.* Putting all this in a shorter fashion, remember the acronym SWOT:

- Strengths
- Weaknesses
- Opportunities
- Threats

The first two refer to your analysis of your business. *Opportunities* are the gaps in the market while *threats* are what the competition is up to.

Cultivate the customer

One key to success in business is, I believe, the way you treat the customer. They are all individuals and should not be sold to *en masse.* One of the best definitions of a customer I have seen was contained in a letter from Graham Brooks, Managing Director of Dowman Car and Trucks of Stockport, printed in *Commercial Motor.* It reads:

> The customer is the most important person in our business.
> The customer is not dependent on us — we are dependent on him.
> The customer is not someone to argue or match wits with.
> The customer is a person who brings us his needs — it is our job to fill those needs.
> The customer is not an interruption of work — he is the purpose of it.
> The customer does us a favour when he calls — we are not doing him a favour by serving him.
> The customer is part of our business — not an outsider.
> The customer is deserving of the most courteous and attentive treatment we can give him.
> The customer is the person who makes it possible to pay our wages whether you are a fitter, office employee, manager or salesperson.
> The customer is the life-blood of this and every other business.

The product life cycle

No product yet invented is not subject to this fundamental law of marketing: every item has a birth, middle age and decline. Youth may be vigorous and death a long time a-coming, but the graph of a product's journey through sales and profitability bears strong similarities to its competitors. Service trades are also subject to the same forces.

Birth bears all the expenses of start-up costs — research, machinery, prototypes, promotion, labour etc. All the money is going out. One hopes Joe Public likes what he sees and buys in sufficient quantity to encourage increased production. The period following the launch should lead through to the time of greatest profitability. Eventually the hump is reached and thereafter sales decline. This could be for a number of reasons. If you have found a genuinely new product and gap in the market then other manufacturers will be attracted to the rich pickings. Price cutting or dumping, combined with heavier promotional spending, may ensue. Fashions may change. Technology may improve or you may have saturated the market.

Stage 1	Stage 2	Stage 3	Stage 4
Birth	Growth and	Middle age	Decline
Investment	maximum profits	Declining profits	Competition fiercer
Probable losses			Margins eroded

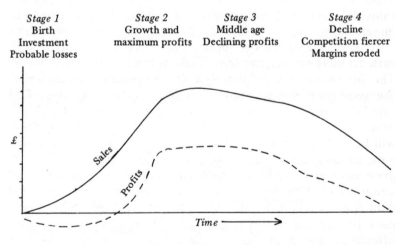

The product life cycle

The decline will continue as long as you are prepared to sink money into it. If you are in shipbuilding this could be for generations — by courtesy of the taxpayer. This cycle goes to the root of marketing, hence the importance of understanding it.

It affects Ford with its revamped Cortina just as much as the corner shop boot repairer. It should remind you to keep looking for new products or ways of modifying existing lines to generate more life and profitability.

Changing a product takes time. A simple task like redesigning a pack can take weeks while disposing of obsolete, overpriced stock in your warehouse will eat into profits.

KNOW WHERE YOU ARE

It is important to recognise where you are on the slope. Going up or over the hump? You must remain alert to what is happening outside your own hectic world. Those who deal solely through agents whom they rarely meet are particularly vulnerable. The further you are removed from the consumer, the ultimate user, the more you are at risk. Markets are fluid, fashions burst on the scene and technology is changing rapidly. The demand for something new all the time seems insatiable. It is important that you attend your trade fair once a year, take an authoritative trade journal and join your trade association to keep abreast of developments.

I despair of firms that boast they never see a representative. Trade reps are your grapevine, not just for scandal, but for valuable pointers. They can also bring you good business and impart sound technical advice.

HOW TO EXTEND THE PRODUCT LIFE CYCLE

The first in the market should make the most profit, provided the goods are readily available and correctly promoted. The price should take account of the lack of competition. If the product is seen to be accepted and profitable, other suppliers will be attracted into the market. Then either more money will have to be spent on promotion and discounts to stockists or price cutting must take place. Inevitably the profits will be under attack. One way of getting more mileage out of the product is by redesign, which can be as trivial as a new colour, new pack or addition of a minor feature. More attachments can be offered to give more benefits. Service industries may have to open longer hours, provide a better guarantee or make more introductory offers.

The additional costs of improving the benefits must be set against the expected sales and profit figures. *Innovation* is the key. Some companies have a heavy investment in research and development and are continually searching for new lines. The British motor cycle industry is the classic example of missed opportunities. In the fifties over 90 per cent of the world's motor cycles were made in the Midlands. The industry was complacent and failed to improve the breed. The Japanese brought out new lightweight machines with innovations such as electric starting, more weather proofing, multi-cylinder engines, and tidied up the general appearance. Good profits made in the boom times in England were not ploughed back into new products. The seventies' oil crisis precipitated the switch back to two-wheeled transport which the home market could not supply.

INNOVATION AND PRODUCT MANAGEMENT

The survival of any company depends on its continued ability to meet consumer needs. Its range of products must retain a competitive edge and must be seen to provide more benefits than the rivals. The product life cycle shows that no business can afford to become complacent or assume that the competition is equally apathetic. Effective product management entails a close watch on the performance of the product and a long-range plan for improvement or replacement to maintain the momentum.

The lesson is very clear. Companies committed to innovation (from a sound base) will succeed: those who rest on their laurels will disappear. The feature of post-war industrialised nations has been not so much the shape of the new technology, exciting as all this is, but the *rate* of change. The computer that filled a room 30 years ago can now fit on a desk.

The search for improvements can be tackled in several ways. First, why not ask your customers what additional benefits they would like? I have owned several new cars in my time but have never been asked how I liked the car or what additional features I would like. The *Guardian* recently asked their women readers to tell them what they would like to see in their next car. This was hailed as a tremendous step forward. Someone had realised that women are different, that they are a growing segment of the market and their needs should be catered for.

A service trade might emulate one bright Hampshire garage. Every car that goes through the workshop has a pre-paid card left on the seat addressed to the managing director. The card invites the client to comment on how well the car was prepared and ask for any improvement he would like to see. The cards are displayed in a rack at the reception, and the owner doesn't cheat and destroy the criticisms. To his credit, the majority praise.

Second, you can ask your own staff. The suggestion box may be a joke in some firms but not in Japan. Honda have a shadow factory set aside to allow their own engineers to produce proto-types and try out ideas. Over 6000 products have been tested and not just for the motor trade. The engineers are given free rein across the field of domestic and consumer products. I am a great believer in involving the work-force. There is nearly always a better way of doing something and who better to ask than the person paid to do it?

Third, you can invest in new products arising from your own research and development (R&D). Depending on the size of the firm, time and money can be invested in the search for innova-tive products. It can be formalised into a separate department with its own staff and budget or fitted in alongside the run-of-the-mill production. In small firms it is simply the boss beaver-ing away at weekends. Part or all of the R&D can be contracted out to specialist companies, universities or technical colleges.

The fourth route is to buy in or license the new technology. A third party may have a valid patent or the know-how which can enable you to side-step years of development work.

There is more on how to benefit from licensing, patents and know-how in Chapter 12.

Costs, price and profit

There are really only three ways you can improve your profit:

1. Reduce your costs.
2. Raise your prices.
3. Increase turnover.

The easiest way to improve your margins is usually by tackling the first option. It is simpler to save money than to go out and earn it. Unless your goods have been consistently underpriced then the usual effect of raising your prices is to reduce sales — unless it is done in such a way that the customers accept you are selling added benefits or value.

All three areas should, of course, receive close attention.

COSTS
Costs can be divided into overheads (fixed costs) and variable costs. Overheads encompass your premises costs (rent, rates,

mortgage), heat and light, plant and machinery, vehicles, salaries and depreciation. The variable costs depend on the amount of production — materials purchased, direct labour involved, machine power and borrowing charges related to those expenses.

The higher your fixed costs the more you must maintain full production. Seasonal service trades must explore every avenue to make some revenue contribution in the quiet periods.

How to cost your output is a complex issue and largely outside the scope of this book. In essence it means taking a rigorous look at whether you are making the most efficient use of your resources. Is the production layout the most suitable, the machines and methods cost effective, the stock levels commensurate with the cost of borrowing and the demands of avoiding breaks in production? Can some items be put out to subcontractors and are you sure your buying is effective? Should you sell the lorry and put deliveries out to a regular haulier? There are innumerable areas requiring close and constant vigilance.

Most common of all, I find, is a delusion that the costs of production are exactly known. Rarely are proper job cards or time sheets kept and an efficiency check made. You must know what each item actually costs to produce before you can think about the price to be charged.

SETTING A PRICE

The price you charge need bear little relation to the *cost*. It should be the highest that the market will accept. The theoretical optimum price level is that at which most can be sold at maximum profit. Too low a price level and you are giving away potential profit: the cash flow will suffer and you could fail to meet your commitments. Too high a price and demand may be lower than anticipated. Every business normally has two choices: to go for high volume at a low price or reduced volume at a high price. It is rare for anyone to enjoy the best of both — high volumes at a high price.

The criterion governing the route is, of course, to maximise profit. High volume usually entails a high capital investment in machinery, premises, and efficient working practices. By that I mean tight control on all processes till the product is sold, and paid for. The margins are usually small and a high and continuous throughput is necessary. The obvious examples are supermarkets, where a vast array of items is controlled and packaged in expensive locations and extensively promoted. The average profit for these giants of the High Street is around 2 per cent.

The high volume route to growth demands expert costing and management controls combined with a strong marketing awareness. After all, you've got to sell that output.

Your *pricing strategy* is often a compromise between the demands of production and economies of scale (keep the machines busy) and what the sales force can profitably dispose of. Sales forecasting is based on the state of the market, competitive price levels and the ability to exploit any gaps in supply.

The major pricing considerations are:

1. *Your marketing objectives.* Slow build-up, quick penetration, low or high profit. The objective could be to attack a competitor at a low initial price, hoping to make a killing later, or to flood the market quickly and pre-empt a new product launch from a rival.

2. *The price you set* often reflects where you believe the product stands in its life cycle. If it is a new product with little competition you should be aiming for a reasonable margin. You must leave yourself room for manoeuvre when competition appears. If it is nearing obsolescence you may wish to clear your warehouse and stockists' shelves with a cut-price offer to make way for the new version.

3. *Your production costs and required profit level.* New businesses, sometimes unwittingly, actually sell at below their own costs of production. It is not until they have been in production for six months and the overdraft has doubled, yet turnover is healthy, that they stop to ask why. While there are often valid reasons for starting up at a competitive level it does help to know your *break-even* point. To non-accountants this is often the easiest target to aim for. Get your accountant to work out how many widgets you must produce and sell over a week or month to cover your costs. This is your break even. Exceed that figure and you are into the profit league.

4. *What the competition is up to.* There are very few unique products: most goods and services have direct equivalents. Unless you are offering something very special you are bound to broadly follow existing firms. The trick in marketing is to so present yourself that the customer is convinced that by dealing with you he is getting something special and will pay a premium price for the pleasure.

5. *Your chain of distribution* has a strong influence on the

price you can charge. Take a maker of sheepskin mittens. He can sell direct from the factory shop and charge a full retail price. He can sell via an agent (who will take possibly 15 per cent) who will sell on to a department store who in turn will mark up 75 per cent. If there is a wholesaler involved he will want payment for his trouble. Selling by mail order will involve different costings again. The manufacturer must judge which method is best to adopt, bearing in mind his own talents and inclinations. Some firms prefer to deal solely with one customer — say Marks and Spencer — in the knowledge that paperwork and chasing for money is simplified. Others will argue that this leaves you vulnerable and you should spread the risk. Your method of selling is one influence on your pricing strategy.

6. *Volume of production and frequency of purchase* are also determinants. If your output is so well made that it never wears out then you must continuously search for fresh customers. This is generally more expensive than capturing and converting a faithful few. The specialist producer of purpose-made ball gowns will have to charge more than the mass producer of little black dresses for department stores.

7. *Positioning* is an in-word among marketeers at present but opinions differ on its meaning. I am happy to believe that it is where you place, or position, the product in the market-place. The price should reflect this place. Furs in Bond Street would possibly not be bought if they were marked at a Petticoat Lane figure. The *haute couture* customer would feel slighted to be asked a mass market price for a unique garment. Customers would not believe that the goods were of merchantable quality. Positioning owes a great deal to the packaging and presentation of the product. Black and gold packaging imparts a feel of luxury — of value rather than price. Image is a strong ingredient.

The UK importers of Audi cars were careful to position the Audi 100 as an up-market prestige car even though it is from the same factory as Volkswagens. In Germany they are used as taxis. Some have argued that it was a mistake to launch the Scirocco under the mid-market badge of VW: sales would have been higher had the four rings of Audi been on the front grille.

8. Those running a *sales force* will come up against the commission element endemic in most organisations. If this is paid purely on a gross sales figure regardless of discounts,

bad debts or returns, then you are giving away profit need-lessly. Better to educate the lads on the road to aim for profitable accounts and tie the commission element accordingly. Anyone can sell given a free hand to strike what bargain they like. Set the sales targets to link with profit as a truer measure of the value to the company.

9. The law of diminishing returns spells out that *ever-increasing turnover* does not lead to a profit rise in tandem. You will reach a point where profits tend to fall off. The continued drive for growth will demand more cash to fuel production, plant and perhaps bigger premises. Labour costs will increase as well. This cash will have to come either from quicker settlement from customers or, more likely, an injection from your friendly bank or outside investment. These not disinterested parties will want a reward for their philanthropy. Growing companies make increasing demands on management time as well, leading either to wrong decisions or to the appointment of indifferent leaders. Your pricing strategy should therefore aim at this level of maximum profit. Unbridled growth does not always lead to a Stock Exchange listing.

10. Look hard at your *discount structure*. Money given away here is straight out of the profit. Discounts are usually given for two reasons: to persuade bulk users to buy in quantity and to encourage early payment.

When customers are scarce it is always tempting to lower your quantity steps and give anyone the bulk rate. Do this as a sales ploy, if you must, but only in the know-ledge of the true costs of producing smaller quantities. Big firms are notorious for taking early settlement discounts but not paying the relevant invoice for months later. There is not a great deal you can do about this if you wish to continue to 'enjoy' their custom, short of writing to them pointing out the error of their ways. Some firms can auto-matically build in an inflated figure to knock off as a dis-count on billing. Again your price structure must take account of this. One successful way of operating a 'rock-bottom' price is a cash and carry price. No dispute — the goods are here — you come and collect and pay on the nail, saving delivery expenses, statements and credit control.

11. *Differential pricing* allows for the same product being packaged differently to appeal to various market segments. I know of one concrete sealer (to stop dust) that is sold

under one name to the trade and under another to the DIY market at several times the cost. There must be many other examples. Differential pricing is also used to encourage bulk users and deter small deliveries.

Everyone has to face *price increases* at some time. Many firms were badly caught out when high inflation was rampant. Some firms were announcing rises every quarter and quotations were a nightmare. The lessons to be learned from this horrendous period are surely:

- Watch your raw materials like a hawk. Never quote for a big order without getting an up-to-date firm price from your supplier — and shop around.
- Keep your prices in step with the Retail Price Index or whatever your trade is governed by. Slip back and you will find it very hard to catch up. It's not being patriotic to hold down prices — in many cases it is plain bad management.

How to present an increase is often a matter of fine judgement. Tackle it in a blunt way and you will lose custom. You must spell out why you are having to raise prices and, if possible, throw in a benefit to sweeten the pill. Wrap it up in a convincing manner. It may be that you can hold the price of other items in your range and emphasise this, rather than have a straight across-the-board rise.

Finally, let's go back and look at the opening statement, and apply the reverse message. There are only three ways to turn loss into profit:

1. Increase volume without increasing fixed costs.
2. Reduce costs without reducing volume.
3. Increase prices *and* maintain sales.

If you cannot do any of these, get out while you are still ahead — if you are.

Forecasting

Predicting market conditions is nearly as hard as weather forecasting. There are so many factors that could affect demand. New products coming on to the market, new materials, changes in fashion, new laws, even political changes or manipulations in the economy will affect market conditions. In this country the weather can create upheavals in many trades from the tourist business to brewing, sports promotion to theatre bookings. A hot summer usually encourages more domestic holidays the following year and vice versa for wet ones. The established business is at a distinct advantage when drawing up a *sales forecast* as it has past experience to go on. You need a sales forecast to plan production and the allocation of resources through the coming year. Most firms now realise the necessity of compiling a *cash flow forecast* as a measure of controlling budgets, profit and placating the bank manager. All the figures flow from the top-line assumption — sales to be achieved. Use the following leads:

1. Statistics from either your trade association or government sources (see pages 41 and 42) may help to establish the size of the market and the brand leaders. You may be lucky enough to find a published market research survey for your interest.
2. What are existing firms doing? All *companies* make an annual return to Companies House (page 49), and while many will be rather out of date, some useful detail should be available.
3. In general terms, a study of the competition will provide clues — life-style of the owner, head count of staff, traffic flow of customers, age of staff cars. Bank and status reports (page 50) can be obtained.
4. Test marketing of samples or of a pilot run is usually valuable. Test the reaction with your prospects — specifiers, wholesalers, agents, local clubs, playgroups, WI or whoever your target audience is likely to be.
5. Some firms will give *letters of intent*: 'We will place orders of £x if . . .'. You may be lucky and get actual orders from prototypes and sample runs. Most big customers plan well ahead as they have strict budgets to adhere to. They may be able to tell you how much they have allocated to spend on items of your type and a target set for your forecast.

One feature of the recession has been to bring about a considerable de-stocking among buyers. Goods are no longer held for months in the warehouse but called off from suppliers in smaller and more frequent amounts. This has made planning more difficult for the manufacturer as long-term contracts have been harder to obtain.

Once your demand forecast has been made, your ability to

produce the goods when required must be calculated. There is no point in chasing department stores if your output is limited to what you and your wife produce, or if limited cash inhibits stocking up before the season.

If you are having to massage the bank manager for funds he will want to see what evidence you can produce to support a sales forecast and to know that you have budgeted for a reasonable sum for marketing.

THE COST OF MARKETING

What should the budget be? Probably more than you are allocating at the moment. Marketing is in the driving seat: it produces the customers, defines the market and derives the profit for future growth. Without a sound investment in research of the markets and the product potential, a reasonable promotional sum and enough for a capable sales effort, the business will die.

Marketing orientated companies regard this charge as vital as that for new plant or increased labour. It is an investment in the future prosperity of the enterprise. But the amount is not an easy matter to decide. The production costs of, say, a machined part can be very accurately costed. From there you add your overheads, profit required and a sales figure is arrived at. The financial return on producing a certain item can be readily calculated. Marketing expenditure is more imprecise. How do you *know* that spending £x on sales staff will produce orders of £y? You may have the choice of a direct mail promotion, an exhibition or an advertising campaign to reach your audience, yet not know what response will be generated. Assumptions will have to be made. To a large extent your own experience with your particular product and manner of promotion will decide what orders you can expect. Certainly, there is a fund of advice and outside expertise to tap (perhaps this book may help) to steer you in the right direction — but the *only test is for you to do it*. All the experts in the world are no substitute for the customer buying the goods in response to your marketing strategy.

There are reckoned to be about 15 different formulae for working out what the marketing budget should be. The most popular are:

1. The same as last year.
2. Last year, plus x per cent (and x can be anything).
3. A percentage of past sales.
4. A percentage of forecast sales.

5. A percentage of gross profit.
6. A percentage of unit cost.
7. The ratio to your share of the market (if you know it).
8. What the competition is thought to spend.
9. What you can afford.

For new firms, it would not be excessive to allocate a 10 per cent budget of gross sales, settling back to no more than 5 per cent when more established. Don't forget that out of this marketing budget must come all the costs of research, advertising, public relations (PR), sales promotion and whatever methods of selling are employed.

THE MARKETING MIX
A major consideration in arriving at the marketing budget is deciding how you will actually market your wares. Marketing is a combination of product, price, promotion and place — collectively known as the four Ps. When you manage to place all these in balance, profitable sales will occur. It is the correct blend of all these variables that leads some marketing practitioners to believe that getting this mix right is a most important element of success in marketing.

Different market segments require a different emphasis. The mass consumer market needs continuous expensive advertising to highlight minute brand differences. *Brand loyalty* is the goal. Industrial goods and services tend to rely on more selective trade advertising and exhibitions to elicit enquiries from which face-to-face selling can take place. Direct mail is very important. The rest of the book will try and point out the correct part of this marketing mix for you.

SPECIAL PROBLEMS OF MARKETING SERVICES
The broad principles of marketing can be applied to products and services but the latter do pose some problems of their own. A product can usually be handled and test sampled. Its performance may be governed by well-known standards and the technology verified. It can often be photographed in use and explanatory promotional material made available.

Services are intangible or, in balance of trade terminology, invisible. The personal repute and track record are everything. More personal face-to-face selling is usually involved, while plausibility and conviction are vital. The growth of the service sector has been far outstripping manufacturing in this country.

In general, less capital is required for plant and premises and staff numbers tend to be small. Start-up costs are therefore kept to a minimum. By extension, competition tends to be fiercer forcing down profits and the failure rate is high. It would be logical, therefore, to state that more care needs to be taken to correct marketing techniques at this lower level of sophisticated business activity to ensure survival. If the business is easy to set up in the first place, it is often equally easy to fail.

Great attention needs to be made in promoting the benefits. The direct personal nature of the service must be stressed. Individually tailored schemes should be offered where possible – the customer must be made to feel special. A caring relationship should be built up with the aim of enhanced goodwill.

The rapid growth of services has led to cowboy operators in some fields. *Codes of practice*, either trade or government instigated, have evolved, with bodies like the Consumers' Association lobbying hard to correct abuses. All this should only help the legitimate business owner as long as he can keep abreast of increasing legislation. The Office of Fair Trading publishes leaflets which inform the trader and customer of their obligations and rights under the Fair Trading Act 1973.

Many *manufacturers* believe they are supplying a product only, but the brighter ones realise that the service element is paramount. It is the intangible nature of what the product can do for the client that is so important. Products are bought to satisfy a need. We expect to be received courteously, treated as an individual, sold the correct solution to our problem and looked after for a reasonable period while enjoying the purchase.

The link between pure manufacturers and the suppliers of services lies in that intangible 'after-sales service'. The Sale of Goods Act 1979 and The Supply of Goods and Services Act 1982 impose the legal obligations of 'fitness of purpose', 'merchantable quality' and 'reasonable cost', but successful businesses will go further than that. After-sales service means looking after the customer with his problems beyond the time he first buys the goods. Reasonable spare part stocks should be retained and trained staff to fit them. Clear guarantee terms should be given setting out what parts, if any, are not covered. The ideal is a 'no quibble' guarantee that is used by some as a sales slogan. The concept can be carried further into running a free advice service, newsletter and technical brochures. Selling has become PR.

Manufacturers could be more successful if they treated their customers in as personal a way as many suppliers of services.

THE PROBLEMS OF A SEASONAL DEMAND

Christmas tree suppliers, swimming pool contractors and winter sports operators have to find something else to do out of season. This bunching of demand makes cash management, staff recruitment and the utilisation of fixed assets very difficult. Some trades solve it by taking on summer students and casual labour, but this still leaves the bank manager to fund the non-selling months. It is the service trades that tend to be more vulnerable.

The holiday industry has set about marketing its fixed facilities with some imagination. Bargain weekend breaks, conference and seminar facilities have all been promoted in the quiet periods. British Rail have helped with their weekend offers and short-term holidays and tie-ups with hotel groups.

Early and late holidays, the 'shoulder' periods, have been directed at pensioners and those not tied to school holidays. Off-season fares can be significantly cheaper, while a holiday in Mallorca or Malta in March can be cheaper than living at home. Ski resorts in the high mountains become hot summer alpine retreats, with chair lifts now being used all the year round. Only the snow is missing. Activity holidays, with people going away to learn a craft, paint in oils, or study old buildings, are less dependent on the weather and can be taken out of the main season. Millfield School, the most expensive in the country, has pioneered the use of its sports facilities in vacation time. The excellent equipment and accommodation are now used to the full with more income for the school, and no doubt for those staff who are prepared to stay on.

Time sharing is another way of spreading the cost. A villa, boat or other luxury item is bought collectively giving each owner the exclusive right to use the facility for a certain period in the year. Many caravan owners use their van only for a fortnight a year. I know of one firm that manages and promotes the use of their van by renting it out to other campers. A full maintenance service is included.

The moral is to develop some attraction, an added benefit, to lure customers into your quiet period. This is usually done by price discounting or manipulation. It is usually better that some income is generated, even at a marginal level, as a contribution to your overall costs.

SETTING OBJECTIVES AND THE MARKETING PLAN

Marketing objectives are no different from financial projections or production forecasts in that they are all exercises in planning ahead to see where the firm is going and setting mile-posts along the way. The objectives should be reasonably attainable and provide a measure of the firm's performance. The plan need not be a lengthy document, probably no more than one or two sides of a piece of paper, but should in essence say:

1. Where the firm is *now* in terms of products and market position (if known).
2. What the objectives are in quantitative terms — to sell 5000 plates or 10,000 flower pots.
3. Where the sales are to be made — outlets, territories etc.
4. The profit to be made from each product. This can be further broken down into segments, salesmen, territory etc as the size of the firm dictates.
5. The product strategy to be carried out — modifications, extra features, new product launches.
6. Research and development (R&D) expenditure related to marketing.
7. Pricing policy — discounts, differential pricing, increases etc.
8. Finally, the strategy to achieve these objectives in terms of advertising, direct mail, sales promotion etc. The dates should be given for specific campaigns and the cost of each calculated.

The temptation is to make many ambitious assumptions and to base everything thereafter on these high targets being attained. New product launches are particularly prone to this optimism. It *always* takes longer than you think. The marketing plan forms part of the overall business plan for your firm and is the chance to sit down and plan where you want the firm to be in the short and medium term ahead. It cannot be cast in tablets of stone but must be flexible and subject to unforeseen market pulls.

The grand word for this strategic view is *corporate planning*. It is the discipline beloved by giant corporations who have sophisticated departments staffed by statisticians and economists gazing into their crystal balls predicting global economic trends that may affect their fortunes. This amount of detail is obviously beyond the scope of small firms, but nevertheless they should be able once a year at least to take an objective look at where they want to go.

YOUR MAIN GOAL

Studies have shown that increasing your *market share* can significantly improve your profits. In consumer terms, it is the brand leader that gets the gravy. The supplier of a very general product that has applications across a wide spectrum will have to spend a long time finding out the profitable avenues to pursue. His marketing efforts will be diluted in penny packets, and the customers' perception will be at a low level. Many suppliers rely on personal recommendation and if the users are split across many segments, sales referrals will be few. Market leaders tend to attract more energetic staff, profits are good and the salaries reflect this position. The price level tends to be set by the dominant producer — others follow. Market leaders also tend to be trend setters with stockists keen to buy their lines. They are the firms that people talk about.

Chapter 2
Market Research

Do you want to buy 6000 plastic toggles? Very cheap. I know a man who developed an article for the home wine maker in which he had great faith. Plastic toggles were an essential part but, unfortunately, he found that it was cheaper to buy them by the thousand than in small packs from the corner haberdashers. When he tried to sell the item he drew a blank and soon realised that a little market research by test sampling would have saved him a lot of money.

Market research is simply a matter of *finding out* as much as you can before launching into full-scale production and investing a lot of money in stock, machinery and finished goods. It is a process that should never stop, as you must never assume that the market is standing still. Customer preferences alter, new fashions appear and competitors lure away regular buyers.

Your research should set out to discover:

1. What does the customer need?
2. Who is the target audience and how much can I find out about them?
3. What is the competition?
4. Are there any gaps in the market?
5. The acceptability of the product by test marketing.

Market research is a major area of expensive and exhaustive activity for big companies. Large departments are continually combing the world markets testing product awareness, customer reaction, advertising recall and buying preferences. Sophisticated statistical analysis predicts sales demands allowing for competitive interaction. Surveys are frequently commissioned by outside agencies with teams of roving interviewers posing carefully weighted questionnaires.

Even the simplest research study seems to cost well into four figures if performed by a specialist agency and I will assume that the small firm reader is more interested in learning what can be achieved with limited resources.

Your research can really be divided in two: local and national.

If you intend purely to serve your neighbourhood then it will not take long. More ambitious horizons will take more time.

Investigations into the existing market — products, customers and the competition — can be tackled by visits to libraries, trade shows and studying the relevant specialist journals.

Where the big firm scores is in its ability to commission what I tend to call *attitude* surveys — scientific predictions of future demand and trends based on qualitative sampling. The expertise required to draw up questionnaires and evaluate the results is beyond the scope of the amateur. Actual test sampling of a limited production run is often the only way to make a trial run, involving a higher proportionate risk to the small firm.

On the other hand, the small firm is invariably closer to its customers and market and able to take advantage of shifts in consumer choice more swiftly. Big firms tend to be far more hierarchical and bureaucratic when it comes to speed of decision taking.

Taking into account your limitations, where do you start? It is a constant puzzle to me why businessmen know so little about what is sometimes the grandest building in any large town:

1. The reference library

One of the most under-used resources in this country is our library service. First it is free which should excite any small firm. Second, most assistants are only too pleased to get a genuine commercial enquiry as a break from kids and their school projects. They know the reference sources and will go to great lengths to hunt out the information.

Counties vary enormously in what they spend on the system. Away from the conurbations, in the shire counties, you may have to travel to the county library to find the best selection.

Well, what's in the library? In the better ones a gold-mine of information on companies, products and statistics produced by government and private sources. Just one day spent going through a dozen trade reference books will yield perhaps a score of names for you to pursue for catalogues and leaflets to *build up a picture* of your sector of business.

To a small firm, probably of least interest will be the government statistics that tend to talk in millions and present the long-term trends. They do need skilled interpretation.

Flag Institute. 1971.
- ■ 8 Newton Lane, Chester CH2 3RB. (0244) 26035. (hsp/b)
  Dir: W G Crampton.
- O *L; information about the collecting, research and usage of flags
- ● Conf - Mtgs - Res - Inf - Library - Flag design service.
- ℓ Fédn Intle des Assns Vexillologiques.
- M 86 i, 10 f, 4 museums & libraries UK / 94 i, 3 f, o'seas.
- ¶ Flagmaster - 4; ftm, £1 nm.
  Booklets on Flag Design, Flying the Flag; 50p & £1.25.

Footwear Distributors' Federation. (FDF) 1941.
- ■ 69 Cannon Street, London EC4N 5AB. 01-248 4444. (hq)
  Sec: A T Robertson.
- O *T; problems common to all sections of footwear distribution.
- ● Mtgs.
- M Multiple Shoe Retailers' Assn; National Shoe Retailers' Council;
  Instock Footwear Suppliers Assn.
- ¶ AR.

Freedom Organisation for the Right to Enjoy Smoking Tobacco.
(FOREST) 1979.
- ■ 3-9 Bondway, London SW8 1SJ. 01-582 4561. (hq)
  Chmn: Sir Christopher Foxley-Norris.
  Chief Exec: Geoffrey Evans.
- O *K; to educate the public (smokers & non-smokers), on all aspects
  of the smoking & health controversy.
- ● ET - Res - Stat - Inf.
- M [not yet available]
- ¶ NL - 3; ftm, £1 nm.

Glass Textile Association. (GTA) 1950.
9th floor, Centre City Tower, 7 Hill Street, Birmingham B5 4UU.
021-643 5494. tx 339420. (asa)

Guild of Television Cameramen. 1972.
- ■ 24 Bonser Road, Strawberry Hill, Twickenham, Middx TW1 4RG.
  01-892 7740. (chmn p)
  25 Carrholm Road, Leeds LS7 2NQ. (0532) 688600. (hsp)
  Chmn: Mike Solomons, Hon Sec: Vernon Dyer.
- O *P; improve the art & craft of television cameramen for broadcast
  television.
- ● Conf - Mtgs - ET - Inf.
- △ Amer Soc TV Cameramen; TVFF (Soc TV Cameramen) Sweden.
- M 500 i, 12 f, UK / 200 i, o'seas.
- ¶ ZERB (Jnl) - 2; ftm, £4 nm. NL - 4; ftm only.

Gypsum Mining Association.
c/o British Gypsum Ltd, 15-17 Marylebone Road, London NW1.

Hairdressing Manufacturers' & Wholesalers' Association.
add Sec: A T Robertson.

Historic Aircraft Association. (HAA) 1979.
- ■ c/o City Deposit Brokers, Royal London House, 22 Finsbury Square,
  London EC2A 1TJ. 01-638 9451. (hsb)
  Hon Sec: A Haig-Thomas.
- O *K; to further the preservation of historic aircraft in flying con-
  dition which involves the provision of a flight safety service to
  the public, the authorities, owners & display organisers.
- Gp Register of pilots.
- ● Mtgs - Res - Stats - Inf. Cooperation with Shuttleworth Trust &
  Strathallan Collection.
- △ Genl Aviation Safety C'ee (GB); Brit Aircraft Presvn Coun.
- M 70 i.

Independent Association of Telecommunications Users. (IATU) 1979.
29 Sackville Street, London W1. 01-439 8505.

Industrial Safety (Protective Equipment) Manufacturers' Association.
add Sec: A T Robertson.
- M 75 f.

industrial Warm Air Heater Manufacturers Association Ltd.
- O *T; manufacture & installation of industrial warm air heating
  equipment.
- ● Conf (irreg) - Stat.
- M 9 f.
- ¶ all 3 publications; £1.50.

Idustrial Water Society.
- 35 Broomfield Avenue, Fazeley, Tamworth, Staffs. (0827) 65089.
  Hon Sec: P E Millington. [(hsp
- X 1979 Cooling Water Association.

Institute of Acoustics.
- ■ 25 Chambers Street, Edinburgh EH1 1HU. 031-225 2143.

Institute of Arbitrators
see Chartered Institute of Arbitrators.

Institute for Architectural Ironmongers.
15 Soho Square, London W1V 5FB. 01-493 1753.
Sec: Peter Spill.
- O *P; interests of individual architectural ironmongers.

Institute of Media Executives. (Inst M E) 1973.
- ■ Ely House, Somerford, Willenhall, W Midlands.
  (0902) 61249. (hsb)
  Chief Exec: J Corbett.
- O *P
- ● ET - Inf (m).
- M 151 i.

Institute of Print Purchasing. (IPP) 1969.
- ■ 24 Aveling Park Road, London E17 4NT. (hsp) 01-432 5111
  Sec: L T E Wilkinson. [(hsb)
- O *P; for those who practice or are directly employed in the
  purchasing of print.
- ● Mtgs - ET - Exam - Inf (m) - VE - Empl.
- M 250 i.
- ¶ Wordspace - 6; AR; both ftm only.

Institute of Vitreous Enamellers.
tel now (0773) 43136.

Institute of Wood Science.
150 Southampton Row, London WC1B 5AL. 01-837 8219.
Sec: Miss J Jepson.

Institution of Industrial Managers
new title of Institution of Works Managers.

Institution of Technician Engineers in Mechanical Engineering.
(ITEME) 1978.
- ■ 8-12 Old Queen Street, London SW1H 9HP. 01-222 0778. (hq)
  Sec: Ian M Barnes.
- Br 7
- O *L; qualifying body & learned society for technician engineers &
  technicians in the broad field of mechanical engineering.
- ● Mtgs - ET - Comp - SG - Inf - VE.
- M 897 i, UK / 41 i, o'seas.
- ¶ NL - 12; ftm only.

Institution of Works Managers
now Institution of Industrial Managers.

Instock Footwear Suppliers' Association. (IFSA) 1932.
- ■ 69 Cannon Street, London EC4N 5AB. 01-248 4444. (hq)
  Sec: A T Robertson.
- O *T;
- ● Mtgs - Stat - Inf.
- M 44 f.
- ¶ NL; AR; both m only.
- X Wholesale Footwear Distributors' Association.

International Baton Twirling Association (British Division). (IBTA)
1973.
- ■ 6 Waterside Road, Paignton, Devon TQ4 6LJ. (0803) 842311.
  Sec: D J Townsley. [(hsp.
- O to promote the highest standards in the technique of baton-twirling.
- ● Mtgs - ET - Comp - Inf.
- △ Nat Baton-Twirling Assn (USA).
- M 2483 i, UK / 45 i, o'seas.

5

Specimen entries from Directory of British Associations
(Courtesy: CBD Research Ltd)

PRODUCTS AND COMPANIES

Almost every trade association produces a *year-book* listing members and their specialities. Trade and product names are often also listed. As some year-books consist only of paid entries they may not be as comprehensive as their title suggests. A reputable publisher will say in the foreword how the entries were compiled. To find what is available look at *Current British Directories*. This lists around 4000.

There are many annual publications of impressive thickness that will help in tracking down companies and who makes what. Some of the standard works are listed here. Inevitably there is some overlap.

Start with *Kompass*. This comes in two volumes, each about 3 inches thick. It is produced in association with the Confederation of British Industry (CBI) and, like the others, inevitably lists the larger companies. One volume is for products and the other for firms. There is quite a clear method of cross-referencing. *Key British Enterprises* claims to cover 90 per cent of the UK manufacturing capacity. It is produced by Dun & Bradstreet the well-known credit agency. There is a lot of information shown that will enable you to determine the size of company you may be dealing with. The top 20,000 UK companies are shown in two volumes. *Kelly's* is probably the oldest street directory published and its past volumes are invaluable for tracking down your family tree! Space is sold by a salesman and it's sometimes difficult to judge the stature of the firm from the entry. The national *Manufacturers and Merchants Directory* is still used by many.

The *Directory of British Associations* is another standard work in every reference library. You can track down thousands of trade and special interest associations. The scope will surprise you. Details given include size and type of membership, secretary's name and whether a newsletter or other publication is available.

Some libraries stock the complete set of *Yellow Pages*: if not, your local Telephone House certainly has them to consult. At the time of writing the new *Thomson Local Directories* do not look like replacing their rivals. Whichever one you use make sure it is up to date.

OTHER GENERAL TRADE DIRECTORIES

There are half a dozen standard reference books worth browsing through. *Stubbs' Buyers' Guide* (Dun & Bradstreet) gives

2 – SPECIALISED

14540
BESA Buyers' Guide.
■   British Electrical Systems Association, 2 Radford St, Stone, Staffs   ST15 8DA.   (0785) 832426.
△   1980.   16 pp.   New ed contemplated, but not in active preparation (Feb 1984).
●   Members AZ (pa, tn, txn); tabulated product index.   Members AZ (pa, tn, descriptions of products & services).

Best of British Pubs, and other Places to Eat and Drink   see   **C.G.A.**

14560
BGA Guide to Business Schools for Prospective Students and Employers.
■   Macdonald & Evans Ltd, Estover Rd, Estover, Plymouth   PL6 7PZ.   (0752) 705251.   tx 45635.
△   1970–   (T).   5th ed, 1981.   £6.00.   118 pp.
●   Incl: Selected business schools in the UK, USA, Europe & elsewhere (pa, d/e, nature of courses, acceptance procedures, teaching methods, n/teaching staff, etc).
NOTE: BGA = Business Graduates Association.

BGMA Buyers' Guide   see   **British Gear Manufacturers' Association.**

14580
BHF Directory: A complete guide to the members & services of the British Hardware Federation.
     British Hardware Federation, 20 Harborne Rd, Birmingham   B15 3AB.   021–454 4385.
△   (Irreg).   1982.   £10.00.   c 65 pp.
■   Members geog (pa, tn), and AZ (pa, tn).

14600
BHRCA Official Guide to Hotels and Restaurants in Great Britain, Ireland and Overseas.
■   British Hotels, Restaurants & Caterers Association, 40 Duke St, London   W1M 6HR.   01–499 6641.
     tx 296619.
△   1928–   (A).   56th ed, 1984.   £5.25; $9.95 (overseas).   568 pp, 47 m.
●   Member hotels & restaurants of the Association, by towns AZ (pa, tn, txn, illustration, proprietors, facilities, capacity, charges, etc).   Line directory of additional member hotels, by towns AZ (pa, tn, charges, etc); AZ index of London hotels.   Line directory of additional member restaurants, by towns AZ (pa, tn, t/cuisine, hours open, charges, etc).   Affiliated associations; member societies of the International Hotel Association.   Motorway service areas geog (pa, tn, operator, facilities, etc).
C/T: Hotels & Restaurants in Britain: The official guide.

Bible Society   see   **UK Christian Handbook.**

14620
Bicycle Association of Great Britain Ltd: List of members.
■   BAGB, Starley House, Eaton Rd, Coventry   CV1 2FH.   (0203) 27427.
△   (A).   Feb 1984.   Free.   4 pp.
●   Bicycle mfrs; accessories & components mfrs; bicycle importers & factors, each AZ (pa, tn).

Big Red Disarmament Diary and Directory   see   **Pluto Big Red Disarmament Diary and Directory.**

14640
Binsted's Bottling Directory.
■   Binsted Publications, 90 London Rd, Hook, Hants   RG27 9LF.   (025 672) 4176/7.   tx 859562.
△   (A–Jan).   1984.   £16.00.   116 pp.
●   Bottlers of beers, soft drinks, wines, spirits, ciders,   brewers, each AZ (pa).   Bottling machinery & materials mfrs & suppliers, cfd (pa, tn, txn).

14660
Binsted's Directory of Food Trade Marks and Brand N: s.
     Food Trade Press Ltd, 29 High St, Green Street G   Orpington, Kent   BR6 6LS.   (0689) 50551 & 53070.   tx 24261.
△   1959–   (Q).   6th ed, Mar 1983.   £28.50.   175 pp.   ISSN 0067–8651.
●   Trade names AZ, with descriptions of goods, name of mfr, London agents, etc.   Mfrs AZ (pa).

62

An extract from Current British Directories
(Courtesy: CBD Research Ltd)

130,000 names across the country. *Sell's Directory* lists 65,000 firms. It has a trade names section that will allow you to trace the maker of a particular product: 25,000 products and services are cross-indexed.

The Retail Directory (Newman) is useful for attacking the consumer market as it lists buyers and the business of several thousand department and multiple stores. There is a separate volume for London giving 27,000 names and addresses.

UK Trade Names (published by Kompass) is helpful in tracking down a company from its product name: 60,000 names. Includes imported goods. If you are selling to local authorities you need the *Municipal Year Book* which gives exhaustive coverage of every District and Chief Officer by name. Don't forget the public sector covers an enormous field — education, health, libraries, refuse collection etc. It is a massively detailed book. It even tells you which authorities use bins and which sacks.

Ryland's, and *Dial Industry* are for the engineering industry. *RIBA Directory of Practices* covers selling to the architectural profession, as it gives every practice and partner by name. And many, many more.

2. Marketing information

Moving from products and companies it is helpful to track down what is happening in your sector of activity. Much of what follows, I must admit, may be of limited interest while you are starting up, but should grow in importance as you expand. Some of the source books will be in the better libraries while the more expensive volumes will have to be borrowed either from the specialist repositories mentioned or perhaps from your trade association. Don't forget that any book published can be borrowed through the inter-library lending scheme. It may take a week or two and reference books will generally have to remain in the library. If in doubt ask the assistants.

The A-Z of UK Marketing Data gives a signpost to the size of individual markets. Basic information is given on market shares, production, exports and imports, forecasts and the brand leaders. Published by Euromonitor Publications Ltd, 18 Doughty Street, London WC1N 2PN.

Mintel covers the consumer goods market each month with

examinations of new product performances and expenditure. Contact Mintel Publications, 20 Buckingham Street, Strand, London WC2; 01-839 1542

Reports Index will enable you to track down what market research reports have already been commissioned and are available. It is always cheaper to buy on rather than start from scratch. The sources are government and private, stockbrokers, trade and professional associations and market research organisations. Published by Business Surveys Ltd, PO Box 21, Dorking, Surrey RH5 4EE.

Market Research Sourcebook by Headland Press is an annually updated book giving wide coverage of marketing information including associations, directories, agencies, libraries and magazines. Included in the price of £39.95 is a telephone updating service.

Key Note publications (28 Banner Street, London EC1Y 8QE; 01-253 3006) produce an in-depth analysis of over 100 market sectors from DIY stores to bicycle traders. The make-up of the industry is examined, market leaders analysed, new developments appraised and products assessed by volume and value. An appendix is given for further reading – press articles and reports. Price £35 per issue. They're not terribly thick but could provide a good introduction.

The government publishes a wealth of statistics on what the country gets up to ranging from coal and steel production to what the average family in the north east spends on sliced bread. The HMSO *Guide to Official Statistics* is your starting point.

Business Monitors are the main barometer to what is happening to the economy. There are three main series – production, service and distributor, and miscellaneous. The quarterly summary is the most useful. Major libraries will stock them.

3. Where to go

Apart from your main library there are 20 or so specialist libraries around the country that specialise in business information. It should be worth making a trip. In London the *Westminster* Reference Library (behind the National Gallery), the *City Business Library* in Basinghall Street and the *Holborn* Reference Library in Theobalds Road, WC1 are particularly good.

The Science Reference Library is in a class of its own. Go here for science and technology, designs, patents and trade marks.

Something like 20 million patents are held here on file. Address: 25 Southampton Buildings, Chancery Lane, London WC2; 01-405 8721.

Warwick Statistics Service based on the University of Warwick, Coventry CV4 7AL;. 0203 418938, will find information for you. They will hunt out data on market share, dig out printed articles, look for sales and price trends. It is not cheap at £20 an hour but if you have a very specific query it could be cheaper in the long run to employ a specialist service like this.

Trade associations, industry and the professions. Trade associations invariably have very comprehensive libraries on their own subject. Non-members are rarely barred but a fee is sometimes charged. I have found that many queries are quite happily answered on the phone: The better Chambers of Commerce — London, Birmingham, Bristol etc — also have extensive resources. Some of the smaller chambers are often useful if they have retained their traditional industries, eg Manchester for textiles. They seem to know every little railway-arch firm. A huge area is industrial and commercial libraries. Every big company has its own internal library and if you ask nicely I'd be surprised if you were refused a browse around.

Don't ignore the professions either. Some years ago I had to do some research on a historical model that appeared in the 1851 Great Exhibition. A trip to the Victoria and Albert Museum library and Institute of Mechanical Engineers' library was most rewarding.

ABSTRACTS

You might by now be wondering how you're ever going to find time to research all the information. Rather than wading through dozens of books, reports and periodicals you could go to an abstracting service. If you give them the subject area they will produce brief abstracts of books and articles sufficient for you to know whether it is worth following up the whole article. It's designed for busy people. There are many abstracting agencies geared to commerce and industry which collate some very abstruse subjects. Your first book to look in is the *Inventory of Abstracting and Indexing Services in the UK* produced by the British Library, R&D Department, Sheraton House, Chapel Street, London W1; 01-636 1544.

Anbar are one of the leading producers of business abstracts. Contact them at 65 Wembley Hill Road, Wembley, Middlesex; 01-902 4489.

The London Business School produce the definitive guide to small business publications. 3000 publications on small firm management are listed in their Small Business Bibliography, updated regularly. Address: Sussex Place, Regent's Park, London NW1 4SA; 01-262 5050.

The Institute of Marketing deserve a place here as the premier professional body for anyone with pretentions to marketing. A number of publications and seminars are available. If you're keen, join as a student member. As you'd expect, it is the repository for a wealth of marketing information. Address: Moor Hall, Cookham, Maidenhead, Berkshire; 062 85 24922. One of their little publicised services is the *Marketing Advisory Service*. You can call on one of 50 experienced marketing members for £15 a day, plus travel expenses. Discuss your requirements with the Director.

Two *government agencies* that can help with advice on marketing, among other subjects, on a face-to-face basis are:

1. CoSIRA (Council for Small Industries in Rural Areas) if you live in a rural area, or in a town of under 10,000 population, in England only. Offices are found in most rural counties (address in phone book) or contact the head office at 141 Castle Street, Salisbury, Wiltshire SP1 3TP; 0722 336255. In Scotland, there is the Scottish Development Agency at 120 Bothwell Street, Glasgow G2 7JP; 041-248 2700, and in Wales the Welsh Development Agency at Treforest Industrial Estate, Pontypridd, Mid Glamorgan CF37 5UT; 044 385 2666.
2. The Small Firms Service, part of the Department of Trade and Industry, if you live in an urban area. Regional offices. Part-time counsellors, usually retired businessmen, do the advising.

If you can afford it you can commission a market research survey from a member of the *Market Research Society*, 15 Belgrave Square, London SW1X 8PF; 01-235 4709. They will provide details of their member consultants' experience and turnover.

4. The trade press

Britain is blessed with a wealth of trade and technical press to cater for every interest. Some 7500 journals, papers and magazines are published every year on subjects from bee-keeping to boxing, craft teaching to catering. Many sectors have two levels

W286300X
COUNTRY LIFE [ABC]
IPC Magazines Ltd, King's Reach Tower, Stamford Street, London SE1 9LS. 01-261 5000/5747. Advertisements: 01-261 5793
For complete listing see entry under General Interest (Consumer section)

●●●● **RATE CHANGE** ●●●●
A284480
DIY ANSWERS—GARDENING
Link House Magazines, (Croydon) Ltd, Link House, Dingwall Avenue, Croydon CR9 2TA. 01-686 2599. Published April 5, other dates on application. Copy – Oct 20. Single copy 95p
Agency Commission 10%
Rate card received December 1983
Standard Rates
page	£650.00
half	£340.00
quarter	£180.00
eighth	£93.00

Series discount available on application
Colour Rates Full colour, full page £1,080, half £750. Spot colour £100 extra
Bleed Pages 10% extra
Special Positions Facing matter 15% extra
Inserts Accepted by arrangement
Mechanical Data Type page size 267 x 190, half 130 x 190 or 267 x 92, quarter 130 x 92, eighth 64 x 92. Col length 267, width 44. No of cols 4. Offset litho
Executives Associate Editors, Roger DuBern and John McGowan. Executive Advertisement Manager, Martyn Silvester. Advertisement Manager, David Beary
Circulation Uncertified

W250150X

| ABC |
Head Office: Link House, West Street, Poole, Dorset BH15 1LL. 0202 671171. London Sales Office: Pembroke House, Wellesley Road, Croydon CR9 2BX. 01-686 7181
For complete listing see entry under Advertisement Only Publications (Consumer section)

●●●● **NEW ENTRY** ●●●●
J284470
EASY GARDENING & HOMECARE
First issue scheduled for April 8, 1984
IPC Magazines Ltd. Advertisements: King's Reach Tower, Stamford Street, London SE1 9LS. 01-261 5622/5000. 4 times a year – 8th April, May, June & Oct. Copy – black & white 7 weeks; 2 colours 8 weeks; 4 colours 8 weeks preceding cover date. Cancellation – black & white 14 days preceding copy date; colours 6 months preceding publication date. Single copy free
Agency Commission 15%
Rate card effective January 1984
Standard Rates
page	£3,200.00
three-quarters	£2,500.00
half	£1,700.00
quarter	£900.00
eighth	£475.00

Cover Rates Outside back cover £5,250, inside front cover £5,100
Colour Rates Full colour, full page £4,800, half page £2,500. Preferred page £4,950, 1st right hand page £5,100, half page preferred £2,750
Bleed Pages 10% extra
Special Positions Preferred positions mono, page £3,500, three quarters £2,750, half £1,850, quarter £975, eighth £500
Inserts £16 per 1,000 basic
Mechanical Data Type page size 273 x 197, three-quarters 273 x 152, half 273 x 96 or 134 x 197, quarter 134 x 96 or 273 x 45, eighth 134 x 45 or 65 x 96. Col length 273, width 45. No of cols 4. Litho
Executives Editor, Jack McDavid. Advertisement Controller, Malcolm Mountjoy. Advertisement Sales Manager (Gardening), David Gannicott. Advertisement Sales Manager (Non-Gardening), Peter McCarthy
Provincial Representatives Manchester: C. H. Watson, Arndale house, Chester Road, Stretford, Manchester M32 9BH. 061-865 0821. Birmingham: J. Denson, Lynton House, Walsall Road, Birmingham. 021-356 4838. Glasgow: D. T. Gilmour, Anderston Quay, Glasgow G3 8DE. 041-221 1879
Circulation Initial Controlled Circulation 500,000 (Publisher's Statement)

Rate card effective March 1982
Standard Rates
page	£180.00
half	£98.00
quarter	£65.00
eighth	£44.00

Series discount 4 – 10%
Cover Rates Back cover full page, mono £275, 1 colour £310, four colour £550
Colour Rates Full colour, full page £410, second colour, page £260, half £175
Classified Rates Wordage 35p (min £6)
Mechanical Data Type page size 183 x 122, half 89 x 122, quarter 89 x 59 or 43 x 122, eighth 43 x 59. Trim size 210 x 148. Col length 183, width 59. No of cols 2. Screen 48. Offset litho
Executives Editor, D. Vagg. Advertisement Manager, M. E. Wright
Circulation Uncertified

M284700
THE GARDEN [ABC]
The Journal of the Royal Horticultural Society
New Perspectives Publishing, Artists House, 14-15 Manette Street, London W1V 5LB. 01-434 2384/3272, 01-437 2091. Monthly - 1st. Copy -black and white 9 weeks; 4-colour 10 weeks preceding publication date. Cancellation - 12 weeks preceding publication date
Agency Commission 15%
Rate card received June 1983
Standard Rates
page	£430.00
three-quarters	£340.00
half	£220.00
quarter	£110.00
eighth	£55.00
sixteenth	£30.00

Series discount 3 – 2½% 6 – 5% 9 – 7½% 12 – 10%
Cover Rates Inside front or inside back cover £451.50, full colour £819. Outside back cover, full colour £858
Colour Rates Full page £780, three-quarters £740, half £400
Inserts Accepted by arrangement
Special Positions Facing matter 10% extra
Classified Rates Wordage 40p, prepaid only. Box No £1.50 extra. **Mechanical Data** Type page size 200 x 118, half 200 x 57 or 98.5 x 118, quarter 98.5 x 57 or 47.5 x 118, eighth 47.5 x 57, sixteenth 22 x 57. Bleed page copy size 228 x 143. Trim size 222 x 140. Col length 200, width 57. No of cols 2. Screen 54. Web-offset
Executives Editor, Elspeth Napier. Advertisement Manager, Christine Guy
Circulation (Jan-Dec 1982) ABC 77,579

	Home	Overseas	Total
Pd (Full)	286	—	286
Pd (Less)	10	202	212
Soc/Assn	70,690	6,391	77,081

M284750
GARDEN ANSWERS [ABC]
Haymarket Publishing Ltd, 38-42 Hampton Road, Teddington, Middlesex TW11 0JE. 01-977 8787. Monthly - Penultimate Wed of month preceding cover date. Copy - 6 weeks preceding cover date. Cancellation - 6 weeks preceding copy date. Single copy 65p. Per year £12
Agency Commission 10%
Standard Rates
	1	6	12
page	£750.00	£713.00	£675.00
half	£390.00	£371.00	£351.00
quarter	£203.00	£193.00	£183.00
eighth	£106.00	£101.00	£95.00

Cover Rates Full colour 15% extra on colour page rate
Colour Rates Full colour, full page £1,200. Series 6 – £1,140 12 – £1,080, half £840. Series 6 – £798 12 – £756. 2 colour (Publisher's choice) full page £975 Series 6 – £926 12 – £878, half £615. Series 6 – £584 12 – £554
Bleed Pages 10% extra
Special Positions 15% extra by arrangement. Facing matter 10% extra
Inserts Accepted £12 per 1,000
Classified Rates Wordage 30p (20 words min). Semi-display scc £8 (min 3 scc). Box No £2
Mechanical Data Type page size 270 x 203, half 270 x 99 or 130 x 203, quarter 130 x 99 or 65 x 203, eighth 65 x 99 or 130 x 45. Trim size 295 x 229. Bleed plates 302 x 235. Screen mono 40, colour 54. Web offset
Executives Publishing Director, Colin Martin. Editor, Peter Dawson. Consultant Editor, Alan Gemmell. Group Editor, Colin Perry. Advertisement Manager, Simon Daukes. Group Advertisement Manager, Nick Horne
Circulation (Jan-June 1983) ABC 60,694

	Home	Overseas	Total
Pd (Full)	56,339	5	56,344
O/Unpd	4,350	—	4,350
RES available			

Part of that invaluable book BRAD, to show the amount of detail given (Courtesy: Maclean-Hunter) of print — consumer and trade. The popular journals are aimed at the man on the Clapham omnibus and many are readily available at newsagents. Alongside are the trade press aimed at the suppliers of those goods. For example, there is *Autocar* or *Popular Motoring* written for the family driver, but if you're trying to attract the motor stockist for that petrol-saving gadget then you need *Autotrade*. The circulations of some specialist journals are quite modest, only a thousand or two, but if they go to that select readership then that is what matters.

There are several directories on what is available. Undoubtedly the most comprehensive and accurate is *BRAD (British Rate and Data)*. This is the ad-man's Bible as it lists the costs of advertising, circulation figure, and often a claimed readership profile. As it costs over £100 for a subscription and little less for individual monthly issues very few libraries will stock it. You will have to make friends with an advertising agency. Slightly out-of-date copies can be bought from the publishers, Maclean-Hunter Ltd, 76 Oxford Street, London W1N 0HH; 01-434 2233 at a reduced price.

If you can't track down *BRAD* there are alternatives: a copy of *Willing's Press Guide* and the *Advertiser's Annual* will probably be in quite small libraries. These give a bare title listing of journals etc. *Benn's Press Directory* gives a little more detail. *Pims Media Directory* is a monthly which gives subject editors or correspondents for media nationwide.

Your market research must include looking through the relevant trade magazines. I suggest you write to the advertising manager for copies. They will probably send you the current issue and a rate card for advertising.

You should always take out a subscription for your trade journal. How else are you going to keep track of what's going on? It will tell you of future trade shows, seminars, legislation changes, firms going out of business, mergers and new products. Many trade papers that carry a lot of advertising are free circulation anyway to those who meet their requirements, usually specifiers.

Scan the ads and use the reader's reply service to write off for product literature. Add new firms and faces to mailing lists. If you're stuck for a product, ring the editors. They've invariably been in the trade for years and know everybody.

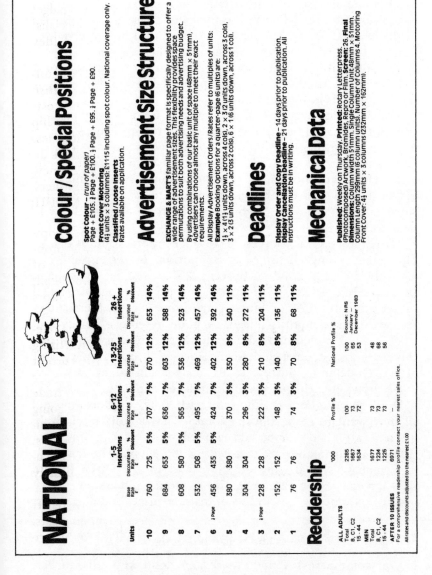

NATIONAL

Units	Base Rate £	1-5 Insertions Discounted Rate £	% Discount	6-12 Insertions Discounted Rate £	% Discount	13-25 Insertions Discounted Rate £	% Discount	26+ Insertions Discounted Rate £	% Discount
10	760	725	5%	707	7%	670	12%	653	14%
9	684	653	5%	636	7%	603	12%	588	14%
8	608	580	5%	565	7%	536	12%	523	14%
7	532	508	5%	495	7%	469	12%	457	14%
6 ½ Page	456	435	5%	424	7%	402	12%	392	14%
5	380	380		370	3%	350	8%	340	11%
4	304	304		296	3%	280	8%	272	11%
3 ¼ Page	228	228		222	3%	210	8%	204	11%
2	152	152		148	3%	140	8%	136	11%
1	76	76		74	3%	70	8%	68	11%

Readership

	'000	Profile %	National Profile %
ALL ADULTS			
Total	2285	100	100
B, C1, C2	1667	73	65
15 - 44	1634	72	53
MEN			
Total	1677	73	48
B, C1, C2	1234	73	68
15 - 44	1225	73	56
AFTER 10 ISSUES	6971	–	

Source: NRS January – December 1983

For a comprehensive readership profile contact your nearest sales office.

All rates and discounts adjusted to the nearest £1.00

Colour/Special Positions

Spot Colour – (run of paper)
Page + £105. ½ Page + £100. ¼ Page + £90.

Front Cover Motoring
(4½ units × 3 columns): £1115 including spot colour. National coverage only.

Classified/Loose Inserts
Rates available on application.

Advertisement Size Structure

EXCHANGE & MART'S familiar page format is specifically designed to offer a wide range of advertisement sizes. This flexibility provides space permutations to suit both advertising needs and advertising budget.

By using combinations of our basic unit of space (48mm × 51mm), Advertisers can choose almost any multiple to meet their exact requirements.

All Display Advertisement Orders/Rates refer to multiples of units:
Example Booking options for a quarter-page 6 units are:
1½ × 4 (1½ units down, across 4 cols), 2 × 3 (2 units down, across 3 cols), 3 × 2 (3 units down, across 2 cols), 6 × 1 (6 units down, across 1 col).

Deadlines

Display Order and Copy Deadline – 14 days prior to publication.
Display cancellation Deadline – 21 days prior to publication. All instructions must be in writing.

Mechanical Data

Published: Weekly on Thursday. **Printed:** Rotary Letterpress. (Photocomposed) Artwork, Bromides. Repro or Film. **Screen:** 26. **Final Dimensions:** Column Width 51mm. Single Column Unit 48mm × 51mm. Column Length 299mm (6 column units). Number of Columns 4. Motoring Front Cover: 4½ units × 3 columns (232mm × 162mm).

Exchange & Mart rate card (details)
(Courtesy: Link House Advertising Periodicals Ltd)

5. Trade fairs

Many new products are first exposed at trade fairs. The manufacturers are test sampling the market to get reaction. There is a trade show for everything. Everyone knows of the massive Ideal Home and Motor Shows either in London or the National Exhibition Centre (NEC) in Birmingham. These are only the tip of the iceberg. There are over 3000 speciality shows reserved for trade only to which buyers are invited. They vary in size from major international fairs such as the Offshore International Exhibition at Aberdeen, the oil capital of Europe, to small gift shows at hotels in Bournemouth.

You will find regional shows catering for a particular area, and mini Ideal Home shows that tour the provinces. There really is something for everyone. Some sectors are well covered. For example, the gift field has over 20 trade fairs from the major Harrogate show in July to the regional West Country one in Torquay in January. Engineers can go to Materials Handling Automation or Powder Technology, both deserving a show in their own right.

There are several sources of advance information available. The most comprehensive is *Exhibition Bulletin* published monthly by the London Bureau, 266 Kirkdale, Sydenham, London SE26 4RZ; 01-778 2288. You can take out an annual subscription for £24 or buy a single copy for £4. Most shows are advised six months ahead. A good reference library will stock it. For agricultural shows the best source is *Showman's Directory* by Stephen and Jean Lance of Brook House, Mint Street, Godalming, Surrey. It also lists steam rallies, airshows, horse shows etc. The price is £3, published annually.

Don't worry about getting *into* trade fairs. Most are free and all they want to see is a business card. They are often relatively sparsely attended compared with rib-crushers like the Ideal Home, but the stands are manned by the people who matter — sales managers, managing directors and so on. Often they're glad of a chat. Shows are expensive to mount and are taken very seriously. Come away with lots of leaflets, prices and ideas.

6. Trade marks, patents and registered designs

If you come across a trade mark and don't know the maker, look in the *Register of Trade Marks* in your library. More obscure ones are in the Trade Marks Registry, part of the Patent

GREAT BRITAIN—continued

LONDON—continued

1983 ★Oct. 11 - 14 London Fashion Exbn.   *Olympia*
Philbeach Events Ltd., Earls Court Exhibition Centre, Warwick Road, London, SW5 9TA   *01-385 1200*

Oct. 11 - 14 Mainseason Fashion Exbn.   *Kensington Exbn. Centre*
Dresswell Ltd., 27 Queensdale Place, London, W11 4SQ   *01-602 7661*

Oct. 12 - 14 Laboratory Exbn.   *Barbican Centre*
Curtis Steadman & Partners Ltd., The Hub, Emson Close, Saffron Walden, Essex, CB10 1HL   *(0799) 26699*

Oct. 12 - 14 Nat. Aids for the Disabled Exbn.—NAIDEX   *Alexandra Pavilion*
Naidex Conventions Ltd., Convex House, 43 Dudley Road, Tunbridge Wells, Kent, TN1 1LE   *(0892) 44027*

Oct. 13 - 15 Design & Technology (for Education & Training) Exbn.   *Wembley Conf. Centre*
International Craft & Hobby Fair Ltd., 3 Rothesay Drive, Highcliffe, Christchurch, Dorset   *(04252) 72711*

Oct. 18 - 20 Computer Graphics European Conf. & Exbn.   *Wembley Conf. Centre*
Online Conferences Ltd., Argyle House, Joel Street, Northwood Hills, Middx., HA6 1TX   *(09274) 28211*

★Oct. 18 - 20 Int. Publishing Exbn. & Conf.—FACE TO FACE   *Intercontinental Hotel*
Face to Face International Ltd., Sovereign Way, Tonbridge, Kent, TN9 1RW   *(0732) 364422*

Oct. 20 - 30 Motorfair   *Earls Court*
Philbeach Events Ltd., Earls Court Exhibition Centre, Warwick Road, London, SW5 9TA   *01-385 1200*

Oct. 25 - 27 London Building & Construction Show   *Bloomsbury Crest Hotel*
Hargould Presentations Ltd., Blairose House, 55 Spring Cross, New Ash Green, Kent   *(0474) 874089*

Oct. 25 - 30 Electronic Hobbies Exbn.   *Alexandra Pavilion*
Reed Exhibitions, Surrey House, 1 Throwley Way, Sutton, Surrey, SM1 4QQ   *01-643 8040*

Nov. 1 - 3 Electronic Displays Exbn. & Conf.   *Kensington Exbn. Centre*
Network, Printers Mews, Market Hill, Buckingham, MK18 1JX   *(0280) 815226*

Nov. 1 - 3 Souvenir & Advertising Gift Show   *West Centre Hotel*
Pressex Promotions, Osborn House, 21/25 Lower Stone Street, Maidstone, Kent, ME15 6YT   *(0622) 671081*

Nov. 1 - 4 Food Processing & Packaging Machinery Exbn.   *Olympia*
Philbeach Events Ltd., Earls Court Exhibition Centre, Warwick Road, London, SW5 9TA   *01-385 1200*

Nov. 1 - 4 London Printing Show—REPRO WORKSHOP   *Barbican Centre*
B.E.D. Exhibitions Ltd., 44 Wallington Square, Wallington, Surrey, SM6 8RG   *01-647 1001*

★Nov. 3 - 4 U.K. Tax Cong. & Exbn.—TAXFAIR   *Cunard Int.*
U.K. Tax Congress Ltd., 20 London Road, Horsham, West Sussex, RH12 1AY   *(0403) 56113*

Nov. 3 - 8 Kensington Antiques Fair   *Kensington Town Hall*
Cultural Exhibitions Ltd., 8 Meadow, Godalming, Surrey, GU7 3HN   *(04868) 22562*

†Nov. 8 - 9 Resins & Pigments Exbn.   *Europa Hotel*
International Symposium & Exhibitions Ltd., Queensway House, 2 Queensway, Redhill, Surrey, RH1 1QS   *(0737) 68611*

Nov. 8 - 10 Software Expo   *Wembley Conf. Centre*
Interco Business Consultants Ltd., 1 Lancaster Park, Richmond, Surrey, TW10 6AG   *01-948 3111*

Nov. 8 - 11 Accountants' Exbn.   *Barbican Centre*
Truemist Ltd., 399a Goldhawk Road, Chiswick, London, W.6.   *01-741 4387*

Nov. 8 - 11 Nat. Graphic Design Exbn.   *Kensington Exbn. Centre*
Project Presentations Ltd., Victoria House, Vernon Place, London, WC1 4DH   *01-242 3621*

Nov. 10 - 20 Caravan Camping Holiday Show   *Earls Court*
National Caravan Council & Angex Ltd., Europa House, St. Matthew Street, London, SW19 2JT   *01-222 9341*

Nov. 12 - 20 "Daily Mail" Int. Ski Show   *Earls Court*
P.A. Int. Ski Shows Ltd., Exhibition House, Lordswood Industrial Estate, Chatham, Kent, ME5 8UD   *(0634) 660852*

Nov. 15 - 17 Electronic Test & Meas'g Instrumentation Exbn.—TEST   *Wembley Conf. Centre*
Trident International Exhibitions Ltd., 21 Plymouth Road, Tavistock, Devon, PL19 8AU   *(0822) 4671*

Nov. 15 - 17 London Midseason Fashion Exbn.   *Kensington Exbn. Centre*
Dresswell Ltd., 27 Queensdale Place, London, W11 4SQ   *01-602 7661*

Nov. 15 - 18 Compec Exbn.   *Olympia*
Reed Exhibitions, Surrey House, 1 Throwley Way, Sutton, Surrey, SM1 4QQ   *01-643 8040*

★Nov. 21 - 22 British Cardiac Society Conf.—Trade Exbn.   *Wembley Conf. Centre*
Swan House Special Events Ltd., Thames Meadow, Walton Bridge, Shepperton, Middx., TW17 8LT   *(03922) 43866*

Nov. 27 - Dec. 1 Wholesale Buyers Gifts Fair   *Mount Royal Hotel*
Trade Promotion Services Ltd., Exhibition House, 6 Warren Lane, London, SE18 6BW   *01-855 9201*

Nov. 28 - Dec. 1 Health & Safety at Work Exbn.   *Wembley Conf. Centre*
Maclaren Exhibitions Ltd., P.O. Box 138, Croydon, CR9 3SS   *01-688 7788*

Nov. 30 - Dec. 4 World Travel Market Exbn.   *Olympia*
Reed Exhibitions, Surrey House, 1 Throwley Way, Sutton, Surrey, SM1 4QQ   *01-643 8040*

Dec. 1 - 4 Wedding & Home Exbn.   *Kensington Exbn. Centre*
Dresswell Ltd., 27 Queensdale Place, Holland Park, London, W11 4SQ   *01-602 7661*

Dec. 3 - 4 Racing Pigeon Old Comrades Show   *Hortic'l Hall*
Racing Pigeon Publishing Co. Ltd., 19 Doughty Street, London, WC1N 2PT   *01-242 0565*

LONDON—continued over

Information obtainable from Exhibition Bulletin

Office (State House, 66-71 High Holborn, London WC1R 4TP; 01-831 2525).

Finding out about existing patents is more difficult. In theory you can yourself search through volumes of patent abridgements held at the Science Reference Library and some other regional centres. Some are held as a computer listing. In practice, while this often makes fascinating and amusing reading, going to a professional searcher is possibly quicker. Once you have the patent number, a copy of the specification is available on payment of a modest fee.

A *design* can also be registered to preserve its unique outward appearance. Unlike patents, you can search the Design Registry yourself. It is a branch of the Patent Office, on the 11th floor of State House, High Holborn, London WC1R 4TP. For more on patents, designs and inventions see Chapter 12.

7. Assessing the competition

As a new starter you must assess what is already available. Rival store groups keep a regular check on what each is doing: they send a junior to list prices.

I'm afraid you have to be a little cunning, like the *Which?* inspector. Do it anonymously. If you're setting up as something simple like a window cleaner, ask the local lad to call. Your neighbour or relation is an alternative. You will be in a good position to judge, not only on his efficiency, but his costs, politeness and whether he wipes his boots.

Let's look at joinery or building. Pick a typical job — porch or kitchen extension. Go through the local paper and *Yellow Pages* and ask your competitors to give an estimate.

Your first impression will be how they answer the phone, a simple enough exercise but very revealing. I can almost guarantee that five out of ten firms will never bother to quote, especially if they are small. It has to be said that many small firms will remain so because they are too apathetic and unprofessional. When you come across one that *cares* it's a revelation. Depending on who comes to quote you will gain another impression. Does he really know what he's talking about? Are the right questions being asked? Is he trying to lead you to something he wants to sell or what you want to buy? Time will pass and the quotes will arrive. The manner of presentation, amount of detail, conditions of sale and acceptance, quite apart from the price, will affect the proposition.

At the end of the exercise you should be in a position to know:

1. The eager competitors, anxious for work.
2. The professionals.
3. Their strengths and weaknesses.
4. Any gaps that you can exploit.
5. Costs.
6. Delivery dates and thus a fair idea of the state of their order book.
7. Methods of selling.
8. Quality of staff.
9. Credit terms offered or deposits requested.
10. Inducements to order (sales promotion techniques).
11. Guarantees.
12. Sales literature.
13. Promptness of follow-up.

If you don't follow the exercise through you won't, of course, know how they actually perform — a vital part — but this you can find out by scouting out past customers.

Some will say, 'That's an underhand way of doing things.' OK, play fair and don't ask for an outlandish amount of detail. But it's still far better to learn before you enter the market than after you're committed. You'll certainly come up against your competitors when you're *in* business, so why not be prepared? Don't forget that the major car companies all buy the rival products and strip them down to learn of new techniques.

PUBLISHED COMPANY ACCOUNTS
Moving on to bigger fish if you are aiming higher and to a more national and sophisticated market, you may like to study company accounts. Information on major (quoted) companies is easy to come by and prodigious. The smaller brethren are more difficult to find and analyse.

Companies House is where, by law, companies have to notify formation and directors' names, and file copies of their accounts. Unfortunately, many companies are dilatory in this respect and you may find the information sparse or out of date. You can see photocopies of what is available either by calling personally at 55 City Road, London EC1Y 1BB or, taking advantage of the postal service, from the Cardiff office for £1. Their address is Crown Way, Maindy, Cardiff CF4 3UZ; 0222 388588.

Who Owns Whom will reveal the subsidiaries of major companies in all their varied disguises.

If you want more depth then you can ask for a detailed report on quoted or unquoted companies. A financial profile and assessment of their credit risk will be given. Three firms offering the service are:

Credit Ratings Ltd, 51 City Road, London EC1Y 1AY; 01-251 6675.

Jordans Business Information Service, 47 Brunswick Place, London N1 6EE; 01-253 3030.

Dun & Bradstreet, 26-32 Clifton Street, London EC2P 2LY; 01-377 4377

On the negative side your own bank, if you ask them nicely, may carry out a 'bad debt' search using one of the national credit agencies like UAPT Ltd, 163 London Road, Croydon CR9 2RP, who have millions of names on file. County court judgements will be revealed and whether they are slow payers. You pay £25 to join UAPT but searches are then fairly cheap — 70p each. A full company status report will cost £11.

The Centre for Interfirm Comparison is useful for comparing your performance with other companies in your field. Companies in over 100 industries, services and professions feed financial data into the centre who, after analysis, pump it out anonymously for comparison. You can thus see a yardstick for your operation against the best, average or worst in your line of country. It is financed by the British Institute of Management (BIM) and the British Productivity Council. Address: 8 West Stockwell Street, Colchester CO1 1HN; 0206 62274. A range of free booklets is available.

ICC Business Ratios do the same for 12,000 leading UK businesses, using a three-year analysis of past results. Not of much use when you're starting off but possibly of interest in the future. Nineteen key ratios are abstracted — profits, gearing, productivity etc. Reports cost around £100 each. The address is 23 City Road, London EC1Y 1AA; 01-638 2946.

Jordans also provide a new companies service which spotlights new formations. The activity, directors, registered office and issued capital are shown. The price varies according to the coverage required: one county or the whole of London. As something like 150 new names are registered each day, a voluminous source of new sales prospects is to hand. Price from £60 per annum.

Testing product acceptability

Having evaluated what is the existing market and formed an idea of where your product should fit in, the step before full production should be limited test sampling. The need for this should be transparent. Intuition has its place but production involving investment in plant, packaging and print must have a more solid basis than 'Aunt Agatha would buy one'.

A pre-production run, produced if necessary by hand or a small batch run, can be shown to potential wholesalers, agents and consumers. Most box makers will produce a sample range on condition they get a proper order in due course. Dummy boxes can be coloured up.

Surveys can be made, either by the time-honoured method of stopping people in the street or loaning for 'wear tests'. Be wary of small samples. Statistically, they are suspect. Try and get a genuine cross-section of your target audience or pick up every tenth person to work the law of averages. A simple example of a questionnaire for craft potters is shown below. Questionnaires need to be carefully framed. Award points that can be taken off the forms and totalled.

- If your product is a knock-down kit, give it to the 'village idiot' and see how well he assembles it from your instructions. You're too close to the job to see the pitfalls.
- Post the item back to yourself and see what the carrier does to it.
- Try a variety of packaging.
- Try a number of product names and see which is the most acceptable.

Almost everything about the product can be tested before it is launched on the market.

The same applies to advertising. Try it in a small way first with one paper or journal before booking space in six and running a campaign. The major companies do it by ITV region — one step at a time. A big advantage of direct mail is the in-built ability to test different headlines, offers and names with a quick response before doing a major posting.

It is far cheaper to change a pilot production than a full warehouse.

A SIMPLE QUESTIONNAIRE FOR A CRAFT POTTER SELLING FROM HIS PREMISES

Are you an old customer?
When did you last come here?
Do you notice any difference in the layout?

For new customers
How did you hear of us?
    Personal recommendation?
    Advertisement?
    Signs?
    Newspaper article?
    Other?
Would you like to see other crafts on display?
Are you buying for yourself or as a gift?
Are you on holiday?
Would you like to see more exclusive and expensive items for sale?
Are there any items not here that you would like to have bought?

Chapter 3
Advertising

Emerson overlooked advertising when he said that the world would beat a path to your door if you built a better mousetrap. The need for advertising must be obvious. Without it you must rely on word-of-mouth recommendation (not to be despised but slow nevertheless) or press editorial. The main force of your sales effort will probably be through advertising of one sort or another. It can be as simple as writing your name on a van, pushing a handbill through the door or buying space in the parish magazine.

Advertising is the link between the supplier and the consumer, communication and information, the medium and the message.

Advertising *by itself* does not sell. It will not shift a bad product (more than once) or create new markets. It must be backed up by sales literature, order forms, a sales force, stocks, distributors and a strategy.

Let's get some of the principles out of the way first. The skill of advertising lies in reducing the global population to your target audience and reaching as many of them as you can at an economic cost. You first analyse the benefits or virtues of your product — isolate the features and translate these into customer benefits. Who has a need for your product? Discover who your potential customers are. Question all the time.

Finally, design the message and pick the medium to reach your target audience.

Think of a customer

The good marketing man is thinking of customers all the time. If company A has found a use for your product perhaps their competitors are worth tackling. And what about others in the group or at head office? Customers start off as unknown names perhaps in a directory. They then become prospects. When they have bought they turn into customers. If you look after them they become key accounts. Finally, some of them will act as advocates — unpaid recommenders of your product to others.

Setting objectives

Never advertise without having an objective. You must have a goal. Effective advertising means always having a clear idea of what you are aiming to do. Advertising is used for a wide variety of reasons. Some are:

1. New product launch.
2. Changing price structure.
3. Exhibition attendance.
4. Recruitment of staff.
5. Sales.
6. Change of premises, enlarging facilities.
7. Charitable, linking your firm with a local good cause.
8. Direct response, to invite enquiries.
9. Trade ads to wholesalers.
10. Appealing for agents.
11. To iron out seasonal fluctuations in demand.
12. Reminder ads — repetitious, constantly there.
13. To announce record results or celebrate an anniversary.

I have listed these to emphasise the many different roles that advertising can play. Don't advertise just because Charlie down the road does or when the local newspaper is doing a feature. There have to be some good solid reasons for investing in a promotional exercise.

The appropriation

Advertising men use this term when talking about how much you should spend. The amount comes out of the overall marketing budget discussed on page 28. What proportion of this should be allocated to pure advertising is where your strategy and marketing plan come in. Advertising is just one method of reaching your prospects that goes into the marketing mix (page 29). The decision will in part rest on what market you are in. The mass consumer market, largely dominated by big manufacturers, has been developed by prodigious sums of advertising expenditure. Brand image is the objective. The industrial market relies much more on face-to-face selling by technical representatives. Advertising is used to solicit enquiries. Exhibitions and a more selective direct mail and technical advertising campaign are used. The amount you spend on advertising will largely be governed by this difference in approach.

The handmade sign for runner beans is entirely acceptable in a country lane, but would you trust your life with the joyflight?

Positioning

Your perceived position in the market-place will determine where your message appears. This is a very important point to grasp. If you've an up-market product then not only must you promote in the right glossy magazines but the style of typeface, layout and presentation must convey an air of grandeur and graciousness.

Let's take a staple consumer product like mustard. The standard yellow Colman's stuff is marketed in a plainly labelled, no frills, clear jar with a no-nonsense label. In front of me I also have a French farmhouse mustard produced by a well-known herbalist with a neat drawing of a chateau on the label and a bit of French thrown in. It tells me that the ingredients are carefully chosen to an old recipe. The jar is a nice, memorable, handy size. The price is almost immaterial. The two products have different market positions, and to reach their sales potential, they are presented and advertised to appeal at their own level.

There is a world of difference, apart from the goods, between say Marks and Spencer and the Co-op. The manner of display, lighting, signs, labels, and layout of the store all serve to distinguish the way they each tackle their respective market.

For years Fords have laboured under the label of being value for money but rather a down-market product. The rather cruel ad of VW comparing the Polo and Fiesta ('But underneath it's still a Ford') highlighted the distinction. The introduction of the Ghia marque with its more luxurious finish has lifted these models into the 'managing director's wife/sales manager' category.

Positioning is basic to everything. You don't find many second-hand clothes shops in the High Street or Jaguar showrooms in the back streets. Visitors to a strange town make for the area where they expect to find the sort of shop they are looking for. If you really think about it, positioning governs everything you buy, often unconsciously.

Charity adverts mustn't be too slick otherwise we'll think the money is going on Mayfair agencies rather than needy orphans. In fact, charity fund raising demands a very professional approach and is one of the more difficult tasks for an advertiser.

Where to advertise

At this stage it may be interesting to think of all the places where you can pay to display your message:

Newspapers, national and local
Magazines, general and specialist
TV — regional and increasingly very local
Exchange & Mart and other pure advertising magazines
Free sheets
Radio
Cinema
Directories and year-books
Yellow Pages
House magazines (eg, bank staff magazines)
Posters, hoardings, transport undertakings
Signs of every imaginable variety, from building boards to
    Piccadilly Circus
Handbills, leaflets, brochures
Litter bins, parking meters, lollipop ladies
Painted buses
Balloons and streamers
Direct mail
Exhibitions
Sports team sponsorship
Packaging
Sales promotion — the fastest growing area
Point of sale material
Give-aways — calendars, wall charts etc
Parish magazines, show programmes
Newsagents' windows

The choice is vast. The problem is deciding how best to reach
your prospect. The criteria for selection are frequency, size of
circulation, coverage, readership profile and opportunities to see
the ads.

FREQUENCY
The copy dates of some glossy monthlies are two months
before publication. This poses problems if you are waiting on a
shipment or uncertain about a product change. Dailies or week-
lies allow much prompter changes. The ultimate is probably
radio where messages can be slotted in on the same day. Many
exhibitions are only held annually, and booking space and
planning your promotion demand several months' notice. Year-
books, diaries and *Yellow Pages* require long forward notice.

HOW MANY COPIES?

Having targeted your audience you will want to know the individual circulations of your advertising media. This is easy when *you* control the output (handbills, direct mail, brochures etc).

A good exhibition promoter will produce certified attendance figures but not all can come up with a profile — a measurement of the calibre rather than quantity of visitors.

ABC (*Audit Bureau of Circulation*) certified journals are reliable for cost comparisons and the figures should be beyond reproach. They can supply an authoritative statement of copies actually sold. You thus know how many readers will see your precious ad. Smaller circulation or secretive publications will have 'Uncertified' beside their *BRAD* entry.

The journal's advertising department will be able to tell you of many special features planned that may be appropriate. Some UK journals have a surprisingly high overseas circulation.

A problem arises with posters and too liberal give-aways. Don't be too ambitious: make sure you can meet a large demand if your message clicks.

Erosion — the numbers game

I recently carried out my own research on the pulling power of the Sunday 'Postal Bargains'. A dozen advertisers were canvassed. I picked out what looked like newish small firms, asking for the response to their ads. The replies seemed to average around 30 per insertion. The moral is clear: don't be deceived by massive circulations.

From a readership of perhaps 3 million with a circulation of 1 million perhaps 100,000 actually saw the ad. Of those, perhaps to 90,000 it was of no interest. The remainder either had one already, thought it too dear or didn't like the colour, were saving up for Christmas or would get around to it 'one day'. Maybe 500 decided they would like one but forgot to look out some writing paper or the husband lit the fire with that issue. Thirty wrote for the brochure and 10 actually bought one. And there are bound to be one or two who returned the product. That's erosion.

COVERAGE

There is a lot of duplication when you use different advertising media. You want to establish how well you reach the audience — the penetration or coverage. A DIY product could be advertised in *Practical Householder*, mail shotted to power drill owners, taken to a trade show to tempt stockists, pushed on TV or any combination of all those. The women's magazine market is a lively and populous one. How many women buy two or more? Which magazine gives the best penetration for your age group? Is *TV Times* a better buy anyway?

The eternal problem with most advertising is measuring the effectiveness. National corporations can afford to have poster displays, bus panels and whole page ads in the *Radio Times* but even they have great difficulty in isolating which medium has pulled in the most response. By definition, small firms tend to be frugal with their advertising budgets, and should avoid any promotions where the results cannot be measured. Their advertising has to be more specific, measurable and *sell*. The favoured routes therefore tend to be ads that use a reply coupon to invite a response or offer a very specific message.

READERSHIP

Readership is always more than circulation, and it varies depending on the type of publication. The classic case is old *Country Life*s which are read years later in dentists' waiting rooms.

You must advertise where your buyers and consumers are likely to see the message. Market research should have told you where your likely prospects lie. Consulting the various publications mentioned in Chapter 2 will enable you to pinpoint which newspapers or journals to aim for. The media data form compiled by the publishers will give a *readership profile*. This is a breakdown of their readers and subscribers by job title (managers, buyers, consultants etc) and often by age, sex, interests (not always the same) and other relevant information for that journal.

Of major interest to some advertisers is the socio-economic classification: AB — Upper and middle classes, managerial, administrative and professional people. C1, C2 — Lower middles, skilled working class. D — working class (semi- and unskilled manual workers) and the poor Es — those at the lowest level of subsistence. This seems to reflect class prejudices but it is important to understand the jargon and reasoning behind it.

The forms are useful but should be treated with common sense and caution. The media reps are in the business of taking your money, after all.

OPPORTUNITIES TO SEE (OTS)

The disadvantage of evening commercial TV advertising is that the shops are closed when the viewer sees the message. Trade buyers are deluged with calendars, diaries, pen sets and message pads in the hope that they will remain in the office at the point of action when a buying decision is made. The more opportunities to see that are given the greater chance that the company name or product will stick. This is why direct mail letters increasingly involve more pieces of literature. The theory (and practice) is that each piece of mailing is looked at before being discarded. It may only be a brief scan but it gives the seller another chance to hook a punter.

The best example I can recall of this was at the last election. My local polling station was the school and in the neighbouring garden a row of posters with one candidate's name was prominently displayed overlooking the playground. Short of being on the polling booth it was the nearest place to be at the moment of decision!

NEWSPAPER AND PERIODICAL ADVERTISING

The two main types are *classified* and *display*. Classified are usually grouped together under a variety of headings. They require typesetting only and can often be rung in quite late to press date. If you run an unusual specialisation ask the paper to put in a fresh heading just for you. It often works and helps to make your ad stand out. The publisher hopes it will attract more advertisers . . . .

Display ads are *designed* and need artwork, headlines, text etc. These will be dotted throughout the publication and generate most of the paper's income. When deciding which paper to go for pick the one with more advertising. Many journals are bought, and read, more for the ads than the editorials. This particularly applies if you're small and can only run to classifieds). Papers which have a very small classified section should be avoided. The ultimate is, of course, *Exchange & Mart*. Remarkably good responses are pulled from quite expensive items. I've even known factories to be let from these pages.

Between the two are *semi-display* used by some magazines. They tend to be small pictorial ads grouped near the classified section.

Trade setting

Pretty well every publication will lay out an ad for you from your rough. If you're desperate to meet a deadline simple ads can be phoned through: there are no doubt some excellent in-house ad-men who will do a competent job. Production costs can be charged as an extra but, in my experience, simple layouts are treated as part of the service. The cost of printing blocks will be charged. Make sure you get the blocks back. But by and large, for imaginative designs you should go to an outside agency or freelance graphic designer.

SLADE and *NGA* are two of the renowned print unions (Society of Lithographic Artists, Designers, Engravers and Process Workers, and the National Graphical Association). Your artwork and blocks may not be handled if they don't bear an approved sticker. Your graphic artist almost certainly belongs.

Some advertising jargon

Buying space. Ads are measured either by fractions of a page — half page, quarter page or by column centimetres. Each publication will have its own layout and a number of column widths.

Space is sold by a standard centimetre depth. Be very careful you understand what you are ordering: a '10 x 2' is probably 10 column centimetres of depth by 2 columns wide. When buying 'half a page' make sure you are getting a horizontal half when you want it, and not the vertical variety. Specify height by width in that order: remember the phrase 'hot water'.

Controlled circulation magazines are common in the technical field. They are issued free (the ads pay for them) but circulation is restricted to those in certain specified positions of influence. There is invariably an application form in the back of every copy.

Copy date is the vital date when the publisher must have camera-ready artwork in his hand to be sent off for printing. It is *not* the date when a rough layout can be shoved in the post. You will miss that issue.

Cost per thousand (CPT). One of the holy grails of advertising, cost comparisons are made to reach a given 1000 readers of each medium. As usual, statistics can mean anything and here the picture is clouded by the intrusion of quality. The cost of reaching 1000 *Financial Times* readers is more than for the *Sun*. The argument was that your average *Financial*

Times reader has more influence in specifying products and contacts than the *Sun* reader.

Never lose sight of your *target* reader: no good reaching a million readers if only 1 per cent is your *audience*.

Editorial. The informative text written by the journalists that separates the adverts. Free sheets tend to have very little editorial and are probably discarded quickly.

Facing matter is when an ad is placed opposite some editorial — as against being submerged in a page of other ads. The space commands a premium price. The opposite is *run of paper* (ROP) where it will be placed anywhere at the discretion of the advertising manager.

Inserts can be very useful. Some magazines will accept your printed leaflet for loose insertion in every copy (or occasionally selected copies to a segment of the circulation in your target area). They'll want prior sight of it and often there is a waiting list. It's cheaper than advertising in the mag (you've paid for the production). If the magazine is in black and white only, this is a way of getting your colour leaflets left over from the trade fair out to the readers.

A media schedule is helpful to plan the preparation of your advertising material and get it off in time. It's really a glorified diary that's stuck on the wall which will reveal to you when your mags and ads are coming out, enabling a continuous programme to be maintained (if that's what you want).

Reader's reply service is widely used to generate enquiries. A pre-paid card is bound in, usually at the back of the mag, keyed in with numbered ads that can produce a prolific number of prospects. There can be a delay before they are sent on from the publisher.

Some *printing* terms are on pages 89-90.

Using an advertising agency

It stands to reason that those who are designing ads every day of the week should be able to come up with better ideas and layouts than raw small firms. Advertising can run away with your money, often to little effect. To understand the nature of the industry, thumb through *Advertiser's Annual* or *Campaign*, the trade gossip magazine. You will quickly grasp that creative directors are the linchpins who move about forming and re-forming agencies and luring old clients in their wake.

Competition is fierce for the big accounts — the FMCG (fast moving consumer goods) spenders with millions at their disposal. Accredited agencies earn commission on their 'billings', the space they buy, that varies depending on the medium used. It averages 10 to 15 per cent. Local papers pay less than nationals. The commission should part offset the cost of using an agency but nevertheless, don't be upset at the costs of employing the professionals.

... AND HOW TO CHOOSE THE RIGHT ONE

Steer away from the big boys. They'll have no interest in small budgets. Find a small partnership, perhaps freshly set up, that is as hungry as you are: not *too* new or you may know more than they do. Ask for samples of their past work. Look at their roughs and try to get them to explain *why* they chose that particular theme. You want to tap into their creative abilities. The advertising jargon and printing terminology can be learnt in time — it's creative talent that you need and should be willing to pay for.

A good agency will be able to advise you on:

1. An objective campaign balancing your various products and resources.
2. Market research; if not within their own partnership, where to find it.
3. Producing the material, booking the space in the most cost-effective manner and evaluating the results.
4. Some agencies will also do PR work and exhibitions here and abroad.
5. They should know a string of reliable printers for brochures and your packaging needs.

It is probably only in the last 10 years that advertising has become professional. It has grown more scientific. Much more testing and measurement of results now takes place: the clients have demanded it. More research and statistical sampling is carried out into what makes people buy and react. The growth of direct response advertising has brought its own discipline. The results of the campaign are soon known. Direct mail can be measured against target very speedily. The agencies have had to revise their beliefs and sharpen their ideas. Clients today want value for money.

Go and see three or four agencies. Take along your product, if you can, with samples of any literature or ads you may have run. Let them do most of the talking. Gauge from their questions how interested they are in you. You're looking for empathy and an understanding of your product and market. A technical product does really demand some knowledge of the habits of engineering specifiers. While it is asking a lot for ad-men to have a complete grasp of the technicalities of your product, there must be some meeting of minds.

Increasingly agencies are specialising. The glamour end has always been FMCG, with industrial accounts looked down on. Be very wary of agencies that have not handled direct mail if that is your direction. That really is one field for the experts. Give them time to think and ask them to produce some *roughs* on ads they would run. Don't expect finished artwork unless you're prepared to pay well for the service. At this stage you are simply looking at how well they have grasped your company and what ideas they can come up with. And then talk about budgets.

Designing your own ads

Despite the obvious advantages in going to an agency, many of you will design your own copy, particularly when just starting in business. I can't turn you into an expert wordsmith in a few pages but the ground rules can be spelled out fairly succinctly. There are many ways of getting the message over and fortunately there is no one sure-fire route to success. It would be a dull world if there were.

Advertising is a transient medium. You don't get more than a few seconds to make an impact. No one is paid to read adverts. They compete for your vision and comprehension along with all the other ephemera of the modern world. Good advertisements follow the formula AIDA — Attention, Interest, Desire and Action. The first requirement, therefore, is to attract *attention*. This can be done either with a headline, a picture, colour (spot or full), special position or novelty. Some researcher has worked out that Mr Average 'sees' over 1000 ads each week — newspaper, posters, TV etc. Your job when designing an ad is to get the reader to stop and digest what you have to say.

The *attention* is best gained by either a headline or a picture. Preferably tell the tale by working both together. Words and pictures in combination can be a powerful medium as long as the story merits it. All too often any old photo is dredged up to fill a space.

Interest. Unless the text appears of interest to the reader, then no matter how beautifully it is put together or how clever the pun, it will be passed over. Length has little to do with it either. Long text *will* be read if it is carefully written and leads the reader on. The subject must be made to look attractive and compulsive reading. The best ads arouse an emotional reaction. You should strive to create *desire* in the reader. 'Yes, that sounds good — I'd like one of those.' It must relate to the reader's circumstances. You must always talk about user benefits not features. And they must be readily apparent.

The ad will have achieved very little if there is no encouragement for the reader to do anything about it. You need *action*. Coupons inviting enquiries for brochures or money off the next order are well tried formulae. At the least, clear instructions must be printed to direct the reader to more information. The old buzz words come in here — 'Limited stocks, Sale, Limited edition to first 1000 callers, Club members' preference, Free trial, Money back guarantee, etc. The best of all is 'New'. Don't fall into the trap of designing ads that are 'all image and no information'.

THE CENTRAL IDEA

The core of any ad must be the product itself. If you can, sit the product on your desk or get a photo and study it. List all the features. How it is made, the material, colour, function, weight and fitness for purpose. Look at taste, texture, packaging, expected life, durability, originality, replacement value and spare parts, not forgetting the price. The list is almost endless. The creative man at the Puffed Wheat agency is said to have toured the factory where it was made. The phrase 'Shot from a gun' emanates from there.

But don't worry about some award-winning pun. Most ads state a fairly basic truth and offer permutations on known and tried reasons for buying. There are supposed to be around a dozen reasons *why people buy* and it wouldn't hurt to pin the main ones up or write your own versions.

1. Self-preservation: to satisfy hunger, provide shelter, to guard health or comfort.
2. Sex appeal: to attract the opposite sex or be narcissistic; glamour.
3. Snob value, keeping up with the Joneses — if not *being* the Joneses. Having the best. Self-indulgence. Greed.
4. Fashion.

5. To satisfy curiosity.
6. To express personality, and build an image.
7. Achievement. To better one's lot. To gain knowledge or skills for self-improvement. Pride and status are at stake.
8. Value for money. The desire to make money.
9. Doing the best for one's family, or indulging them.
10. To satisfy a dream.

These are all psychological or emotional reasons. The most successful advertisements play on these motives. Some years ago a detergent ad ran based on a shining white knight dashing round the kitchen dispelling washday blues. It was excruciating to watch night after (k)night but sales blossomed. It was in fact just what the housewife wanted. It bore no resemblance to the product or reality. Drayton Bird in his original book *Common-sense Direct Marketing* quotes his own idea for an encyclopaedia ad. He shows a child running up the path shouting, 'Mummy, I've passed.' What parent wouldn't be touched by the *emotion* generated in that picture and caption?

KEEP TO THE THEME
Advertising men love to talk about campaigns. That sounds a bit grand for small firms. I prefer to think about themes, objectives or the strategy.

Before you get down to designing what an ad will say you must decide on your central strategy. New product launches, clearance of old lines, moving up-market or that old stand-by 'rationalisation' will each need a different emphasis and handling. Unless you are running the same layout continuously, which is a bit uninspiring, all your ads should have a common theme linking them together. There should be a family resemblance. If the reader bothered to cut them all out and place them side by side it should be apparent without looking at the company name that they all originated from the same source.

This goes beyond using the same type-face and border. The use of illustrations, the appeal and phrasing of the headline and the manner in which you spell out the sales message should all read in the same tone. It's common sense, of course. If you regularly wait for the No 17 bus, you would be confused to see a yellow one come along when you're expecting one that is red.

So each time you design an ad, lay out the previous efforts and pick up the threads. Ideally, before you place the first one you will have thought out what the next six will look like. But don't run it for ever: change when results start to drop off.

Nor should you change for change's sake: why alter a successful formula? Inevitably all strategies need revamping from time to time.

REMEMBER THE BASICS

All marketing revolves around those eternal questions Who, What, Why, Where and When?

Who is your target audience? What are they interested in and what are their needs? I've read of a Fleet Street editor who kept a blow-up of a section of the Cup Final crowd on the wall. When a bright sub presented him with some high falutin' copy, he would swing round to the wall: 'There's your audience — never forget it!'

What are the benefits? Don't try and trot out all 33 but hone them down to three at most and headline *one* — your *unique selling proposition.*

Why should they buy it? What is your offer? The big world is a competitive market and in your ads you must try to put a convincing reason for immediate action or response. Use those buzz words. Alastair Crompton in his excellent book *The Craft of Copywriting* draws a distinction between two sorts of product. Some you can really say quite a lot about (DIY products or household gadgets and many technical products, for example) but what can you say that's new about springs, or screws or stout for that matter? Guinness has been produced for well over 100 years so they have to resort to all manner of fanciful things to attract attention and be memorable. They use showmanship and jazz it up.

If your product is in the same category — a regular mundane type that has been around for years — then I think you almost have to forget about looking for distinctive features and go for the razzmatazz. Dreary products can produce tired ads so why not recognise it from the start? Nudes to sell oil filters is corny: use a bit more imagination.

What to include

Get a pad in front of you and play around with various ideas. Draw the exact size of the ad to prescribe the boundaries you have to work in. Lay out the paper or journal in which the advert is to appear to get a feeling for the style and readership of your audience.

HEADLINE

Your first task is to decide on your *headline*. Too clever openings will confuse. Various techniques can be used to encourage the reader to pause and read on.

A favourite is to ask a question.

Where do you find the quietest dishwasher?
How do you break into a bank?
What have you done to low tar?
Which is the newer car?

Explanatory headlines perform the same role:

How to stop smoking.
How to save fuel bills.
How to stop paying tax.
How to beat Ford's price rise.
Five reasons why you should use Whoppit.

TEXT

If you adopt a telegraphic approach to all your writing you won't stray into unintelligibility. Use short concise words rather than the journalese so beloved by politicians and trade union officials. Say what you mean in direct, simple language.

Remember that 1 million British citizens are illiterate and many of the rest receive their view of the world via the *Sun*.

Make every word mean something. Most of your first efforts are capable of condensing, I am sure. Don't forget you are paying for that space — wasted words cost money and squeeze out those that *do* count.

THE OFFER

If you can make a good offer this should be your headline. Offers can be anything you like, such as 'Two for the price of one', 'Free trial', 'Free credit', 'Instal now, pay later', 'Beat the budget', 'Prize draw' and so on. In inflationary times a powerful argument is 'Buy now at the old price . . .'.

USP

Unique selling proposition: no prizes for guessing where this magic phrase came from. There is a school of thought that says people buy and choose from competing products because of one major distinction. Isolate that benefit and not only will you hit on the customer's trigger but will establish the plank for your advertising. It *can* lead to absurd themes being pushed, but the idea is good. People don't remember 28 punch lines in an ad or leaflet. They haven't got time and you haven't got the money to take whole page adverts.

Pick out the main strength of your product and work your headlines around it.

I'm working at the moment on a bath renovation service. The price is not significantly cheaper than buying a new suite, but there are other attributes:

- The showroom prices quoted in the builders' merchants for new suites don't include installation.
- There is all the fuss and mess involved in heaving out the old suites, some of which will be cast iron, and replacing with new.
- The renovation service offers a wide choice of colours, some of which will harmonise with the client's existing tiles and fashion.
- Some people don't believe in the throw-away society and have a fondness for the old styles.

All these different selling points need condensing and a bit of honest market research done to establish a clear USP.

REMEMBER THE BENEFITS

You and I buy things because of what they'll do for *us*. With the sole exception of charity offerings, and in that I include Scout sales of work and PTA Christmas card drives, we part with money because we can see a use for the product. A particular shampoo is not bought because it contains malathion. That's a feature. The benefit is that it kills nits! The benefit of a tungsten-tipped saw blade is that it lasts longer, saves downtime on changing over, and reduces sharpening costs.

It is very easy to fall into the trap of always talking about the features of your product and particularly of a service. It is of little interest that your service vans may be connected by two-way radio to save van mileage: the benefit to your customer is a prompt round-the-clock attention.

By and large, your customers are not interested that you may have a spanking new factory with the latest in computer controlled machine tools. That is *your* benefit. They are concerned that you can meet delivery dates and produce the goods at a competitive price.

Price can be a benefit. If you are selling a product that is going to save someone money, then multiply the savings up. Fifty pence a week is neither here nor there, but £26 over a full year is a headline! Few would go out and buy an encyclopaedia on French cooking, but if it is sold every week as a partwork — 'only' 80p every Friday — you've captured an audience. Petrol-saving devices are pushed on the same lines. No one notices 5 per cent off a gallon of petrol, but projected over a year's motoring of 12,000 miles, the savings (in theory) are memorable. The Man-from-the-Pru relies on the same maxim by a weekly extraction.

All your advertising should be looked at in terms of customer needs.

Some advertisement techniques

Copy writers use a variety of techniques to get the message over in an effective and memorable manner. A straight headline and text would be confused with the editorial, so papers now insert 'Advertisement' over layouts of this type. Convention has defeated imitation.

USE WHITE SPACE

There is always the temptation to fill every bit of usable space on your dearly bought ad with persuasive text. The vast majority of newspapers and journals are printed in black on white paper and therefore carry advertising matter in the same restrictive medium.

By leaving a generous margin around the actual copy you can make *your* ad stand out: simple and very effective in a mass of otherwise anonymous grey text. Test it for yourself. Reach for your local paper and open it at the classified section or any other that carries a lot of advertising. When you open up a paper you tend to do so at arm's length and scan before homing in on what looks like an interesting item. Those that are more likely to catch the eye, I would suggest, are the few that stand out clear from their neighbours.

The concept has, of course, been carried through with whole page ads and even posters. Large areas of blank or single-colour paper surrounding a short message act as a focus.

BEFORE AND AFTER

This treatment has many applications. My bath renovator will do well to show two pictures, one an old scummy, chipped relic

Reversed type.
If it's hard to read it won't be read.

Which is more important,
the firm or what it does?

One that tries to be different,
but I'm not sure whether it will
get read.

Not quite sure what is on offer here.

Humorous yet telling headline.

No headline at all.

and next to it a bright, gleaming creation portrayed after the treatment. Anything that offers a face-lift can be illustrated: window replacement, lawn fertilisers, carpet shampoos, loose covers and many others. The treatment is particularly effective for services as distinct from products. There must be a strong visual treatment with first-class illustrations. Bear in mind that newsprint does not take half-tones very well. Don't ask too much of the medium.

SELL THE EXTREME
Often the best way of selling the benefits of a product is to show it in action. And don't stop at the natural use. Go to the extreme. If your paint is weatherproof illustrate it on a lighthouse or North Sea oil platform. I can remember a new type of toughened glass coming out years ago. It was pictured supporting an elephant. No one would use it for that but the absurd combination made the point very effectively. People will think, 'If it's good enough for that it must be OK for what I want.'

ENDORSEMENTS
We can't all afford television personalities to push our double glazing but there are homelier ways. Extracts from letters from satisfied customers, 'Mrs S of Worthing has told all her friends to rush out and buy Bloggit since this cured her aches' can work wonders. Endorsements are probably more easily used in direct mail because you have more room to quote long extracts. ('The original letters are on our files and open to inspection.') The pools promoters use endorsements widely. A picture of Mr Y from Burnley clutching his cheque for half a million and grinning from ear to ear tends to personalise the message: 'That could be me.' Technical products lend themselves to endorsements as well. 'As used by Rolls Royce' or even by a defence contractor implies some standing and credence. Obviously, get the firm's permission first.

COMPARISONS
The selection of products is all a matter of comparison. The consumer does it when deciding which product to buy. He looks at the features and benefits. However, until recently it was considered unethical to indulge in comparative advertising — 'knocking' copy. The motor trade seems to have adopted this method completely with adverts continually running down the opposition. They should surely be able to find enough reasons to buy on their own merits.

Comparison advertising can be successful and ethical if carefully handled. I wouldn't mention competitors by name, as the motor trade does, but by implication. A local double glazing firm competing with the nationals could stress that, 'The money you pay goes into the goods, not to pay for TV advertising, commission salesmen or celebrities.'

NEWSWORTHINESS

This is very difficult to achieve with long copy dates but the weekly or daily papers will allow your ads to have a *topical* flavour. You could hit the bull's-eye with this if you look ahead and plan. Changes in legislation, budget tax changes, royal events are all fairly predictable. A carefully worded ad placed on the same day will attract attention. It all needs flair, imagination and sometimes a bit of luck.

NOVELTY

An ad can stand out by being out of context. Some unexpected feature pictured in the layout can highlight your message. We're not necessarily back with the nudes but anything you can legitimately pull into your advert that would not normally be expected to be there can be successful. It's our first rule of advertising — attraction. Smirnoff do it with sky-divers, White Horse Whisky with white horses. You don't have to go to such extremes. A man knitting or even cooking is worth a second glance. Perfectly reasonable pursuits but not within the normally accepted way of portraying domestic chores.

PEOPLE MATTER

Try and portray the product in action, in a real environment. Kitchen designers tend to show yards of gleaming cupboards and shelves with not a soul in sight. Put a bright young housewife preparing food in the picture and it comes to life. OK, so you lose a bit of the product but you gain in appeal.

People identify with the subject portrayed. Figures in ads tend to be younger, more handsome and virile than in real life. That's poetic licence. The women's lib organisations are always complaining that you never see a tired harassed housewife with buttons missing selling products. The reason is that people believe scruffy people sell scruffy goods. Perhaps we see what we want to believe. It's all a fairyland world.

Your characters should be believable, with a touch of dressing up. The person using the product should be closely associated with your type of audience. If it's a DIY gadget, pick a man who looks like a time-served tradesman as the model. Capable, gnarled, expressive hands do a lot for a photograph. The way he handles a tool will say a lot.

If you're using a factory shot, make sure you observe the Health and Safety Regulations — no machines left unguarded, and employees wearing the right headgear, goggles and footwear. Anything else looks sloppy and will be picked up.

Babies are a sure-fire attraction especially if you're selling to mothers. There can't be many household products for which you can't work a good baby shot in somewhere in the life of the campaign! Animals are worth the same treatment. How many products can you think of that have had a backcloth of rustic simplicity — a nice clean field of Jerseys or Friesians?

HUMOUR

Anyone who has struggled this far with the narrative will realise I'm a firm convert to a touch of humour: perhaps not in ads for undertakers but that still leaves plenty of scope. As not everyone laughs at the same things it does demand a light touch. The launch of a new business can be announced in standard dry formal tones or treated as the stork in the picture opposite. The response from the clients was exceptional.

CARTOONS

Picture stories can be very successful. I don't know whether that is a reflection on the low standard of education of the readership or that cartoons do tend to stand out on a page of otherwise regular text. You don't have to go the whole hog of commissioning a cartoonist to draw up a full strip. A cartoon character, ie one single figure or caricature, can act as the lead in introducing the text. That can become your logo, your instantly identifiable feature. Such logos tend to be animals of the lovable sort — bears, dogs and other household pets. I suppose Robinson's golliwog is one of the oldest, with Fox's Glacier Mints polar bear a close second.

Illustrators tend to be a freelance breed and most towns have one. Naturally, there is a concentration around London where most work is. Your better local printer should be able to suggest one or two.

ILLUSTRATIONS

That every picture is worth a thousand words is as true in adver-

ANNOUNCING
A NEW
ARRIVAL

tising as anywhere else, even more so when space is at a premium. Newsprint takes a poor photo and with many papers still clinging to letterpress results are often disappointing. Most technical publications use a fair quality gloss paper which reproduces well. Unless you're a pro leave photography well alone. Most products demand good studio conditions, not propped up on the garden bench for a snapshot.

Line drawings are a good substitute and cut-away subjects can often be portrayed only in this way. Technical illustration does not come cheap, quite rightly, as it is a highly skilled art. If you have the choice, go for photos every time — they are more believable. The illustrations must complement the headline. The two must work together. Don't use the headline as a caption to explain the photo. That treatment belongs to the family album.

If the picture needs a caption to explain it then you're using the wrong picture. A telling caption can add dramatic or emotional emphasis. Of the two the headline is more important. That's your attention grabber that must give a 'come-on' to make the reader stop and want to know more.

Don't neglect the picture agencies who can supply photos (for a fee) much as libraries supply books. You don't have to commission a photographer to take that special shot.

COUPONS

This much used word in marketing can mean redemption coupons for goods or services or address coupons for enquiries.

Let's look at *money off* coupons first. Ignore the mass market soap packets. You need a sophisticated handling system, invariably put out to one of the specialists, plus a fast moving product. No, the principle has wider interest for small firms. My local restaurant regularly runs a £1 voucher discount for family meals at off-peak times. The plant and staff have to be there so why not maximise the investment and bring in new clientele at slack periods? The coupon is all part of the ad. The idea has plenty of applications: dry cleaning, garages, wine trade, theatres, stately homes, the list is endless.

Address coupons undoubtedly increase response. Your ad need give no more than the bare bones to entice custom. Fuller details, no doubt with decent illustrations, will follow on receipt of that little coupon. Experience has shown that the larger the coupon (within reason) the better the response. Many people do not have nice neat writing and genuinely have difficulty in getting their name and address in little boxes. You have to make it easy for them. If they have to hunt for a piece of paper and enveloped to reply, many people will put it off and forget. Put a nice enquiry coupon on the bottom of the ad and many will fill it in there and then. If you want to use a coupon, position is important. Coupons printed in the 'gutter' or binding of the journal are more difficult to get at and decrease response, whereas the best place is a convenient right-hand bottom edge. 'L'-shaped ads are also worth a run with the coupon as the 'toe'.

You'll get your fair share of loonies — 'Mickey Mouse', 'Mrs Thatcher' — of course. The harder ones to spot are educated children filling in for things they *would* like. Every encyclopaedia salesman can tell of weary evenings going round housing estates to find that Tommy has been indulging in wishful thinking.

When you've been at this lark for some time you will develop a nose for the spurious enquirer. The postcode will be wrong or the franking on the envelope does not marry up with the reader's address. Keeps you on your toes.

MONITOR FOR RESULTS

Log all your returned and keyed coupons plus all your telephone enquiries in a *sales enquiry book*. Columns should be ruled for every method of promotion you undertake so that a check can be kept on advertising expenditure. Make sure you include 'personal recommendations'.

You can check response in a number of ways:

1. You ask. On the phone after taking details say, 'Oh, by the way, how did you come to hear of us?' Most people are only too pleased to let you know.
2. Keying all your ads (see page 168).
3. Printing a line of boxes on your order form, one for each medium.

> It will be very helpful if you would please indicate where you saw the advertisement:
>
> *Exchange & Mart* □
> *Radio Times* □
> *Practical Householder* □
> *The Observer* □
> You are an existing customer. □

Watch the conversion rate. One ad may pull a lot of enquiries but few orders. Prune accordingly.

POSITION

The position of your ad is very important. The best and most expensive places are the covers. These are usually booked up for some time ahead and are probably beyond the reach of most small firms.

Local papers love to run features on everything from spring weddings to changing your car. The editorial matter is sometimes painfully thin. The sprat is to hook advertisers to buy space round the article. Be wary. It's your money they're after.

There are different schools of thought about whether a right- or left-hand page is better. Next time you pick up a magazine see which way you flick the pages: from the back or the front.

A good spot is next to the *reader's reply service* if they run one. Cheapest position is 'run of paper' (ROP) which is anywhere the make-up man can fit it in.

Trade directories and year-books are rarely worth advertising in. Some trades have thousands of entries. How are you going to get noticed? Unless you can get the spine or the bookmark then forget it.

SIZE IS NOT EVERYTHING

Research has shown that ads do not pull in proportion to their size. A whole page does not produce twice the number of responses as half a page, but only about 70 per cent more and so on pro rata. That's a comforting thought to those on limited budgets.

By extension I would rather have two one-eighth pages placed separately in the journal than just a single quarter page. This gives scope for trying different messages in the same journal and testing your ideas quickly. Alternatively, I believe you will get a better run for your money by spreading the campaign over a long period than sinking it in bigger ads over a shorter period, unless your objective is to make quick sales. The old adage generally holds true: repetition is reputation.

How do you say it?

Having covered some of the techniques I must come back to the language you use. Advertising is salesmanship in print. The most successful adverts have been those in the language we speak and use every day. It's the natural way. Just because you go into print doesn't change the manner of presentation. You're not a script writer for the six o'clock news. Forget about that classical pun or double entendre. You must think about the *product*, your *audience* and what the customer *needs*. Those are the three vital elements. Avoid words that have become distorted or played out through over-use: fantastic offer, unrepeatable bargain, exceptional opportunity, and unique. Would you use those words in speech? Try and find something *new* to say in your copy. Make it interesting and lead the reader on — inform. Nobody reads dull ads. Always be truthful and don't make claims you can't substantiate. Wild and extravagant claims will be seen to be just that. People must believe in the product.

Write in the present tense and assume the consumer already has the product.

'This hedge trimmer will save you hours of arm-aching work.' Better is: 'This hedge trimmer saves you . . .'.

Don't talk in terms of price — talk about *value* and worth. The price of a pressure cooker may be £20 (or rather £19.95), but its value is a saving in time to the busy housewife, a reduction in fuel bills and a versatile extra pot for the imaginative chef. There is a saving in vitamins as well. A product can be dressed up in seductive packaging to seem worth many times the price asked. The humble electric drill is worth hours of sweat over the old primitive hammer and chisel method of knocking holes in a wall. It is an absolute boon to the home handyman.

David St John Thomas (of David & Charles) tells of the care needed in designing a book. The pages must be carefully weighted to give the right feel, and to be seen to be worth the price asked. Books can be dramatically thick or thin depending on the paper and binding chosen yet still have the same content.

It is often in this critical area of how you present value that sales are made or lost.

Cooperative advertising

Newcomers to marketing quickly realise that more than half the cost of promotion often lies in the idea and origination. It is not much more expensive to order 5000 leaflets than 1000. How much better then to club together and form cooperative groups and attack the market under one heading or brand name. The motor trade have done this for years. When a new model is launched the manufacturer buys a large amount of space and gets the dealers to buy a portion of the ad for their own location. Collectively, perhaps 30 dealers in the franchise can make more impact than any one individually.

It works particularly well in the tourist trade. Farm holiday operators can form a group in a region and produce a joint leaflet, but only one reference point is given for bookings. It is a simple matter for one person to allocate parties to separate farmhouses and it makes booking quite attractive for the clients.

The same thing can be done for other tourist attractions. A town or region can produce its own tourist guide covering all the attractions — hotels, guest houses, camping sites, tea rooms, historic houses, museums etc. Together they can make it seem an area bursting full of delights and draw tourists in. Hotels can form a chain and pass bookings on without any other formal linking.

One street in Oxford that is a little way out of the centre has produced its own booklet listing the attractions. This is freely available in information centres and undoubtedly must pull in a large number of strangers to the city. There are lots of opportunities in cooperative advertising that have been barely touched. Garages that rent out part of their forecourt to allied activities like valeting, van hire, trailer manufacture etc could combine to draw more prospects to their doors. Non-competing industrial products could be combined in mailings and part of the packaging can be sold to other producers to advertise their products.

The whole attraction of this field lies in gaining more mileage for your money.

Project a corporate image

You may be a brand new small firm but you can still have a corporate image. This grand term describes the face you present to the world, usually in terms of printed material — posters, letter-heads, sales tickets, brochures and signs — all of which conform to a master plan. Some extend the term to describe the company philosophy — the *corporate identity* — that covers staff selection, training and attitudes. Clean overalls, perhaps with the firm's name on the pocket, are effective if they are regularly laundered. Small firms are usually content to stop at the printed matter.

It is your house style. The same colours will be used for print, van, even uniforms. There will be a single style of lettering and logo.

Most firms grow haphazardly. The first item of print is

Company stationery projects the corporate image.

invariably a business card, often produced in a rush, sometimes by a friend. Little thought is given to style. Letter-heads and invoices follow, perhaps from another printer, who will produce his own version. And so it goes on.

How much more professional if it were all planned from the start! Strangely enough, it hardly costs any more, but your image is greatly enhanced. There is a feeling of hanging together, belonging in one family. People recognise your literature without actually reading it. Try it yourself. We all recognise the Ford or Boots sign long before we can actually read the word, as the shape and outline are familiar.

Presentation is very important. For mail order, where the customers never see the proprietor, the sales letter, design and weight of paper are vital. It always depresses me to see good products under-sold. For small runs — 5000 or so — the cost differential between a good paper and a poor one is slight but the advantages enormous.

WHAT'S IN A NAME?
Corporate image starts with the *trading name*. Many proprietors simply trade under their own name. Fine. If you are well-known locally, why throw away that advantage? Otherwise try and convey in the title what you are doing. Somerset Wholesale is not very illuminating but Somerset Electrics is better. 'Crafts' is becoming a bit of an overworked word. If you are only dealing in your own locality build a local feature into your title.

A memorable title without being too obscure is worth aiming for.

Business cards should be brief and encapsulate your activities. Thermographic printing used to be the rage. This is a method of raising the surface of the lettering which was (and still is) expensive. It is said that sharp buyers used to refuse to see reps who called without producing the superior card.

There are several firms who will print your picture (if you are vain) on the card as well as your name to help recall. Better perhaps to portray your product. Flashy cards can be supplied on metal, photo-etched or on gold and silver foil. Take your time and look around.

COLOURS
Colour is important. Browns, greens and yellow generally denote rural simplicity not to say folksiness. The deep purples, reds and black generate wealth and opulence. The dayglo

colours should be left to trendy sock manufacturers. If you are an exporter check that the theme colour you are using means the same thing abroad. White in Japan means death. Packages for display in supermarkets should be sensitive to the lighting.

DON'T HIDE YOUR LIGHT

Few firms have no form of transport but there are a lot of anonymous grey vans running about: trade vehicles with all that lovely bare space demand imaginative signwriting. People pay good money to have their name on a bus. You have the choice of a vinyl stick-on or magnetic sign that can be transferred from van to van. This does make it easier to resell but tends to be rather utilitarian. Estate cars can carry a board in the rear side windows.

Once you've paid for the display — keep it clean.

A painter and decorator asked me to help once. I asked about his board and he ruefully produced a filthy battered object with one side hanging off. Not the best advertisement for his trade.

Put your visitors at their ease. Display some product samples or pictures of completed work in the reception so they can learn about you. If you don't manage to sell them anything first time at least they'll go away with a pleasant image of harmony, competence and professionalism.

Keep the outside of the building swept and free from rubbish. Tidy the front office and don't let mechanics sit on the front office chairs in their greasy overalls. That visitor may 'only' be a rep — but he'll carry away an image of the firm that could make or mar your business. He could even be that buyer you've been trying to hook.

PREMISES SIGNS – WHAT YOU'RE ALLOWED TO DO

Signs outside the premises are also important for your image but are often neglected. Every potential businessman should try acting as postman for a week. It is important that your premises are clearly signed. The planning authorities control what you are allowed to display through the Advertisement Regulations (part of the Town and Country Planning Acts). Some signs are deemed exempt from control. These are:

1. An advertisement sign on your own premises giving the name and description of what you do. To avoid putting in an application, the highest part of the sign must be below the first floor window sill. In certain Areas of Special Control — conservation areas for example — the area of the

Examples of good signs

sign must not exceed 10 per cent of the wall surface up to 12 feet above the ground.

2. You are allowed two signs if there are two frontages to your premises.

3. Do not use letters or figures more than 2 ft 6 in high (or 1 foot in an Area of Special Control).

4. A single flag-pole (why not?).

Illumination requires permission.

Highway signs are something else. Tourist enterprises in particular rely on clear advance warning and directional signs to pull in passing trade. There is invariably conflict between the highways department (at County Hall), the owner of the business, local planning officers and the inevitable do-gooders in the village. Apart from certain permitted signs for stately homes, youth hostels, licensed caravan sites and the like, *all* other directional signs need planning permission. Practice seems to vary between counties, and even districts on how blind an eye they turn to rogue signs. You stand more chance of success if you produce a well designed sign, not too flamboyant or large, placed in a friendly farmer's field rather than the highway itself. Never tack it to a telegraph pole or highway signpost. Signs on the highway, as distinct from the other side of a hedge or ditch, are controlled by the highways department who tend to take a much stricter view than the local planning authorities.

Your county tourist officer may have worked out an official policy on paying for authorised signs. In consultation with the highway men (I don't mean it like that) they may allow you to pay for a proper blue and white sign. You have to convince them that there is a reasonable throughput of visitors and that people would have difficulty finding you otherwise. As ever, road safety is paramount.

I should add that every planning officer dreads questions on the Regulations. They are terribly involved and arguments often centre around the minutiae.

Buying print

Your corporate image depends largely on the quality of your printed matter. Printers are a fortunate breed. Every business needs them. If it's only a humble business card and a letterheading then a printer has a job. Unfortunately, a mystique has grown up around printing which the industry has no interest in dispelling. Despite advances in electronics, the printed word is likely to remain the main method of communication for sales and marketing techniques for some time to come. Printers come in all shapes and sizes. Top of the list are the book printers who can turn a roll of paper into a paperback on one machine. Like the rotary presses of Fleet Street, these goliaths need to produce thousands of copies in one operation to make them economic. At the other end of the scale are back-room part-timers with a Roneo turning out the parish magazine or raffle ticket. It is important to understand that 'horses for courses' was rarely more true than for print.

THE JOBBING PRINTER

Always ask to see samples of a printer's work. You will only get a feel of his technical ability, flair and level in the market by studying completed jobs. You may not be aware yourself what good print looks like or how a simple leaflet can be turned into an attractive, arresting piece of propaganda.

Unfortunately, many small jobbing printers have been crushed to boredom by years of churning out jumble sale leaflets and school programmes. They've forgotten how to dress up a mundane product with a bit of sharp artwork. Their type books were bought 30 years ago. Everything has the same ruled border. And don't talk about colours other than black! Perhaps it is unfair to blame printers too much. The margins are very slim at that end of the game and the client is usually only interested in one thing — the cost.

THE KEY TO GOOD PRINT
If you don't know what good printing is go and see some *graphic designers*, the freelance variety.

They have to live by their skills and most are way ahead of your back-street printer. The cost of printing lies largely in the origination — the artwork, design and preparation for the camera. The actual machine time is of less importance unless you are into long runs. Once you have the artwork this forms the basis for all your printing. The letter-heading design can be carried through to your business card, invoices, compliment slips, delivery notes, packaging etc. You may get years of use out of some original designs.

DISCUSS THE PURPOSE
Printers will usually tailor the job to your price providing a sensible job can be done. Let your printer know your budget. He will ask the purpose of the job: no point in running expensive handbills if they are to be given away at a children's funfair.

Paper sizes will be discussed, and weight and surface. You have the choice of one ink colour (usually black) or several. Sometimes the addition of just one 'spot' colour will highlight part of a brochure very effectively.

You could well use several printers for different items. Few small printers handle colour work and large firms would rather not know about business cards or letter-headings. They will possibly take it on, sub it out and add a handling charge.

Don't be mean with printing costs. Most of this book is geared to harbouring your money but I don't believe that pounds skimped on print is ever worth while. It shows. This is not to say that every job needs the full colour treatment — far from it — use the most appropriate image. Full colour brochures will be expected for an up-market kitchen designer but a handbill giving notice of an opening sale can be treated more economically. Think hard about the number of leaflets that you will need. The first 1000 will be the most expensive because they must bear all the costs of artwork, colour separations, plate making etc. The run on will be considerably cheaper, perhaps two-thirds of the first cost. There is no point in running back to the printer each time you want a further batch. You will be paying for setting-up time, cleaning down the machine, folding and guillotining on each occasion. Work out a sensible requirement for the next 12 months.

HOW TO COMPARE COSTS

When estimating, visit several printers and ask for a quote but on a written basis. It is unfair to compare without explicit instructions covering the text (number of words), size and weight of paper, number of pages, illustrations, binding etc.

If you are happy with his stock type-face you'll save time and money, otherwise the work will have to be sent to a trade setter.

If you are supplying the copy will it be 'camera ready' or are you expecting him to lay it out?

But price is not everything. What is the delivery like? Is he reliable? Above all, can you detect flair?

PLAN AHEAD

Never say you want the job done 'as soon as possible'. All jobs are like that. It will simply go to the bottom of the pile. Give the poor man sufficient time to plan his work and do the job justice. Remember he has to set from your copy, deal with any illustrations, perhaps order the paper, put out the colour separations, line up a binder and allow you time to proof-read and correct any alterations.

As with most things a little planning goes a long way. When you book space at an exhibition think about what extra sales literature you will need.

A one-colour leaflet shouldn't take more than 10 days. If the printer can't do it before then — move on. Be a bit careful of these instant print shops springing up on every street corner. They tend to be managed by people who have had a crash course and the quality and originality are rarely there. Their prices are sometimes not that cheap either.

Half the mistakes occur with poorly prepared copy. The temptation is to get it away to the printer and feel it is 'under way'. You will only be compounding your errors if you do so. Always give *typewritten* copy to your printer. Keep corrections to the absolute minimum.

Corrections before platemaking are usually simple. Never

proof-read on the printer's premises unless it is a very simple job. Take the proof home to a quiet room. Check and recheck. There is nothing worse than having a misspelling staring at you after the job has run. Double check phone numbers. And don't just check from your typing — check with your source. You may have transposed a number. The printer should provide a slip to say that you have proof-read so there can be no dispute later.

Don't forget to match your leaflets to a standard envelope. There's nothing more infuriating than folding a nice brochure into a tight envelope. With increased paper standardisation this problem is not as frequent as it once was, but occasionally a designer will come up with a very long or wide design that will give problems in the post.

Price-lists are better printed on a separate sheet and slipped into a brochure. Otherwise, what do you do with perfectly good stock when the prices go up? Alter your nice leaflet in biro or throw the lot away?

If you need an elaborate *brochure* ask for a dummy to be made up and get the feel of it. Weigh it against the postage steps.

There are two alternatives to full colour. Print on a tinted paper with two colours for text and headlines. Don't overdo the tint. If you have a limited requirement then a very reasonable choice is real photographs stuck on a plain printed leaflet. The cost can be as low as £5 a hundred from a photo laboratory.

At its simplest level there are several instant art books available where you snip out a design and paste it up.

HUSBAND YOUR ARTWORK

Keep rigid control of all your artwork and illustrations. Unless anything is said to the contrary you should retain ownership. Original artwork can suddenly assume almost priceless proportions in an emergency. With most jobs now produced photographically, the artwork and text *must* be perfect. The camera will not hide imperfections — it will magnify them. Unless you are a graphic designer leave production of the artwork to a freelance or printer. Letraset may look simple but you can still produce a less than perfect finish. All your origination must be first class — colour work demands excellent transparencies and this usually means employing a professional photographer. Take photocopies of what you have sent to the printer so that when he rings up with a query you know what he is on about.

Don't handle the artwork more than absolutely necessary. It must be kept spotless. Take copies, then anyone can scrawl all over them.

Some printing terms

While any knowledge is dangerous, the following common terms may help you to communicate better with your printer.

Artwork: The general term for the output of a studio — graphics, illustrations etc. *Camera-ready artwork* means everything laid out and pasted up ready for the camera.

Bleed. Not a nursing term but an extension of the print area to the edge of the page, in fact beyond, as the excess will be trimmed off: hence 'bleed off'. Usually used with a solid colour or photo.

Colour separation. Photographic copying through colour filters to provide (usually) four negatives from which colour blocks or plates will be made. The quality of colour work depends largely on the skill with which the separations are matched and balanced.

Copy. Textual matter provided for typesetting; the 'body'.

Four-page cover. A baffling term — refers to the cover of a brochure which wraps around front and back. It comprises four pages referred to as cover 1 (the front), cover 2 (inside front cover), cover 3 (inside back cover), and cover 4 (outside back cover).

Half-tones. Black and white illustrations that have been photographed through a screen and a block or plate made. The size of screen will determine the quality of the finished article, depending on the paper used.

Justified type. Type which is spaced to leave straight edges on both margins. Formerly used for all printed matter but it is now quite common to see much of today's material (except books) left unjustified on the right, ie ranged left. Some (expensive) typewriters will produce justified type. Occasionally the left-hand margin only will be left unjustified — called 'justified right' or 'ranged right': regarded as 'arty'.

Landscape. Illustration in which the width exceeds the height; 'portrait' is the reverse.

Letterpress can be likened to your John Bull printing outfit as it uses raised type individually set by hand and clamped in a forme, or frame. Alterations are more easily made than with litho but still cost money as it is time-consuming to go back. Dying out, but has its uses.

Lower case. Small letters, not CAPITALS (or caps) which are called upper case.

Offset litho. The most widely used method of printing today. A thin metal (or occasionally paper) plate is photochemically prepared from your artwork or text via a process camera. Once the plate is made there can be no alterations to it, so corrections must be made early on if great expense is not to be incurred.

Page. In printers' terms one surface of a sheet, thus one sheet of paper equals two pages. Be careful when numbering. Technically, every page will be counted even if not printed, so the front cover of a paper-covered brochure will be page 1 and the first right-hand interior page will be number 3. Bad numbering causes mistakes!

Paste up. The process of assembling all the artwork elements of the page — text (or copy), headings, illustrations, borders and rulings.

Perfect binding. The final process after printing that glues the pages into the cover. Often carried out by a specialist trade finisher.

Plate. Thin aluminium-coated sheet that carries the image used in litho printing. Cheaper paper plates can be used for short runs, but it shows.

Print size. The measure of type size. 72 points make 1 inch, so 6 point type is 1/12 inch high. Different measures may be used overseas.

Proof. The first sheet of the finished set job, to be read through for mistakes.

Ream. 500 sheets.

Reverse type. Type which is reversed out, ie, white lettering on a black background. Harder to read, especially in small letters.

Saddle stitched. The common form of stapling a leaflet on the centre fold, unlike stab-stitch where pages are stapled near the left-hand edge.

Screen. A glass screen inserted between the process camera and the photo to produce the negative for plate or block making. This breaks up the picture into dots (or occasionally whorls) or lines. The higher the screen number the finer the screen.

Type-face. The style or design of the type. Times Roman, Helvetica, Univers etc. Type also comes in different *weights* or thickness. This book is set in 11 point Baskerville.

Photography

Closely allied to printing is photography. You will need photographs of your product for your leaflets and when you come to exploit the media, but photography is a specialist field and not for the Instamatic user (sorry, Kodak). Black and white prints will probably fulfil most of your requirements and *outside* shots can be taken by most practised amateurs. Use black and white film, not colour film printed in black and white. The normal rules of photography need to be followed. Get close in, avoid fussy backgrounds, show some human interest, beware reflections and shadows. Most important are prints of good contrast (muddy prints don't reproduce) and needle sharpness.

Above all, make photos interesting and tell a story. I can recall a major company sending in a photo of their latest export order. It showed a pile of crates on the dockside! Goodness knows what was inside.

Interiors are much more tricky. Lighting needs to be professionally managed. Some objects such as jewellery, glassware and architectural models are extremely difficult to bring to life. Anything involving machine processes requires a lot of experience to make interesting. The standard retirement presentation is invariably depicted with the managing director and old faithful staring into camera.

Black and white prints need to be no larger than half-plate size (or 5 by 7 in), glossy and double weight. Colour magazines need transparencies. Don't send B&W printed newspapers, transparencies or colour prints and expect the publisher to take a B&W print off it. Keep staples and pins well away from prints. Use a self-adhesive label on the back of the photo with the details to identify it: never write directly on the back. It may show through or transfer to the next print, particularly if it is resin coated.

Photographers tend to work alone. Go for a commercial or industrial specialist rather than the home town weddings man. As usual, ask to see samples of his work. *Try* and retain the negatives otherwise you'll have to go back to him for continual reprints. Some tend to charge a fairly high fee for this whereas if you have kept the negatives you can then go direct to a local photo laboratory. If you are really impoverished, go along to the local amateur photographic club. There are bound to be some keen lads looking for some revenue to offset an expensive hobby. But, as in life, you get what you pay for.

Finally, if you are in the field of producing one-offs, be it furniture or specialist joinery, pictures or pots, build up a port-folio of *record* shots that you can show future customers. Get yourself a salesman's sample book, the photo album approach, which you can produce and carry around with you. It will be invaluable as the years go by.

Chapter 4

Public Relations

Previous chapters have hinted at what most of us do without thinking — try and present a favourable image to the world. PR is the fancy name for this commonsense activity. To the purist it is 'a conscious planned campaign of informed communications to induce a favourable climate of opinion'. By itself it is not a selling medium but can prepare the way for an advertising campaign. PR and advertising often work side by side. It should project your corporate image.

Internal and external PR

Good PR can be internal and external.

Internal PR means keeping the work-force informed, involved and happy. It implies good communications between management and the lads: there should never be a 'them and us' feeling. It is surely better that they know from you what is happening to the firm rather than pick up rumours in the pub. Your own employees should be the best advocates: if they can't project the business, who can?

It was probably the Japanese who first brought in a set period for discussion each month for management to outline the company's plans. It is the time for you as boss to encourage a no holds barred debate on the problems and solutions to progress. You should encourage openness by talking about orders in the pipeline, targets to be attained, prospects that are being chased.

Then is the time for you to shut up and listen. Everyone from the youngest recruit to the foreman has something to contribute. There is nearly always a better way of doing things and often those performing the actual task are the best ones to ask. Encourage suggestions and pay for any cost savings. Make everyone feel important and that they have a part to play. The time may come when you have a vital deadline to meet and require Sunday or bank holiday working. Without staff loyalty and involvement you will always find it an uphill struggle.

External PR is largely involved with using the media to good effect. Never lose the chance to publicise the firm's activities. It need be only one paragraph tucked away on an inside page. A regular mention will retain your name in the public eye. It need not cost a lot of money — just a little time and keeping an eye to the news value.

You *can* employ a professional firm of consultants but really you, as a small businessman, are the best person to perform that task. You know all about your activities and after a little practice in writing press releases the chore should become easier. PR is all about contacts. There are plenty of freelance journalists and writers about who can help you if you still feel timorous. Compared with the technicalities of advertising, PR is much simpler.

PR objectives

All your PR activity should have a planned objective. Think of the people whom you wish to influence: they are your target audience in the same way that advertising defines your market. If your market is defence equipment there is little point in cultivating the local free sheet. The public you are seeking to influence could be the local council, factory neighbours, buyers and consumers, your banker and your employees. The information you put out should be strictly factual and not an attempt to gloss over some shortcoming in your service. Too often 'a spokesman said' is the ill-considered front for some disaster.

PR should be planned on a long-term basis: it is not something that can be generated overnight. Frequently it involves showing social responsibility — providing heaters for flood victims or drawing paper for the local kindergarten. The costs involved need not be large, it is the thought that counts. At present the farming community does not have a good image. The public in general thinks of the destruction of hedges, straw burning and butter mountains and relates all that to the cost of the Common Market. Instead of concentrating on the efficiency of farm production in this country and benefits in terms of self-sufficiency and low food costs, the media have been obsessed with broiler chickens and nature conservation. Whoever handles the PR for the National Farmers' Union has a long struggle.

PR for the local community can take the form of modest sponsorship for the school lollipop ladies, old folk's outings, 'keep our village tidy' bins, loan of the firm's pick-up truck for the cricket team roller and all sorts of other innocent causes.

The small business columns of your local papers are always ready to print good news that shows your efforts in a favourable light. There is so much gloom in the country that a cheerful item should find ready acceptance.

Understanding the media industry

To get maximum impact from your PR activities it is important to know how the media go about their job. It is a sophisticated and highly fragmented industry with considerable expertise at your disposal if you know how to tap into it.

You should first understand that, with the exception of the national press, the local media (press, radio and television) have very small news-gathering staff. They rely on being fed stories from the community.

All operate broadly in the same way, ie they all have reporters, sub-editors, a news desk and an editor who decides the overall balance. Where they differ is how they like the news presented and in the matter of deadlines. Unless you have a major story it is rarely worth sending to the national papers. The exceptions are the increasing number of specialist columns on women's interests, food, motoring and the small-business page. They will pick up very small-firm happenings if there is a good story with a message.

The centre of any paper is the news desk. The editor lays down the house style and the journalists write in that vein. Short punchy sentences with no long words will tend to be used in the popular tabloids. More in-depth detail and analysis are the prerogative of the heavies.

The sub-editors are the linchpins. They cut and rewrite the stories (if they have the time) to fit the space available. That is where the pressure is. You may come across researchers (particularly for the BBC) who work some way ahead of the programme, digging out background material. The lowest are the cub reporters who get lumbered with attending the local council meetings, quarter sessions and MPs' fête openings. Every paper has its 'stringers'. These are freelance journalists who feed several papers, and possibly a national, with their own local news.

THE LOCAL PRESS IS THE MOST IMPORTANT
Everyone reads the local press because, unless we're hermits, we

like to know what's going on in the area. Where's that by-pass going and did Councillor Harris really pass building tenders to his brother-in-law? While Fleet Street has faltered, the local and regional press have gone from strength to strength. They've been the first to instal modern machinery and to some extent keep clear of the worst Fleet Street practices. Apart from the gossip news the pull of local papers lies in its advertising. The classified small-ads are a mine of information to bargain hunters. However, one threat has been an explosion of free sheets — pure advertising hand-outs with a minimum of editorial. This is often bought in as a ready-made 'drop in' feature. The proprietor simply pastes up a 'Wedding Page' or 'Motoring Tips' and then persuades local traders to buy space around it. The local press are countering this by launching free sheets of their own.

Newspaper proprietors are in business just like you and are out to make a profit by increasing sales. They will not achieve this if the stories are stale, inept or inaccurate.

WHAT THEY'RE LOOKING FOR

What makes news? Topicality, originality, personality and sometimes humour. You must find a *topical peg* to hang the story on. It's not news that your business is making, say, coffins, but it will be if it's your tenth anniversary or you have just taken on your fiftieth employee, or sold your thousandth coffin or had an order from Russia . . . . There's a story everywhere if you look with a journalist's eye.

I once put out a story that a local cabinet-maker had made magicians' tricks as a sideline for years. That by itself was not news. The impact was that his main customer was giving a show at the local theatre. The regional TV station wanted to lock him up in one of his own trunks! The story got him half a page plus picture and many nice direct quotes. All for free.

The only space where you can get away with a less noteworthy story is the local features page. Many papers have a women's page, craft or business section where an in-depth story can be laid out, but these opportunities are rare.

The press release: telling the media

It is perhaps not generally realised how much of a paper's output comes in unsolicited. Many reports are straight reprints of stories that are fed in. These come in the form of press releases sent in by individuals, associations and firms. Because the press work to deadlines, *your* news stands more chance of getting printed if you observe some basic ground rules.

1. The item should be *typed* on a sheet of A4 paper headed up 'Press Release' or 'Press Information'. Address it to the 'News Editor', 'Newsdesk' or a named journalist.
2. Double spacing should be used to allow room for alterations at the desk. Wide margins should also be used for instructions to the printer. Keep to one side of the page. Paragraphs should not be broken at the end of a page.
3. Date it and put a headline on to identify it. Don't worry over much about a witty gem of a headline. Invariably the sub-editors will write their own even if yours is brilliant.
4. Most stories can be told in three paragraphs. The meat should come in the first one. If space is short then the sub's blue pencil will delete from the bottom. Even if the bulk of the story is cut, at least the main facts will get printed. The first paragraph must say 'Who, what, why, when and where', and succeeding paras can expand and colour the detail.

   The papers are always looking for fillers — short items that can be dropped in at the end of a column. A brief story has a very good chance of getting published as it stands, if it is simply written in plain English.
5. Your story should contain at least one direct quotation or comment. Not from that dreary spokesman but a named individual of some standing or relevance.
6. Keep it simple and write for the readership. Reserve technical jargon for the technical press who will understand, indeed require, the detail. In the popular press an announcement that an improved car jack has been produced can simply state that it will aid the elderly. Motoring magazines will want to know whether it is hydraulic, pneumatic, what psi it will work to, if it's of chromed steel or a painted pressing.
7. Abbreviations are the bane of life today. Some, but only a few, are well enough known not to need spelling out but most will. NATO or EEC are all right but NUT (National Union of Teachers) or MAA (Motor Agents' Association) will take the full spelling. Every industry has its jargon and you should remember that *what is familiar to you may be incomprehensible to your readers*. You need only to spell it out the first time — successive mentions can be left as abbreviations. You can also get round it by saying: 'The

P H Coate & Son   **Willow Grower and Merchant**

PRESS RELEASE

Japan buys Somerset baskets

A small firm of Somerset basket makers has just won its first export order to Japan for 150 baskets. PH Coate and Son of Stoke St Gregory, near Taunton, employ only four basket makers although several more work in cultivating and processing the willow that grows all round this quiet village.

One of the partners Chris Coate says, 'Our industry has been decimated by imports from the Far East and today we are down to perhaps a tenth of the size from before the war. Imported baskets tend to use split cane and willow, and although they can be more ornate than ours, they definitely don't last as long. We believe they liked the rugged strength of the traditional Somerset basket.' Coates won the order from Hankyu a large department store at a trade show in Bristol. As they ordered 15 different types, from picnic hampers, bread trays, log baskets and fruit pickers, Coates are hoping that more orders will follow from the best selling lines.

PH Coates are no strangers to exports in other fields. For some years they have been developing markets for artists' charcoal also made out of the willow that they grow. They have been supplying the national names for some time but in the last three years their high quality product has been boxed under their own brand to eight countries. Willow growing is now almost exclusively found in England in a small area to the east of Taunton, centred around Athelney where Alfred burnt the cakes. As the craft is still entirely produced by hand, Alfred would appreciate the skills today.

ENDS

Enc 1 photo of basket maker.

Further details from: Chris Coate, PH Coate & Son, Meare Green, Stoke St Gregory, Taunton. Tel North Curry 490249.

mineworkers' president, Mr Arthur Scargill' rather than 'Mr Arthur Scargill, president of the National Union of Mineworkers'.

8. The local press can be distressingly parochial. The classic story of 'local man lost at sea' instead of '*Titanic* sinks' has its parallels today. They are more likely to print a story if you can tie in to a local dignitary or personality. My local paper is obsessed with everything that the Mayor does. The poor fellow can hardly blow his nose without a picture appearing. If you can rope him in somehow you're almost guaranteed coverage.

9. An *embargo* is a request to the press not to publish before a stated date. You can put an embargo on your release to prevent prior announcement of your earth-shattering speech, but at the same time alert the press to be ready for it. In practice it can be abused for trivial reasons. There is no point embargoing a church fête opening but there could be some point at a new product launch. With differing copy deadlines it is sometimes helpful to issue a release to a variety of media safe in the knowledge that most will play the game. It is helpful to them if they are given advance notice of a major announcement or personality appearance. At the top of your release it should therefore say either 'Release immediate' or 'Embargoed till 12.00 July 31st'. Use the device sparingly.

10. Finish with a contact for more information. Give a phone number at work and out of hours. This will tend to be used only if a gap appears in a radio broadcast schedule and a journalist is looking for more detail.

11. All the media work to strict *deadlines*. Be aware that if you ask television crews to appear in the middle of the afternoon you will be very unlikely to make the six o'clock news or magazine programmes. Many locals sold on a Friday are printed on a Tuesday or Wednesday morning. A release that fails to make it by then will probably be spiked — a euphemism for 'filed for later use'. The national dailies, of course, have more flexibility and often have several editions. At the other end of the scale many colour supplements and monthly journals have a cut-off date six weeks in advance. If you're planning a Christmas story think ahead.

That covers the basics, now let's look at what and how to write.

WHAT MAKES A GOOD PRESS RELEASE?

You must steer away from *selling* your firm and product, and write *news*. Anything else is advertising and will be discarded. You're not writing an advert, you're telling a story to interest the readers. A simple attractive statement of facts is all that is needed. Cut out the waffle and come to the point in the first sentence. Nobody's going to wade through six paragraphs to find out who did what and when. Editors are busy men — they just won't bother.

The *introduction* is the most vital part. You should ask yourself, 'Will it make the reader want to read on?' Avoid detail and side-tracks. The paragraphs should have bite and flow. Keep the sentences reasonably short. State the main point of the story early on and isolate the news. For example: *not* 'Delegates from 20 countries watched as the Lord Mayor opened the first International Congress of Snuff Taking at the Wigmore Hall', *say* 'The First International Congress of Snuff Taking was opened today by the . . .'.

Quotations from your speaker should never open the story. The reader's impression of the *value* of the remark entirely depends on the standing of the personality. You must know *who* is speaking before any weight is put on the reported remarks. 'British coal is too dear,' announced by Arthur Scargill would be sensational but the same remark by the Electricity Board Chairman would be more understandable. Put the speaker's name first. There is another rule to remember: statements of *opinion* should be printed in quotes " " or ' ', statements of *fact* should be left alone.

Don't say: 'Small firm bankruptcies exceeded 5000 a month for the first time in 1983,' said Ron Parker, Chamber of Trade Chairman. Instead say: Ron Parker, Chairman of the Chamber of Trade, declared that small firm bankruptcies exceeded 5000 a month for the first time in 1983.

Watch the tenses when changing a statement into reported speech. Avoid starting the story with a present participle or 'As', eg, saying, telling, announcing etc. It's a poor way to begin. 'Announcing the start of the Round Britain Wheelbarrow Race, the Sports Minister foretold a big demand for cornplasters'.

Finally, try and keep lengthy titles, official bodies and complicated names out of the introduction. Write with a light touch and save the essential details (if any) until further on in the piece. Don't discourage your readers too soon.

Good pictures are always welcome

Every picture is worth half a page of text if it's a good bright subject. News photos are definitely best left to the professionals. Editors are always on the look-out for good examples. They must be glossy prints, double weight and of good contrast. And make sure they are sharp! Seven inches by five is quite large enough. Don't forget to label the reverse of the photo when sending it in. Modern resin coated prints don't accept many inks and ball point pens show through. If you forget to identify the print, your release and the photo will separate in a busy newspaper office and ne'er the twain will meet. Use a self-adhesive label on the back and never use pins or staples. Paper-clips are the only practical method of attaching the print to the press release.

If the story is strong enough the paper will send its own photographer. Don't forget to ask for several copies — always useful.

Once in a lifetime you'll come across a scoop picture. Always keep a camera in the car. Fleet Street will readily process the film for you immediately if you tell them what you've got. A member of the public did that once when Labour leader George Brown ran his Jag into a bus — rotten luck for G Brown but rewarding for the amateur photographer.

Occasionally a *press pack* is called for. This is not just the release but supporting literature on the firm, background notes on the directors, product leaflets and photographs. Wrap it up in a nice folder. There are several specialist binder firms who can do a very professional looking job on very short runs using hot melt glue or slide binders. Save it for the *big* occasion. Press packs can tend to be pretentious.

KEEPING UP THE MOMENTUM
Once you start getting results you'll want to keep it going. Try and find a story regularly for the local press and get to know your local journalists and editors. Perhaps there is a news agency in your town that sends stories off to the media. They can be very helpful as they earn their money by the number of lines that get published or seconds on the air. If they do their job properly they will be on intimate terms with all the right people. There's no charge to you.

Always be frank and helpful and *available*. If they ring you and you're at a meeting, make sure you always ring back. This applies even more so in adverse times. Don't pump them with material in good times and expect them to print it if, when a bad story breaks, you pass a 'No comment'. The local press in particular will rarely wish to knock a local firm. They know that jobs and prestige are at stake. They are very much part of the community themselves.

Most important: always be truthful. Half-truths will always get found out.

One company near me *always* gets a piece in the paper every week. It can be something as riveting as one of their drivers being awarded a ten years' accident free certificate or a gold watch presentation. It's rarely of desperate news value – they happen to have an active press officer.

On the other hand, I've been told that if you overdo it then when a press release with something really of value comes in it may well be overlooked. You've got to *study* your media and learn what style of items get printed. If your paper habitually prints trivia then make the most of it. You're simply keeping the firm's name in the public eye and for the price of a stamp that can't be bad.

THE TRADE PRESS
Research has shown that 40 per cent of buying decisions made in large firms are based on information gathered from the trade and technical press. It is therefore very important that you regularly send press releases to your relevant journal. Details of how to find them are given on pages 42-4.

For these journals you can spell out the technical performance in the expectation that the readership will not only understand but wish to know more, particularly if it's a new product.

But still don't fall into the trap of writing a 'puff' for the product. The *advertising* manager will be more interested in grabbing your money. You can spell out the specification without saying that it's the best since Edison. It is a difficult art to write a story about your product that is newsworthy yet does not read like an advertisement. The tone must be more flat and subtle.

Personnel changes, factory openings, mergers, trade shows, unusual jobs either by design or speed all warrant an airing in your trade journal. Study what gets published. Your stories all help to build up an image, inspire credibility and improve awareness. You will then find it's easier getting in to see the buyers.

THE NATIONALS ARE DIFFERENT

Don't waste too much time on the national papers. You'll have to do something fairly sensational to excite their attention.

You do stand a fair chance if you concentrate on those quality papers that run a small business page, such as the *Guardian*. Otherwise they will tend to pick up items of bizarre interest. A South Wales factory that ran keep fit exercises before they started work made the national news.

The Press Association (PA) is a wire feeder agency that is worth putting on your mailing list. If they pick up a story it could finish up anywhere. They have some provincial offices.

If you think all this is a bit of a hassle then let me relate two stories.

1. I know of one small firm that produces cassettes of a mother's heartbeats that is played to soothe fractious babies. It works. The story was circulated and picked up via the *Nursing Times*. Enquiries came from the Middle East and Australia.
2. A plastics firm makes reproduction rainwater goods imitating lead hoppers and downpipes. Press releases to architectural and church magazines brough forth 400 enquiries.

PRESS CONFERENCES

Beloved by politicians, they are rarely appropriate for the small firm. Once only you may have something particularly newsworthy — an innovative product, Queen's Award, new premises etc. The story must be good to lure busy newsmen away from more exotic happenings. Invitations should be sent well in advance with a map of how to find you and an indication of what it's for. If you can rope in a prestigious local celebrity to present whatever it is then so much the better. If your factory is unavoidably grotty, hire a local hotel room. Choose a place with good access and parking.

The time of day is important. Contrary to popular belief, journalists would rather not be forced to sit and eat a lavish midday meal at the end of which are some perhaps dreary speeches and finally the hard news. Offer an 11 o'clock start with no more than light refreshments. Most stories can be told in half an hour and the media men plus photographers can be off and on to the next one. If they are invited to a 12 o'clock 'do' they *know* it will drag on and most of the day will be wasted. Consequently, many won't bother to attend.

Hand out your actual release or press pack *after* the speeches or demonstration otherwise you will be competing for their attention. Radio in particular will appreciate a quiet room for interviews.

All your staff must be well primed on what is expected of them. Give your girls a hair-do and if it's a factory tour, launder the overalls. Sweep up! Identify your staff with name badges. Warn your colleagues not to indulge in any 'off the record' witticisms. An open press conference is not the place to impart background confidences.

If you're launching a technical product, have a layman's introduction. Not everyone went to Imperial College. If you can spare them it's nice to hand out samples.

Presentations can be as involved or as simple as you like depending on your audience, as long as they're not too drawn out.

You can spend a lot of time preparing for a press conference but rarely can you predict who will turn up. It may coincide with the Falklands War (as mine did once). You may be clashing with a bigger news story or your idea of a hot item may be cold turkey to the editors. Finally, check off those papers who didn't come and send on your press pack. Get photos from all the photographers for your files. They will certainly have taken some which weren't published and copies are cheap.

Going on the box

All the experts are predicting that there will be an explosive growth in small television stations over the next ten years. Already most of the country is served by truly local studios with quality in-depth programmes being shown every week on local issues. The broadcasting media are always on the look-out for able businessmen to present the business community's side. It is an opportunity you should be prepared for.

Ninety-seven per cent of UK homes have television, making this medium far more intrusive than any newspaper. Paradoxically, unless you manage to capture anything other than a fleeting slot few, if any, sales will come as a direct result of this laudable exposure. The advantage of a *newspaper* mention is that reference to the address and other details can be easily made. The interested TV viewer has to chase up the studio if he really wants to find out more: television is all part of the active small firm's PR armoury.

You may court the producers with a normal press release or

they may come to you for an expert opinion. *Never* turn down the opportunity to appear. The first time will probably be nerve-racking, but successive occasions will be more enjoyable.

Television is run like a newspaper. Journalists gather news and there are editors and producers. The deadlines tend to be more exact, and there is certainly more pressure and organised chaos in a studio than a newspaper office. Local stations go for the parochial flavour leaving the nationals to supply the bulk of documentaries and hard news.

Because there is less air time available for 'small town' news your story must be good and, of course, preferably visual. Often relatively trivial stories with a twist finish the six o'clock magazine regional programmes.

Send your release to the news desk in the usual way in good time for them to plan their schedules. With distressing regularity, I have found they will do nothing until the morning of the broadcast when you will get a phone call and be expected to drop everything and come into the studio. They seem to believe that it's all very easy.

WHEN THE BIG MOMENT COMES
Let's look closely at what to do if you get asked to appear.

1. Ask the researcher or whoever invites you what the *angle* of the broadcast is likely to be. What is the story? Why have they asked you? If the format is a discussion or documentary it is essential to find out who else is taking part. You don't want to be confronted with a militant trade union official without being prepared. It could be a pressure group who have got wind of your new extension that might pump out smutty fumes.

   You should be aware of the style of the programme and interviewer. Are they in the Robin Day style? If so, you need to really do your homework. Ask how long the item is likely to be. A 90-second slot will not give you much time to air your arguments.

2. If the area of expertise lies with someone else in your company, it is wiser to pass the chance on.

3. Ask whether it will be a live broadcast or recorded. There are few live broadcasts today but go for that if you get the chance. Filming beforehand gives scope for editing and loses you the chance to ensure that what you really want to say goes out. Live broadcasts also have more bite and impact. I am reminded of one businessman who did two

broadcasts in a week. One was recorded. I told him to wave his leaflet about in the live broadcast and he had an extremely good response. There was nothing they could do about it.

4. If the filming is done at your workshop don't be put off by the numbers who may descend on you. The record, I think, goes to the BBC who have been known to send *ten* for an outside broadcast to film one man. ITV are usually more frugal.

5. Take some *visual aids* to the studio — some of your products or leaflets.

6. Armed with the general framework of the programme you are now able to *plan* what you want to say. Professional interviewers will tell you how rarely people think what they're going to say. It is *your* business — no one knows better than you what makes it tick. The programme is about *you*, not the prejudices of the interviewer. You should go along determined to get over your main points — don't surrender the ground.

7. Fix no more than *three* points that you must get over. It is no use launching into a great involved spiel with all sorts of subsidiary points. The viewer will certainly not take it in, assuming that the interviewer lets you ramble on. While he is not bound to tell you in advance the exact questions he will ask, in the interests of fluid programme making he should give you an outline. Don't be surprised if one is slipped in to throw you. It all makes for good television. Unless it's a 'Checkpoint' style of programme, they're not there to show you up in a poor light.

8. Make sure you can find the studio and park easily. Dress soberly, eschewing bright colours, especially reds. Steer clear of loud checks and lines and avoid wearing a dazzling white shirt. They can all affect the picture. You will undoubtedly be warm under the lights so make sure you're comfortable.

9. Check your dress for loose buttons, tie and zip! You may get the odd dab of powder if your nose is shiny. Check your hair.

10. Don't drink before the broadcast. You will be tempted — to steady the nerves — but leave it alone. A clear head is essential.

11. If you get time, ask them to show you the cameras and control room as it helps to remove the mystique. Meet the

interviewer and run through the format — don't start till you're happy. Don't *slouch* in the chair — lean forward or sit on the edge — it will keep you alert.

When you start look at the interviewer, not the camera. There will probably be three cameras, one for each side and one for a combined view. The one that is actually on vision has a red light showing but don't try to follow the light. Even experienced hands get confused. It is more common now to have an attached throat microphone rather than one on a desk.

When you are talking try and remember that you're not talking to millions but one person or a family in their homes. Television is an intimate medium. Don't forget to use that human touch — the smile.

Most people tend to talk more quickly than in normal conversation. If you're a gabbler try and calm down. If it's being recorded don't worry too much about the 'ers' and 'ums' and pauses. Most will be edited out. If you are stuck for a reply pause a little, polish your glasses or blow your nose (not too ostentatiously).

12. Avoid mannerisms if you can. Scratching your nose (or worse), twitching, wrinkling your nose, tugging your moustache will all distract and irritate the viewer.

HOW TO KEEP CONTROL

If you think the interviewer is missing the point there are many ways of *avoiding* the question and bringing it round to your way. Some examples:

'What I would really like to say is . . .'
'That's a good question, but don't you believe . . .?'
'You must remember that . . .'
or that old stand-by — 'The fact of the matter is . . .'

Some articulate politicians will get their prepared points over whatever questions are asked! Remember, when all is said and done, it's the image not the detail that counts. Next day nobody will remember what you said but they will recall whether you were a 'nice guy'.

ABRASIVE INTERVIEWS

Once in a while you may be unfortunate and be really hounded. The only way to handle such interviews is by thorough preparation.

1. You must be truthful if asked direct questions but there are ways of wrapping it up!
2. Find some new *fact* in your favour, a government report or survey that may be unknown to the interviewer. Don't reveal it before the interview when you can fire it straight back: could floor him. Always be courteous and never look smug.
3. One trick is to give a short answer and then *shut up*. He will be waiting for you to put your foot in it — but keep quiet. He will *always* start another question.
4. Alternatively, if you're being prevented from making your point, keep talking — even over the interviewer. He will shut up as it makes bad television for two to be talking at once. You will win the *sympathy* of the audience.

   This is really the nub of abrasive interviews. You are out to be the wronged guy and generate sympathetic audience reaction. So don't come over as a bolshy, short-tempered individual. Always keep control. The interviewer would sometimes love to see you flip your lid — it makes for good television.
5. Answer a trick question *with* a question. Turn it back. 'Do you really believe that?'
   'Why don't you ask . . .?'
6. Don't let him put words in your mouth. Correct at once if you are misquoted. Always be courteous and look eager and alert.
7. Don't forget it is better to *repeat* your three points than move on to others.

Final summary
- Ask why they are interviewing you.
- Plan what you want to say.
- Find out the format.
- Memorise your three points.
- Get there in plenty of time.
- Don't smoke or drink beforehand.
- Avoid loud clothes.
- Go to the loo beforehand!
- Relax and enjoy it . . . and smile.

Radio

Much the same rules apply to radio broadcasting as to television. As there are more local radio stations you have a better chance of getting air time. However, there appear to be few serious attempts to get beyond constant music, and business matters are not given much space on local radio. Because of its relative simplicity it is being used for instant comment. You are most likely to be called up for a contribution at five minutes' notice. Recordings are increasingly being used 'down the line', ie on the phone, so a little briefing on this should be helpful.

The first warning you may get is a journalist ringing you saying, 'I'd like your comment on the proposed increased bin charges by the council.'

Don't rattle off a snap reply. Ask a few questions on the programme and find out what else will be raised. And *ring back*. Give yourself time to think and plan what you want to say. Those few minutes will be vital. Move into a quiet room, stop the machines and typist and if you've other phone lines take them off the hook. Ring the studio back and keep your notes in front of you. Don't turn them over, tap pens or count your money.

LEARN THE TECHNIQUES
Radio interviewing demands a bright varied voice. Avoid monotones. Try and lighten your voice in pace and emphasis. Although no one can see you, learn to smile on the phone — it will get a chuckle into your voice.

Don't try and listen to the broadcast as you speak. You'll create feedback howl. They'll probably play the broadcast down the phone before your introduction.

If you're called to a *studio* the recording conditions there are, of course, far more responsive. Every inflection and gasp will be picked up. The mikes are extremely sensitive. You will be told how to direct your voice to the mike and a voice level test will be carried out. If you are reading from a script make sure it is typed and on one side of each sheet only. Lay them out side by side.

Breathing is important. Don't take great gasps or bother about drawing breath through the nose and out through the mouth. Do whatever comes naturally to you. Pace yourself. Count one-two after full stops.

PHONE IN PROGRAMMES
These are becoming increasingly popular as a way of encouraging the audience to speak to experts. Once you can get accepted on your particular topic it could lead to a regular

engagement. This is a marvellous PR exercise. It will, of course, be live and you must be able to think quickly. Take along some standard reference books on your subject to refresh your memory. If you are uncertain of the right answer it is better to say so than give out false information.

REMOTE STUDIOS

Up and down the country are specially set up rooms used for remote broadcasts. They are linked by land line to a major studio and give broadcast conditions. Some are unmanned. You may be told to get the key from a police station and find a box-like room. There will simply be a phone, the microphone and obligatory coloured lights. You will sit down on your own in this rather eerie atmosphere and watch the green light. This is to get ready. When the red light comes on you're 'live' and should start reading. Don't cough or say 'that's it' till the red light goes out.

Lock up and take the key back to the keeper: all rather disembodied. The same thing may happen with television. You may be interviewed at a distance and only see the speaker on a monitor. Sound will come to you via an ear plug. You have to choose to look either at the camera or the monitor but don't chop between the two. Hopefully, the monitor will be very close to the camera, giving a frontal shot. If they are wide apart then you should try and look straight at the camera. You won't of course be alone on this occasion but you will be apart from the interviewer, who could well be talking to three or four others at the same time: definitely more gruelling.

And the fee

Television and radio both pay for appearances but they may forget unless you ask. Naturally, you get more for going on the screen.

Other PR techniques

There are many subtle ways of engendering a nice warm glow about your company, and not all of them are expensive. One delightful example from a factory with social awareness comes from Hinton Poultry at Norton St Philip near Bath. The factory has been successful and grown rather large for the village. Last year they sent the following letter to all the local children:

Dear Children,

Would you like to own a tree? Hinton Poultry would like to give a tree to each of the children in Norton St Philip. Lots of trees will be planted between Churchmead and the chicken factory. They will be quite small when they are planted, and you will be able to watch your tree grow, as you grow yourself. I expect you all know Dr Peter Thompson of Oldfield Nurseries. He is going to plant all the trees and he will plant your name on the sort of tree you choose. The trees will be quite delicate for a few years and Dr Thompson will look after your tree for you.

Factories are dangerous places and we do not want any of our children to get hurt, so I thought the best thing to do would be to have a special day each year for all the children to look at their trees.

May 2nd is a school holiday and a factory holiday, so on that day, I shall arrange a picnic for you all and you will be able to see your tree. May is blossom time, so the little trees should be very beautiful. We shall have a special day every spring when you can look at your tree.

When you have decided which kind of tree you would like to have, please fill in the form. You can take this into the Norton St Philip Post Office. Mr Peter Walker will pass it on to me.

I shall write to you again soon to tell you all about the picnic.

I am really looking forward to seeing which kind of tree you choose. Please let me know soon.

With love from:

Yvonne Boore

The result was overwhelming. Probably every child in the village (125 of them) chose a tree but grandparents also wanted their grandchildren, living out of the village, included as well. The annual party with an entertainer, tea and presents must be the highlight of the year. The goodwill now generated must make it all very worth while.

The motor trade has become adept at trying little stratagems to win appreciation. One I like is to leave a tissue in the car after a service with the printed legend, 'The steering wheel and controls have been cleaned by our mechanic but this tissue is for your added convenience.'

Still with the motor trade, I know another garage who always leave a bouquet of flowers, attractively presented, on the rear seat of each new car sold, addressed to the lady. They have a regular contract with the local florist which keeps the price down. Believe me, the new owner values that personal touch out of all proportion to the cost.

They also send a birthday card on the anniversary of the purchase assuring the customer of their continued interest. Figures show that people tend to change their car when the HP or bank loan is nearing completion. A timely reminder at this stage can be very cost effective, but send it three months before the loan runs out — people do plan ahead.

I've heard of a restaurant that asks when any children present have their birthdays. A note is made of their address and a card is sent on the due date. The crafty host encloses a voucher for their meal. Naturally their parents have to come too . . . .

On a humbler note our local butcher keeps a box of sweets under the counter to be given out to toddlers. Of course, the kids always want to drag their parents into that shop.

CHARITY WORK

Every business seems to get tapped into supporting the local cause. More often, causes in the plural. It's a fact of life and unavoidable if you set up in a small community. Try and be fair to everybody and let it be known that the same, probably small, amount goes to them all. It can very easily get out of hand. Look on it as your PR contribution. A little can go a long way. Why not present a trophy to the local Guides' sports? It might become known as the Smith Cup? If you are a builder, giving away demolition materials to the Scout hall can do your image a power of good, or lending your portable heaters to the old folk in a power cut.

OPEN DAYS

These are a good PR exercise for your customers, prospects, local dignitaries, suppliers, neighbours and the media, not forgetting the wives and husbands of staff. Choose something interesting to show and talk about. Provide a light buffet and some liquid refreshment. Keep someone working the machines to bring a bit of life to the place. The motor trade do this rather well when a new model is launched. Get the local beauty queen or sports star to grace the occasion. It need not cost a great deal at all but the benefits could be many.

SPONSORSHIP

The *Guinness Book of Records*, Michelin Guides, Cornhill Tests are all sponsored events right in the mainstream of PR in that they generate goodwill in a pleasing, innocuous way and keep the sponsor's name in front of the public. Small firms can cover a little bit of the same route in their locality by more modest means. Every village has its cricket or football team and no one would turn down sponsorship of the match ball in return for a little publicity. There are always apprentices grateful for help with tools. A bursary for which deserving causes were invited to apply annually would receive mileage in the local press.

There are lots of permutations on this theme. School prizes for accomplishment presented by the local store or a photographic competition on an industrial theme will reflect goodwill.

BECOME AN AUTHORITY

Never turn down a speaking engagement. There are masses of clubs and societies always on the look-out for a guest speaker, from Rotary Clubs to the WI, wine circles to bird-watchers. It's all good PR. You never know who might be in the audience and what it may lead to. Take along some slides and samples and tell them all about your speciality. Don't forget to leave a few discreet leaflets behind. These sorts of things can never be anything other than sowing the seed but can be very rewarding.

On the same lines, if you really are an expert submit learned articles to the appropriate magazine. The simple byline mentioning which company you are from will bring forth some business. One thing will lead to another: very good for service trades and professionals.

WHEN YOU ARE ONE

When you have survived your first year in business hold a birth-

Minehead Shoe Co-operative birthday celebration
(Photo: Paddy Mounter, Langport)

day party! Have a cake, ask along anyone who has helped you in any way — suppliers, builders, the landlord, clients etc, not forgetting the bank manager. And the media: it could make a lovely story. I did the same thing with a shoe cooperative and for an expenditure of under £100 coverage was obtained on three TV channels and half a dozen newspapers.

RUN A NEWSLETTER

The subtle way to increase product awareness is by producing your own newsletter. Subtle? If you simply fill it full of praises for the product it will never get read. The newsletter approach can be successfully used where:

1. You have a wide and increasing range of products.
2. Your product has many applications.
3. You have a wide range of clients in many different activities who have but a spasmodic use for your expertise.

I believe it is particularly suitable for a *service* trade. You can preach by illustration and example what others are doing and how they are benefiting from your particular skills.

It helps if you have a known client or prospect list that you can mail on a regular basis. The advantage that a newsletter offers over advertising is that there is more room at an economical cost to display and expand your message. Good photographs can be used with a technical explanation of why you were able to help. Above all it should be interesting and newsworthy. Put in a few jokes or cartoons borrowed from trade magazines. Most journals will gladly give permission for short extracts to be reprinted if due acknowledgement is made.

Let me relate my own experience. I used to be involved with the marketing of industrial and architectural models. Our clients ranged from consulting engineers, architects, oil companies, advertising and PR consultants, exhibition promoters both here and abroad. To reach them all by advertising would have meant taking space in a dozen journals at inordinate cost. Even the most productive client rarely ordered more than one model a year. By adopting the newsletter method, 400 specifiers were gently reminded of our talents every quarter. The latest model was shown with the name of the client and an explanation of the project was given. Very soft sell. There were usually about ten good enquiries as a result. Total cost? About £50.

You could do the same with, say, stone restoration. Various examples of churches before and after would soon get the message across. Or outside catering — different grand houses with marquees on the croquet lawn. Or interior decorating. The list is endless.

EPILOGUE

If you are still confused over the difference between advertising and PR let me relate from Michael Bland's book *Be Your Own PR Man*.

'There's an old saying that if, at the end of a candlelight dinner, you tell a girl that you are fantastic in bed, that is advertising. If you tell her she desperately needs a man and you are the right one, it's marketing. But if at the end of the dinner *she* says that she's heard you're a great lover, and please can she go to bed with you, *that's* public relations.'

Chapter 5
Selling

The world can be divided into those who can sell and those who are doomed to be buyers. The owners of small businesses must ensure that they fall into the first category.

If there is one common thread among small firms it must be a hatred and fear of selling. But sell you must. Production is useless unless the goods are sold. Large firms have the extravagance not only of sales departments, but managers and a trained professional work-force calling regularly on old customers and generating new prospects. The small firm has none of these luxuries. The proprietor not only has to decide how best to produce his goods but must also dash around drumming up business. You *can* appoint agents but you still have to convince (sell to) them and you will surely not want to leave *all* of this vital area to third parties. There will, for instance, be trade shows and important distributors that you will want to chivvy along. A knowledge of selling techniques is vital to survival. You cannot abdicate all responsibility — not if you want to grow that is.

Few proprietors in my experience adopt any formalised approach but attack the market in a well meaning but increasingly frustrating way. Salesmanship is a skill, whose techniques can be learnt and applied just as readily as those of production. And they do have to be learned, practised and persisted with. You won't make sales with every call — far from it — but a systematic approach, going through a sequence of logical steps, will bring results.

Prospecting for customers

Your previous market research (Chapter 2) identifies where to put your efforts. All the time you are looking for *names*, the first ingredient in selling. You are out to identify buyers, specifiers by name if possible, who are potential users of your product. Titbits of information — new contracts, diversification, more staff — are ammunition for your attack. You are after a snapshot of the company.

People who buy people

The first rule of selling is to sell yourself. The product is very much second. If you don't like meeting people and learning what makes them tick then you'll never enjoy or be any good at selling.

A knowledge of psychology helps. People are different, everyone is different. The same person is different at nine o'clock and at lunch; over a drink, cold sober or talking about work or his hobby; on a Monday morning after a weekend with in-laws or on Friday thinking about that business trip to the Caribbean.

This is the fascination of selling. People buy people first. The product comes later. Watch a real professional salesman at work. All the time he is looking and listening. Looking for reactions, the eyebrows, the shrug, inflections in the voice. Looking for an opening, a buying signal, a chance to sign up an order.

Try and *be yourself* — don't adopt a stance or affect to be more knowledgeable or polished than you are. Selling is a conversation but one where you are controlling the direction. Take care over your appearance — no one takes to a scruff — but a pin-stripe talking to farmers would be out of place. Wear clothes you feel comfortable and happy in yet which carry an air of confidence. Suit your clothes and tactics to the situation. Bank managers are fond of relating stories of small-firm owners dressed up to the nines, obviously ill at ease, who have come to raise some money.

Honesty is the only policy. If you don't know the answer, say so and make sure you come back promptly with the information.

You are allowed just two lies: 'It's my fault' and 'You're right.'

Setting objectives

The profession of selling enjoys little status in the UK whereas in the United States the value of good salesmanship is recognised as a vital part of growth companies.

Many salesmen in this country drift round firms like milkmen. They call on the same people week in, week out. 'Nice day,' or 'How's trade?' or more daringly 'Same as last time?' They are order takers. They make no attempt to develop their business or show an interest in their clients. The only people they listen to are their own voices. They are defeated before they start. The buyers are the enemy. Secretaries are fair game, and a warm office is definitely to be preferred to knocking on strange new doors.

But you can afford none of this. Every hour away from base must be cossetted. The object of selling is to get orders. Each face-to-face call must have that end in view. Perhaps not on the first visit, but each call should end with a new bit of information of use along the road. Good accounts need working on. Remember, there is always a competitor in there already, possibly cheaper, invariably satisfactory but above all — known.

If you do walk out with a large order first time there is probably something wrong. The suppliers may have stopped credit or your prospect may know of a price rise on its way.

The reason for setting objectives is two-fold. It gives you something to aim and plan for as well as a fall-back position. Don't set too high an objective or you will easily get discouraged. If you aim to sell 500 items, can they take half at once with the balance over three months? Work out a trial offer: sale or return, perhaps, or a promise to tender next time. Even as low an objective as more contacts within the organisation can be worth while, keep your spirits up and make you feel you have achieved something. You have to find ways of keeping *your* motivation going. Aim high but not at the moon.

Know your product

As proprietor you should be fully versed in all your products: their performance, quality, reliability, cost, delivery, after-sales service etc. It is no good setting out your stall without all these facts at your fingertips. Is your sales literature correct with the up-to-date prices? If you are going to demonstrate the product, does the sample work?

Don't forget to check an old customer's account before pumping more into him. Has the last order been delivered without any hiccups? You don't want egg on your face.

Planning saves time

Get a map and divide the territory up. It may help to run a circle around your base representing one hour's driving time, then further circles beyond that. Try and avoid dashing about haphazardly as time between prospects is dead time. In a city

119

use public transport, if it is physically possible. Your first call should be made after 9.30 am unless specifically arranged. It will give the buyer time to sort out the post and get the day under way. Different trades require a different approach in your timing. Publicans, doctors, vets and headmasters have a 'best' time to call.

Don't always call in the same town on the same day of the week. That way you may switch early closing day and catch that buyer who is always out. It is strange also how different places look on other days of the week.

If you can afford to go out every day then work on a rotating pattern. This will shift the week on. Friday afternoons are generally a poor time to call. Leave them for your record keeping and paperwork.

I think you have to discipline yourself to allocate a set time each week or month when you will go out selling. This will vary if you are a brand new business or well established. But the time never to neglect calling is when you are busy. Your spate of business won't last and trying to establish fresh customers when you are in a slump is too late. The time to establish contacts is at the crest not the trough.

YOU MUST DEVELOP A SYSTEM

Drop in your local commercial stationers and get a good loose-leaf binder. There are several on the market that take 200 sheets (400 sides) and will slip in your glove pocket. Use it to record your prospects' names. Unless you adopt a routine approach to your canvassing from day one you will get into slipshod and wasteful ways. Don't write the names alphabetically but group them in towns or convenient, logical areas. Using this method will give alternative choices to plan your calling time, rather than thumbing through all your records to pick out the appointments.

On each sheet record the exact name of the firm (for invoicing purposes), the address and phone number, buyers, product lines and who does the existing business. List the delivery address if that is different. Record the date of your call and any other relevant information, which can be the name of the secretary or receptionist (most important − courtesy is the great door opener) and topics discussed with the buyer. Staff come and go so jot down not just the name of the buyer but his exact job title. It could be 'Consumables' or 'Fasteners' or 'Plant Manager'.

As a further refinement a diary note should be made for a

follow-up. This can be literally in a diary or in a multi-pocket file. For the latter you will need 43 pockets — 31 days and 12 months. A reminder can be slipped in either the next month's pocket or, if you want to be more exact, the correct day file. Don't leave your binder in the phone box. It could be invaluable to a competitor and you'll be lost without it. Write your name and address (private home) inside.

How to get past the secretary

Cold calling (ie without an appointment) is rarely rewarding. Buyers are busy people who generally abhor door knockers. You won't always be able to make appointments and indeed, some firms are relatively easy to get into without that magic phone call, but your time is valuable and your car costs a lot to run.

The more people you can see in a day the more chance you have of making a sale, so make an appointment where you can. Ask for the buyer and make sure you record the name. If you are stuck for the name it sometimes helps to make one up. Say: 'Mr Johnston the buyer, please' to which the receptionist may reply, 'Don't you mean Mr Whiteside?' or whatever.

In some firms the buyer's secretary guards her boss like the Crown jewels. Offer *alternatives*, and always be positive and self-assured.

'Good morning. My name is John Richards from XYZ Company. I am in your town next Wednesday and Thursday morning. Which day is more convenient for me to see him? I have a proposition I would like to put to him which will take no more than 15 minutes.'

Make sure that you are seeing the *right* person. Many large firms split buying functions right down. Finally, when you do get an appointment make sure you understand where the prospect is situated.

If you are fobbed off, be persistent yet firm, and always be polite. They may genuinely have completed their buying for the season, or only work on annual contracts. Never put the phone down without having learnt something of value, some extra fact that you can come back on. You must leave yourself with a lead-in for next time.

The presentation

At last you've arrived for your appointment in good time, well groomed without being flash. Don't block the fork-lift, park in the chairman's spot or scratch his Rolls (nearest you'll get to one, I know). In your case you will have a notebook and pen (that works), brochures, your diary, colour photos of your product range or past successes that aren't in your leaflet, samples if size permits, and your order book (why not?).

Put your cigarette out and greet the receptionist. Study any display products or company results displayed in the foyer while you are waiting. Never talk down to anyone — that man sweeping the floor might be the managing director. I know of two very successful firms where one manager *likes* to sweep up and the other types all the firm's letters. Some salesmen adopt a very superior air to those they consider to be their inferiors. The traps in this strategy are:

1. You rarely know exactly to whom you are talking.
2. Anyone in the firm can be a source of useful information.
3. Cultivate the receptionist — she can get you in to the boss ahead of the competition, and inform you of his interests and busy times.
4. It reflects ill on your firm.

And remember the old adage — be nice to people on the way up, you may need them again on the way down.

When you are shown in, introduce yourself, shake hands — and *smile*! The smile is the ice breaker, it shows you are human, just like the buyer. A smile means warmth and understanding. It relaxes tension and removes the worry lines round your mouth. A smile is also the shortest distance between two people.

BREAKING THE ICE
First impressions are most important. Remember that you never get a second chance to make a first impression. The rules of the game allow you first bite to get your presentation under way. Keep pleasantries to a minimum. Don't throw that advantage away by rambling on about the weather or admiring the buyer's rubber plant. And if the prospect is a girl, avoid looking down her cleavage or at her legs (female readers please reverse roles here).

If he is not familiar with your company, a thumbnail sketch of the set-up, personnel and specialities is in order. Starting on a subject you are totally familiar with helps to break your nervousness and encourage a natural flow of words.

Your whole manner should be positive, enthusiastic without being overbearing, sensitive to responses from your audience and on a stance of equality. An attitude of craven humility or the reverse can be equally disastrous. It will be difficult at first to sound natural but strive to conduct your sales pitch as a normal conversation, for this is, after all, what salesmanship is all about. Ask questions — *open* questions. By that I mean questions that can't be answered simply by a 'Yes' or 'No'. For instance, 'Shall I send you some?' can only provoke either yes or no and if it's *no* then you've rather run out of steam.

Probing questions like, 'How many do you use in the course of each shift?' or 'What do you look for when you buy this product?' will involve the other person. It ceases to be you spouting at a blank face but changes to a two-way conversation. He has to think and give intelligent replies. You are showing an interest in his business, his problems and his successes.

By shifting the emphasis you should develop the sales patter into a discussion, not about you but about his world and how your product can help him *make more money for his company*. Questions should be aimed at discovering whether and in what quantities he uses products similar to yours. The old standbys of what, where, how and when will do very nicely.

The buyer

Look at it from the *buyer's* point of view. If he's doing his job properly he must always be on the look-out for products that will do the job more efficiently at better cost from a reliable supplier. They must meet the company's quality standards and be available at the right time in the correct quantities.

Once the buyer has found a supplier that meets perhaps very exacting requirements it is human nature to stick with him rather than be chopping and changing about. Unless you can offer some very cogent reasons why he should change, then the *status quo* will prevail.

LISTEN TO THE BUYER
When you're talking you're not listening, when you're not listening you're not learning. A good salesman is a good listener, not necessarily just a good talker as popular assumption has it. How many hear without listening? You listen to promote

dialogue, for *buying indicators* and points you can pick up for leads and decisions.

Many salesmen have their set patter which defies interruption. They have to go through the routine trotting out all the selling points regardless of the buyer's reaction.

The worst example I have heard of was a doorstep salesman who produced a portable record player (this was before cassettes) carrying the message.

THE QUESTIONING BUYER
Old hands at buying can sometimes floor you by repeatedly asking questions. Turn it back and answer a question with a question.

> *Buyer:* Why should I give up my existing supplier I've known for years?
>
> *You:* When did you last get another quote?
>
> *or*
>
> Don't you think some competition is good for everyone?

WHEN SILENCE IS NOT GOLDEN
One of the hardest buyers to sell to must be the silent or 'grunt' type. Your spiel produces no interest. The only way to draw him out is to keep asking short open-ended questions. If you have a product that can be demonstrated, then encourage discussion by involving the prospect.

OPENING DOORS
Occasionally you will come across a buyer who just will not see you. If you are really convinced that you can save his employer's money and that he may be lining *his* pocket from the competition, try writing to his managing director with your proposition. Obviously, don't spell out your other suspicions. You won't make many friends in the buying department but you *may* get the business.

On a slightly different tack I'm reminded of one salesman who could always get in to see the buyer but never really gained his confidence. He eventually learned that the buyer was very fond of poodles so he borrowed one and just happened to bump into him on the daily walk. A common bond was established and the business was speedily obtained. That was professionalism – and persistence.

Buying indicators

All through your presentation you should be looking for buying indicators. If not green lights then there are amber lights to say: 'Right, I'm interested, sell me some.' The amateur salesman will tend to trot out all the selling points, steam right through and out the other side. In many cases it is just not necessary and sometimes self-defeating to keep in top gear when the buyer has given a hint that he is interested. *Talk too much* and he may change his mind or think of a good reason why he won't buy any.

Examples of buying indicators are:

'What are your deliveries like?'
'Do you do them in red?'
'We've tried similar products in the past.'
'Do you do trial offers?'
'What's the minimum quantity?'
'How much does it cost?'

The new salesman will not recognise these as intimations to buy but treat them as a series of questions and simply make the appropriate reply. He should be reaching for the order book.

The buyer, perhaps unconsciously, is coming over the brink to a favourable decision. The poor man needs reassurance; he needs help to coax out a 'Yes'. The reasons for that decision are worth thinking about. The buyer may genuinely like you and your product and be impressed by your sales pitch. Alternatively, the timing may be just right. You may be the last rep at the end of a long day and he hasn't the strength to argue. His existing supplier may have just let him down. He may want to ginger up an existing supplier by alerting him that he's not the only fish in the pond. It may even be a case of internal politics that he wants to needle a colleague by breaking the patterns of supply. Once in a while you will get an order out of pure sympathy that he senses you are new and perhaps nervous. Don't count on that more than twice.

Other products and other customers

Before you go into the buyer you may have decided that one particular product line is the one for him. Run through your presentation but don't forget before you leave to ask two questions:

What other products are they interested in?
Do they know of other prospects that you could see?

If you don't ask, you may not be aware that their buying patterns have changed or new processes have been installed. *They* may not be aware that you carry other lines. But don't carry this to excess – leave something for your next visit.

Other prospects could be buyers at head office or another division that uses the same products. There's nothing like a referral from one buyer to get you into the magic sales office. Don't forget your stock in trade is *names*.

Concessions

Never make a concession without asking for something in return.

'If I discount by 5 per cent will you order 1000 instead of 900?'
'If I . . . will you . . .?'

Handling objections

Objections to buying are your *opportunity*. Quite simply they are reasons that you can fasten on to and turn to your advantage. Let's look at some common objections and ways of getting round them.

Buyer: I've always dealt with XYZ Co.
You: I'm not after *all* your business. Give me a trial order and see how we perform. It will be a valid comparison with your existing supplier. Suppose they have a fire or strike and can't deliver. When did you last compare quotations? Even Fords buy components from several suppliers.

Buyer: It's too dear.
You: Are you sure you're comparing like with like? The benefits I mentioned will give longer service and save you money in the long term.

If price is the cause of objections, then switch from price to value. Rolls Royces would never sell on price alone. They are bought because they last 30 years, everything works superbly, they have 30 coats of paint, are hand trimmed and sail through the traffic because of their status.

If you are selling volume items it sometimes helps to quote unit costs or break the cost down to so much a week.

Buyer: You can't meet my delivery times.

You: How critical are those delivery dates? Can we part deliver and produce the rest at weekly intervals?
or
If we could meet your delivery how many would you like?
or
Let me ring the works and talk that over with my colleague and see what we can do.

Buyer: You're a small firm and we only deal with established contractors.

You: Everyone has to start from somewhere. Being small means that we can adapt more quickly to pressures and switch over to rush orders. You can pick up the phone and speak to me, the boss, with no difficulty. Our overheads are lower than large suppliers and the benefits are passed to you.

You can also throw in good labour relations and the absence of a closed shop if that's relevant. Be careful though. Some large firms are under orders not to accept work from non-union subcontractors.

Fortunately, the problems of being small are not quite as daunting as before. Even the government is streamlining its procurement procedures and is trying to encourage a proportion of supplies from the small firms' sector. Several large firms now have a deliberate policy of encouraging small local suppliers.

Ring the changes and find out if the objection is genuine or if you are simply being fobbed off.

Buyers often raise objections on price because they are undecided. It is the easy way out. Move on to delivery or after-sales and other benefits and find if cost is a genuine reason. If it still is, then you'll have to bring in other arguments and probe deeper.

Never *argue* over objections. Reason and put your point of view but don't lose control of the discussion. And never enter into a slanging match!

Always be on your guard not to disclose confidential information and never use derogatory tones about others. The buyer may well think, 'If he says that about them, what will he say about my firm?'

It's also easy to be unwittingly pumped about the buyer's competitors. Use discretion. The odd name dropped with care can sometimes help with clinching an order. Farmers in particular tend to imitate their more go-ahead neighbours and want to know what is happening on the other side of the hedge.

A final important reason why you get objections is that the buyer often has to convince his superiors and perhaps a committee that his decision was the right one. He is using you as devil's advocate. His own integrity and judgement are at stake and he must be assured that all the possible objections are covered. It would amuse you to see the reversal of roles later on when *he* argues the points to his colleagues.

Second sourcing

Unless you have a genuinely unique product, the main objection presented to you will be an existing supplier firmly entrenched. Every firm has suppliers that you cannot budge, and for a new small business to oust existing loyalties, great patience and persistence are required. Several key points can be raised with the buyer:

1. How long would it take you to replace your major supplier if they had a fire, strike or merger? What would be the effect on your business?
2. Wouldn't it keep your other supplier on his toes if he knew there was someone else knocking on the door? Competition is a marvellous shatterer of complacency. It's an insurance policy.
3. What were the reasons for placing the business with them in the first place? Isn't the position similar now?
4. When did you last compare prices?
5. When did they last let you down on delivery or quality? (Every firm does at some time.)
6. Put 'suppose' questions. 'Suppose you landed that big contract, could they meet all your demands?'; 'Suppose the pound drops again, do they have enough stocks to fulfil the quantity?'
7. Fords always have several suppliers for identical components.

Closing the sale

While many of us will have a fair stab at getting out a run of selling points, the main difference between an amateur and the professional salesman is his knowledge of closing techniques. Closing the sale simply means getting an *order* — the whole point of this exercise.

All through your presentation you should be alert to those buying indicators and looking for a quick close. You don't have to go through all the merits of your wonderful product if you're getting good signals. Close the sale there and then.

The techniques of asking for an order are many. Some salesmen claim to know and use over 15. I'll not pretend that you need to be fully conversant with all of these, but being prepared may open your eyes to what can be achieved. Having more than two means you do not continually have to steer the discussion around to your pet phrases.

Two vital points must be grasped:

1. A closing question is any question that you ask, the answer to which confirms that the buyer wishes to buy.
2. Whenever you ask a closing question — *shut up*!

If you keep quiet then only one of two things can happen: either the customer goes along with you and you have an order, or a reason is given that you can discuss.

THE DIRECT APPROACH

Why not ask for an order? That is what you're there for after all. They can either say 'yes' or 'no' and if it is 'no' then you have an objection you can get to work on.

An objection *can* be a buying signal. Some buyers are indecisive and want to be helped in making the decision. There might be a doubt on some detail that needs clearing up.

THE ORDER FORM CLOSE

This is the most well used of all. Get an order pad out on your knee and during your discussion ask the customer questions filling the answers in on your form.

'What is the delivery address? Where should the invoices be sent?'

Unless you are stopped, they've bought, haven't they? The *assumption* is made that they are going to buy but you never actually ask the question.

ALTERNATIVE CHOICE CLOSE

There was a hamburger bar that wanted to increase sales of eggs. As customers walked in, they were asked, 'One egg or two?'

Few stopped to consider whether they wanted an egg at all. Your closing questions give the *choice* of buying this colour or that, with wheels or not. The choice is not between whether you want any or not, but assumes that you are certainly going to have *some*, the only decision is what variety.

'When do you want delivery, before Christmas or after?'

Alternative choice questions are invariably prefaced with, 'Which do you prefer?' or related to those old friends when, what, where and how. The questions must always be assumptive.

SHARP ANGLE CLOSE

The best salesman I know claims he first learnt this technique as a lad watching the Birmingham costermongers. He relates the story of a woman asking: 'Are those oranges sweet?' To which came the irrefutable reply, 'Would you like some if they were?'

Save this technique for when you are asked:

'Can it do this?'
'Will it run uphill?'
'Will it stay clean?'

Reply (sharp angle back) by saying, 'Do you want it if it does?' instead of tamely saying, 'Yes, it does.'

When you've agreed that the customer wants it if it does, then you've made your sale.

SECONDARY QUESTION CLOSE

It goes like this: 'As I see it, the only decision you have to make today is whether you have the order this week or next. By the way, do you want to use your pen or mine?'

There is an alternative choice here, but the trick is splitting the decisions into major and minor. It is a distraction. When the prospect has made the minor decision, he has made the major as well!

QUESTION CLOSING

A simple technique that is often missed. If you are asked, 'Can I get the delivery in seven days?' don't say, 'Yes' but close the sale by asking, 'Do you want delivery in seven days' time?' When the customer has said 'Yes' he's bought, hasn't he?

CALL BACK CLOSE

We've all heard the line: 'I'll think it over. Call me next week.' It's a polite way of saying 'No!'

When you do call back, *never* start by saying, 'Well, did you think it over?' because the likely response will be – 'Yes I did; no thanks.' Instead, try: 'I am sorry but the last time I called I forgot to tell you . . . .' It doesn't matter what it is. Continue by saying, 'Let's run over what we agreed last time,' and go through the whole presentation as before, the only difference being that you will now say, 'As you remember,' 'You will recall,' 'We said that,' and then go into the normal closing techniques. *Never* ask whether he has thought it over.

OBJECTION CLOSE

If you come across a client who continually raises objections which you then defeat, ask him: 'Tell me, is this the one final objection?' If it is, then you have made a sale.

SUMMARY QUESTION CLOSE

To be used on the prospect who waffles and won't come to a decision. You allow the subject to use 'no' when he really means 'yes'. An example:

'Just to clear my thoughts, what is it that you're undecided on? Is it our delivery date?'

If he says, 'No' it means he accepts the delivery date and that is not a valid objection. So continue with all your selling points one at a time.

'Is it this?' 'Is it that?'

Every time he says, 'No' you have got a 'Yes' out of him. If he says, 'No' to all of your 'Is its?' he has bought! If he says, 'Yes' you have pinned him down to a definite objection that you go to work on.

ENDORSEMENT CLOSE

Bring in a *true* story of someone who has used your product and benefited from its use. The knack is tying it in with someone the buyer can relate to. Alternatively, tell a tale of someone who *didn't* use you and suffered as a result. This close is widely used in the insurance field.

THE FEAR CLOSE

This should be used with discretion. The object is to plant a seed of doubt or fear in the prospect's mind: a fear that if he doesn't order today then the chance will not recur. If the prospect says he will order 'next time' then you have to say he will not be able to order at the same advantageous terms. That statement must be transparently accurate.

Examples

'Sign now and you'll get £100 off.' Much used by double glazing salesmen.

All the more suspect when used by itinerant tarmac gangs: 'We've just finished resurfacing the road round the corner and we've got a few barrows left. Not worth taking back. Shall we do your drive now, missus?'

Never!

Like all management techniques, they must be practised. One top man practises on his wife . . . .

The dangers of sale or return

SOR is a common practice among craft shops, largely, I suspect, because most are under-capitalised and do not know their market. For the new craft producer the offer is tempting. Everyone wants their goods on display in the High Street so why worry? You haven't made a *sale* until the money comes in. The goods could very well be damaged or soiled and unsaleable, if they come back to you. What check have you whether the goods have been sold anyway?

The whole area is ripe for disputes, although it does have a genuine place for the experimental piece or single expensive sculpture or picture. It is entirely legitimate that the gallery owner should hang and display works of art on an SOR basis if they have a limited but defined appeal. Otherwise the money please, Mr Shopkeeper.

SOR goods must be the subject of a written agreement. You will need to cover:

1. Insurance — at whose risk are the goods on display?
2. Commission — at what rate?
3. Terms of payment.
4. Packing and carriage — who pays for the return?
5. An agreement that the goods remain your property until paid for.

Away from the craft field, SOR is widely used as a sampling method to get goods out on the shelves. New products are often launched in this way to tempt the stockist.

Many large firms have built up their business by sending out goods 'on approval'. The customers can try the goods in their homes without having to pay first. The dangers are obvious to small firms on restricted capital: there is the risk of never seeing your money (small debts are not worth chasing), the return postal costs and damaged unsaleable goods. I believe it is a path to tread with caution and only attractive if you enjoy a very good margin.

Beware the Unsolicited Goods and Services Act 1971 which was brought in to discourage wholesale distribution by 'inertia' selling practices. It allows people to retain any goods sent to them for which they didn't ask and prevents the sender chasing for payment. Fines could amount to £400.

The art of demonstrating

A product that can be demonstrated requires its own technique. Practise first how and what points you are going to highlight. Check out all the components before you set up each and every time. It is not sufficient to put it away and take it out next month without a dry run.

If it is an audio visual (AV) presentation run through the slides and see that they are in sequence and the right way round. Don't do what I did once and leave the projector in a cold car till just before the meeting. When I switched on the slides I had great difficulty in focusing the image, which had me baffled. Someone with a knowledge of humidity pointed out that the lenses were steamed up.

The art of demonstration should involve the following features:

1. While you are actually showing the product — keep quiet. The client can't listen to you and look at the features.
2. *Respect the product*, don't dump it on the table. Even if it's only a cheap item, bring it out of a decent box, remove the tissue and give it a polish. Handle with care and reverence — all part of the image.
3. *Involve the customer* and let him handle the goods. But if there is anything approaching a knack to any operation, keep him away. Encourage questions. Try and leave the goods for the client to play with, if that is appropriate, on a trial basis. It gives you another selling opportunity when you call back.

133

4. If the product is too large to carry round, give one of the cheapish audio visual presentations using slides or video. This can be very effective. There's nothing like a bit of movement and colour to attract attention. Once you have paid for the video, you can use it for other occasions — trade shows, agents' meetings, shop windows. You can even hire it out to other interested parties.

5. Working demonstrations for plant and equipment can go down very well. Farmers love to try out a bit of new apparatus on their land. Get a group together with a chemical firm or your big local contractor and you've got the right atmosphere to generate some business. Don't forget a reasonable amount of food and drink.

Telephone sales

Selling by phone is hard. Think of the *disadvantages*: no eye to eye contact; it's hard to tell the buyer's reaction and there is no product demonstration. They can always put the phone down on you. No leaflets to see.

On the other hand, there is no tiring driving between visits, no parking problems and no traffic snarl ups.

They say that a rep on the road costs £20,000 a year. How many clients can you see in a day? Five? There is an old joke that if someone stopped a cinema matinee performance and asked if there was a salesman in the audience half the people would put up their hands.

Telephone selling can be very cost effective. Direct mail rarely achieves more than a 2 per cent response rate, but the vast majority of us will accept a phone call. Don't we get out of the bath to answer the phone? This compulsive nature of the beast is its attraction as a selling tool.

VOICE TECHNIQUES

Given that you can't see the other person, you can quickly form an impression of his personality: whether he is excitable, young or old, thinks before he speaks, is bored or tired or just 'a nice guy'.

As with all selling you sell yourself first. Your enthusiasm will be projected over the phone just as clearly as if you were sitting in the same room. The listener will form a mental image of you from your speed of delivery, mumbling or clear diction, forcefulness or tardiness.

Clear diction, meaning and sincerity are therefore vital points to practise. *Smile* on the phone. Have you ever heard a voice that isn't smiling? It's surly, discouraged and defeated. Why should you *buy* a voice like that?

PREPARATION
You will be working from a prepared list of prospects with the usual background details. Some practitioners go so far as to suggest a written script. That I find is a bit extreme, but use one if it helps you. At the least you want a short list of the main selling benefits.

GETTING PAST THE SWITCHBOARD
In a depressing number of companies the switchboard girls are trained to fight off salesmen like the plague, so avoid referring to selling or any other close relation like market research or surveys.

Describe the nature of your call:

'I'd like to discuss a new technique in adhesives' or
'I'm sure he'll be interested in profiting from a new discovery.'

There is no point in launching into a sales pitch with anyone other than the decision taker.

WHEN YOU SPEAK TO THE BUYER
Good telephone selling revolves around bringing out an interest in the prospect's company.

'I notice that you won a nice order from Kuwait the other day.'
'I see that you are exhibiting at the next trade fair.'
'Your trading results had a good press on Sunday.'

Open out the client to get him talking and look for opportunities to inject some sales points. Use the regular techniques — what, when, where, how and who? *Why* tends to lead to rather abrupt remarks and may seem to be too probing. Telephone selling must always be the model of courtesy. No hard sell here.

Radio actors should make good telephone salesmen. They know how to sound interesting and convincing, when to pause and vary the pitch of the voice. Practise by yourself into a tape recorder by reading from a script. Get some variety and persuasion into your voice. Go on a telephone sales course.

OTHER USES OF THE PHONE

Don't neglect *incoming* calls as a sales opportunity. They may be ringing up for lengths of timber. Ask about stains, fixings and cutters and the like. The idea may not have occurred to them. They may not even *know* that you stock such lines.

Take a hard look at your sales route. Could not those *regular* customers be just as easily serviced by phone? It could be easier for them and certainly cheaper for you. It would leave you more time to call on fresh prospects. Train other staff to handle all telephone sales. Pick a girl with a bright cheery personality and she might develop more business than you the boss.

The most profitable way of expanding your sales is by selling more goods to your *existing* customers. That should be writ large in every sales office. You should be thinking all the time, 'What else can I sell them?' We are all creatures of habit and tend to go back to the same shop or supplier. If you keep up a smart service and look after people, it is far less time-consuming to sell to existing customers than chasing round looking for new faces all the time. And the easiest way to do this is by phone.

... AND ABUSES

1. Keeping the customer waiting without explanation while the extension or buyer is tracked down. If there is likely to be a delay, promise to ring back — and make sure you do.
2. How often do you ring a firm to hear, 'Abrgwtyrurlifod Company'? The person is so used to answering the phone that the firm's name becomes incomprehensible.
3. A common fault in engineering firms is to locate the phone in the noisiest part of the works. At least that's how it seems. It's sometimes more interesting to listen to the conversation and hubbub in the background than the caller.
4. Good bosses tell someone when and for how long they will be out.
5. Try and avoid putting the phone down before the customer does. It's a subtle point but hearing the 'click' is somehow impolite and disconcerting. It sounds as though you are glad to be rid of him.
6. Anyone who answers the phone should have a basic grounding in what the firm does. Whoever answers the phone *is* the firm to the caller and an indifferent voice is no help or image builder.

7. *Identify the caller* before quoting a price. He could be a large trade customer who deserves the best price.
8. Chain a pad and pencil to the phone. How amateurish to be asked to 'Hold on a tick while I find a pen.'

If you have an answer-phone you will know that many people (especially the older generation) refuse to leave a message. All you hear on playback is the click. Try *opening* your recorded message with a quip. Instead of, 'This is the Mayfair Widget Company on 234 67845,' try — 'Yes, I hate these things too,' or 'I quite agree. These machines are dreadful.' It does work by breaking the ice with a human touch.

TELEPHONE SALES COMPANIES
Finally, there are now many specialist telephone sales companies who will canvass for you. You agree a script, supply the outlines of the target market and let them get on with it. It is probably more successful for getting you in to major buyers than actual selling, though some claim to be able to sell impressively expensive items over the phone. At first sight, they look very expensive to employ, but may be worth looking into. They are widely used in the United States and rapidly gaining ground over here, especially in London for selling insurance.

Quotations, invoices and terms of trading

Gentlemen's agreements should have no place in your sales pitch. Although the law says that a contract can be made verbally, with or without a shake of the hand, if things go wrong it is awfully difficult to prove what was agreed. The magistrate will decide by who keeps the straightest face. It becomes a case of 'his word against mine'.

Some golden rules:

1. Never accept an order without confirmation in writing.
2. Never order materials before you get a written acceptance.
3. Don't accept an order over the phone without a written order.
4. Don't vary the order or accept additions without the same procedure. Each variation is a fresh order.

An *estimate* is a well reasoned guess at what the job is likely to cost. You are allowed to alter the final figure.

A *quotation*, on the other hand, is a firm figure at which you undertake to complete the work. If that figure is accepted you have made a contract. If you break that contract either by poor performance or non-delivery you could be sued.

Always put a *time limit* on your quote for acceptance: 'This figure holds good for 30 days,' or whatever. In days of high inflation it is folly to give either long fixed-price contracts or undated quotations. Some sectors use a known cost of materials index — architects and builders for example.

Make sure you get a signed *acceptance* in an approved form. The simplest method is to get back a signed copy of the quote or equip yourself with a duplicate book from any stationers.

References should be taken for new customers before committing yourself to large or special orders. Any professional trickster always keeps a couple of tame referees available so it helps to *ring* rather than write. Speak to the other firm's credit controller — you should be able to pick out the dubious characters. Credit agencies (page 50) and your own bank can also help with inside research. Ask your bank manager to explain the nuances of the reply as there are sometimes coded warning signals to the initiated. If you are uncertain send a *pro forma* invoice that must be paid before any goods are delivered.

Always be suspicious of large orders dangled before you for no sound reason.

A *specification* should be given saying what you are supplying. You may need to supply drawings, dimensions, samples and detail any special finish. Reference should be made to a British Standard colour chart and the relevant BS or Ministry of Defence standards if appropriate.

Your *invoice* must be addressed correctly as this is what passes title in the goods. The wise builder doing conversion work will invoice the husband and the wife. It has been known for the property to be in the wife's name and the husband refusing to pay. For small firms make sure you distinguish between sole proprietorships and those with limited status as invoicing in the wrong name could make later legal actions difficult. For large firms always quote their order number and any other detail required. Mark it for the attention of the authorising person. Include your VAT and the number. Don't give them any excuse to delay payment.

Terms of trading should be stated on the invoice. When is payment required? In 30 days? On delivery? And do you mean 30 days after delivery or after the date of the invoice. 'Monthly' could mean either the end of the month after the month of delivery or a month after delivery. Complicated, isn't it?

When you date the invoice is important. Many large firms regard the last day of the month as sacrosanct. If you deliver on the last day of the month and invoice religiously on the first you'll lose 30 days in your cash flow. Most firms like to pay at the end of the month after the month of delivery.

With the advent of computers many companies now close off the books on the 25th of each month or thereabouts. Miss that cut-off point and you'll have to wait a further month to get into the system. If you are dependent on several large firms, find out how their systems work. Fit your invoicing and deliveries to *their* scheduling — not yours. In the interests of cost cutting many firms are no longer sending out *statements*. If you are following the trend make sure that your invoice is clearly stamped, 'Please pay on invoice — no statement will be sent.'

Delivery and *advice notes* should state after what period damage claims can no longer be entertained.

Deposits should always be taken with orders for specials or one-offs from unknown customers. The amount should preferably cover the cost of materials.

Conditions of sale are the small print on the back of your order form. They should cover damage claims, dispute and arbitration procedures, supplier's liability and payment terms among others. The Institute of Purchasing and Supply puts out specimen contracts or you could copy one of the big boys'. One point to watch: by accepting an order you are bound by *the customer's* conditions of sale *unless* you point out the contrary. It is then up to them to accept your amended conditions or refuse the contract. It would be surprising if you managed to get a large firm to amend their conditions of sale unless it were for very minor reasons.

Overdue interest on unpaid bills is now more popular following Inland Revenue practice. The finance houses have done it for years. As an inducement to prompt payment some firms offer *discounts* of 2½ or even 7 per cent for settlement in seven days. The problem comes when large customers deduct the early discount and still pay in three months.

Satisfaction notes signed on completion of an order do not hold the force of law. The customer can still claim against you afterwards under the Sale of Goods Act 1971 for fitness of purpose. The mere signing of a note does not relieve liability.

The *Romalpa* case caused a stir in 1976. This brought a whiff of continental usage to this country. Briefly, the result has meant that if, in the event of *insolvency* of a debtor company,

139

Terms and Conditions

1 COST VARIATION
Quotations are based on the current costs of production and are subject to amendment by Uniprint at any time after acceptance to meet any rise or fall in such costs. Work for which the customer receives no quotation will be charged in accordance with Uniprint's prevailing prices where applicable. Should expedited completion of work be agreed and necessitate overtime or other additional cost an additional charge may be made.

2 VALUE ADDED TAX
Uniprint shall be entitled to charge the amount of any Value Added Tax payable whether or not included on the quotation, price list or invoice.

3 DESIGN WORK
Preliminary or design work produced, whether experimentally or otherwise at customer's request will be charged for.

4 PROOFS
Customer's corrections on and after first proof, including alterations in style, format or layout, will be charged extra. No responsibility will be accepted by Uniprint for any errors in proofs submitted to the customer for approval.

5 PAYMENT
Unless Uniprint has agreed to credit terms in the case of any particular customer or payment has been made in advance payment shall become due when the goods/work are ready for collection or delivery and will not be released to the customer until payment has been made.

6 ACCOUNT CUSTOMERS
In the case of agreed credit customers of Uniprint payment shall be made by the customer not later than the fourteenth day of the month following the month when the work is completed and ready for collection/delivery.

7 COLLECTION AND DELIVERY
Unless Uniprint has expressly agreed to deliver the goods/work to the customer they must be collected by the customer from Uniprint's premises upon notification that they are ready for such collection. In the event of Uniprint delivering the goods/work to the customer whether agreed at the time of placing order or otherwise an additional charge will be made.

8 VARIATIONS IN QUANTITY
Every endeavour will be made to deliver the correct quantity ordered by the Customer but Uniprint reserves the right to deliver up to 10% for overs or shortages the same to be charged or deducted.

9 CLAIMS
Claims by the customer against Uniprint arising from damage, delay, partial loss of goods in transit or shortages must be made in writing to Uniprint and the carrier (if any) so as to reach them within three days of collection or delivery and claims for non-delivery to be made within twenty-eight days of dispatch of goods. All other claims must be made in writing to Uniprint within ten days of the date of collection/delivery. In the event of a customer failing to make such claims to Uniprint within the times herein stated the customer will not be entitled to recover any damages, loss or compensation from Uniprint and shall be liable to pay the full invoice price for the goods/work. In the event of Uniprint at the request of the customer dispatching goods by post or by independent carrier the posting or the delivery of the goods to the carrier shall be deemed to be delivery to the customer and the customer shall not be entitled to make any claim against Uniprint in respect of damage and/or partial loss of goods in transit or for non-delivery so long as such goods have been posted or delivered to the carrier as aforesaid.

10 LIABILITY
Uniprint shall not be liable for any indirect or consequential loss or for any loss to the customer arising from third party claims occasioned by errors in carrying out the work or delay in delivery and shall not in any claim brought by the customer against Uniprint for loss, compensation or damage be liable to pay more than the invoice value of the work/goods in respect of which such claim is made.

11 STANDING MATTER
Artwork or other work belonging to the customer may be destroyed immediately after the order is executed unless written arrangements are made to the contrary. In that event rent for storage may be charged.

12 CUSTOMER'S PROPERTY AND MATERIALS SUPPLIED
(a)   Customer's property and all property supplied to Uniprint by or on behalf of the customer will be held at the customer's risk.
(b)   Every care will be taken to secure the best results when materials or artwork are supplied by customers but responsibility will not be accepted by Uniprint for imperfect work caused by defects in or unsuitability of such materials or artwork.
(d)   Where the customer supplies materials adequate quantities shall be supplied to cover spoilage.

13 GENERAL LIEN
Uniprint shall in respect of all unpaid debts due from the customer have a general lien on all goods and property in its or the customer's possession and shall on the expiration of fourteen days' notice in writing to that effect be entitled to dispose of such goods and property and apply the proceeds towards the discharge of such debts. Such notice shall be deemed to have been validly given if posted by pre-paid post addressed to the customer at his last known place of business or the address appearing on his order to Uniprint and shall be deemed to have reached the customer in normal course of post.

14 CANCELLATION OF ORDERS
Uniprint shall be entitled to withhold delivery, stop production or cancel any order if the customer fails to pay any sum owing on the due date of payment on any order and in such event the customer shall be liable to pay for all goods delivered or work done at the invoice rate and be liable to Uniprint for any additional costs, expenses, losses or damages suffered as a result of such withholding of delivery, stopping of production or cancellation of order.

15 ILLEGAL MATTER
(a)   Uniprint shall not be required to print or copy any matter which in its opinion (as to which Uniprint's opinion shall be final and conclusive for the purpose of this clause) is or may be of an illegal or libellous nature.
(b)   Uniprint shall be indemnified by the customer in respect of any claims, costs and expenses arising out of any illegal or libellous matter printed or copied for the customer or any infringement of copyright patent or design.

16 PERIODICAL PUBLICATIONS
A contract for the printing of periodical publications may not be terminated by either party unless written notice is given as follows.—

Nature of publication	Length of notice
Weekly	One month
Fortnightly	Two months
Monthly	Three months
Quarterly	Six months

Notwithstanding this provision Uniprint shall be entitled to withhold delivery, stop production or cancel the order in accordance with condition 14 herein.

17 FORCE MAJEURE
Every effort will be made to carry out the contract but its due performance is subject to cancellation by Uniprint or to such variation as we may find necessary as a result of inability to secure labour, materials or supplies or as a result of any Act of God, War, Strike, Lockout or other labour dispute, Fire, Flood, Drought, Legislation or other cause (whether of the foregoing class or not) beyond our control.

Terms and conditions of sale
(Courtesy: Uniprint Ltd)

and payment has not been made, your goods can be identified, then you, as the seller, can uplift the goods. You must have included an appropriate clause into your conditions of sale. Your claim will have preference over that of other creditors. In essence, the wording should run, 'Title to the goods does not pass until payment has been made.'

There has been insufficient case law as yet but it would seem that subcontract or component suppliers will be at a disadvantage if the goods supplied have already been fitted or absorbed into other finished products.

Finally, for further enlightenment, Ewan Mitchell has written a very readable book, *Draft Contract Letters* (Business Books), that could be very useful for disputes involving contract and many other business legal matters. If in doubt contact a good commercial solicitor.

Selling to the big firm

The dangers of getting too reliant on big contracts should be obvious but the temptation is often there. The advantages are:

1. Long production runs.
2. Prestige.
3. Bigger orders than might otherwise be the case.
4. A chance for a rapid increase in turnover.
5. A reduction in paperwork — fewer invoices and simpler credit control.
6. Sometimes a free issue of material, ie the large firm actually pays for the raw material and supplies it to the subcontractor for machining.
7. Larger orders usually mean that materials can be bought at the bulk rate.

But the dangers are:

1. Vulnerability to sudden switches in demand and buying policy, or failure of a major customer.
2. In manufacture the tendency is to farm out the awkward, unprofitable, one-off jobs and retain the steady, repetitive work in-house. This can be a useful role for the specialist contractor but all too often the price charged is too low.
3. Too many large firms are immoral when it comes to prompt payment for the work. You are often left with the choice of suing and never working for them again, or carrying an increasing financial load. You have a hold on

141

the firm only if you are the sole producer of a vital component that is holding up delivery of their production. I have heard of one firm who threatened to destroy the technical drawings if payment was not made.
4. Being tied to long fixed-price contracts. Take a hard look at the customer's tender forms and avoid agreements without a price adjustment clause.
5. On long production runs check the batch size as this will determine when you get paid. You must also be certain that your own quality standards can meet your supplier's demands. Rejections could be ruinous.

THE COMPANIES TO AVOID

Some large firms continually play one small firm against another, driving the price lower and lower. When work is short it is very difficult not to take on the production just to retain the loyalty of the work-force. I know of several cases where the ex-works price is multiplied by five by the time the goods appear on the shelves. And the firm has been screwed down by pence to get the job. Large organisations also use every trivial error to excuse late payment. Such firms are mostly wealthy, highly profitable organisations with impeccable Stock Exchange credentials. The laws of libel forbid me to list such companies but they are well-known in their trade. In my experience some good firms to deal with are John Lewis, Liberty's, Harrods and Shell. They have an enlightened attitude and seem generally keen to encourage small suppliers.

UNDERSTANDING THE LARGE ORGANISATION

Having sketched out some of the black spots, it may be helpful to outline the way to tackle the large firm, because if you can get on a good footing it can undoubtedly give you stable growth.

Anyone who has worked for a large company knows that it is intensely hierarchical, departmentalised and indecisive. A small firm owner will probably order the supplies, vet the quality and pay the invoice. In a large firm these three basic functions may be performed by:

1. A team of buyers.
2. A quality assurance (QA) inspector.
3. A warehouseman, who may be hundreds of miles away from the buyer.
4. An invoice clerk.

5. A department head who passes the bill for payment.
6. The computing system that spews out your cheque.

Any hiccup in this long chain and your cheque could be delayed until next month's payments. All large firms employ professional buyers who belong to the Institute of Purchasing and Supply. It is rightly recognised as a most important function.

FIRST STEPS
Before approaching any big company you must find out and understand the market they are in and the way they are structured. Send for their annual accounts which will often give quite detailed breakdowns of their main activities and subsidiaries. Shell, for example, issue a special booklet on how their purchasing is arranged. If you are selling to a major store, pay a visit and spend some time going round the various departments to get a feel for their merchandise. All large stores try and portray a certain image, style and price range. Your offerings must be compatible.

The next step is to phone and find out which purchasing department you need and which buyer (by name) is likely to be the right contact.

In most firms the chief buyers (who may be known as 'procurement', 'materials service' or 'directors of supply') have an overall control and tend to reserve contracts over a certain ceiling, say £500,000, to themselves. They will have many buyers under their control who each look after a limited range.

Write for an *appointment* giving full details, technical literature, photographs and perhaps a sample. It is no use just turning up on the off-chance: they are all busy people with appointments booked up. It looks very unprofessional to adopt a casual approach. Spell out why you think they would benefit from your goods or service, quote prices and name other large firms you supply. Harrods, for example, will be looking for some measure of exclusivity. If you are in the defence, aerospace or oil supply fields, be prepared to wait from six months to a year to be financially and quality vetted. Small component suppliers must convince their customers that their background and future are soundly based to assure continuity of supply. A detailed QA inspection may follow.

TENDERS

Most buying is done on regular contract or tender for a given period. The major problem for new firms is to get on the tender list. Inevitably there are many firms ahead of you on the list either as existing suppliers or hopefuls waiting for next time round. The standard brush off is to say, 'Yes, I'll put you on the list,' but you never hear another thing. Some companies do have a regular switch round to keep existing suppliers on their toes but all too many have a cosy relationship.

There is no easy solution, but as with all selling, you must maintain regular contact with your potential buyer and keep him informed of new products.

GETTING PAID

We all hear the horror stories of people waiting months to get paid but forget that the vast majority of companies do pay their bills regularly. I believe that small firms fall down largely because of their own inadequacies. The golden rules are:

1. Send out your invoices promptly (many don't).
2. Quote order numbers, despatch dates, missing items and any other ingredients that your customer expects.
3. State your payment terms and any early settlement discount offered.
4. Make sure that your invoice matches any offer made by your salesman!
5. Most important of all, ensure that you understand the client's cut-off date for the computer. Many firms close the payments ledger around the 25th of each month and if your invoice is not through the system by then it will wait till next month. *Find out this date* for all your big customers and make a large note on the wall for all to see. Survival depends on your cash flow.

Your most important ingredient for success in this area is your relationship with the buyer you deal with. Many are genuinely interested in helping you to grow, to your mutual advantage, so make a friend of him and involve him in your progress. Try and bypass him and you will usually put his back up. If you are really stuck for payment I can recommend three courses of action:

1. Send a telex. The junior will broadcast the message all through the office which usually embarrasses all but the most thick-skinned firm. There are telex agency offices if you don't run to your own machine.

2. Write to the managing director or chairman at his home. You can usually track down his address through a combination of the *Stock Exchange Year Book, Who Owns Whom* and various books listing directorships.

3. Give them seven days to pay then sue. You can do this yourself through the local county court. The formalities are simple and the summons fee goes on the costs. The limit is now £5000; above that you must go through the High Court — definitely a job for your solicitor. I have always found the magistrate's clerks helpful in filling out the forms.

    Leave this as a last resort.

THE GOVERNMENT

One buyer you should not have to sue is the government. This market is vast as it encompasses the Ministry of Defence, National Health Service, Property Services Agency (PSA), HM Stationery Office (HMSO) and many others. Unlike the USA, the UK government is still feeling its way towards a positive buying policy in favour of small firms. The systems, because of the complex nature of the contract tender paperwork, tend to favour firms with plenty of experienced office staff.

The biggest spender of all is the Ministry of Defence but because of the generally sophisticated and expensive nature of the required equipment, most purchases will inevitably be direct with large organisations. Your opportunity will be with components via the back door of a major company, unless you have a unique product in demand. As a main contractor you will have to meet stiff quality standards which can be very expensive to install.

The basis of most procurement is by competitive price tendering from approved firms on a tender list, which brings us back to the old problem discussed earlier of how you get on the tender list. It could be a long wait. You may stand more chance by cultivating purchasing departments that are situated regionally, eg health authorities and the PSA. There are also various MoD research establishments scattered around the country that specialise in peculiar methods of waging warfare. If you can interest a local expert by solving his problem it could give you a way in.

Two free booklets worth reading are *Tendering for Government Contracts* which is available from the Small Firms Service (freefone 2444) and *Selling to the MoD*. The introduction to this reads, 'Small firms should always remember that MoD buys not only sophisticated weapons but also everything — from boots to breakfast cereal — needed to support the Armed Forces in peace and war.' It is obtainable from the Industrial Policy Division, Room 2328 Main Building, Ministry of Defence, London SW1A 3HB.

The pattern of distribution

Before any serious marketing is attempted it is important to study the pattern of distribution in your trade sector. Accepted trade practices vary and you would be wise to follow the herd while you are small. Pioneering is best left to those with money. This overcrowded island is well served with wholesalers-cum-distributors. Carriers are plentiful and now that the motorway network is nearly complete delivery is speedy. The wholesale trade is, however, under attack after years of inflexibility. Existing patterns are changing with the rapid growth of multiple chain stores and cash and carries, but for many small firms wholesalers remain the most sensible way of selling and distributing their products.

ADVANTAGES OF DEALING WITH A WHOLESALER
1. They buy in bulk, meaning fewer distribution drops for you.
2. They break bulk and sell on through their sales force.
3. They hold a buffer stock.
4. They collect accounts — you are saved servicing a multitude.

Wholesalers enable a small firm to reach a large number of retail outlets or smaller trade customers and save you the expense of calling on many otherwise unprofitable accounts. They are able to do this, of course, by carrying a large number of lines of which your item may be only a tiny fraction. Van sales with racking supporting hundreds of lines can tour a dozen outlets a day.

Credit control and cash flow should be improved. There should be minimal paperwork, fewer invoices, delivery notes or statements. The wholesalers tend to be long established and possess an in-depth knowledge of their customers and market. As, generally, far more capital is needed to set up as a wholesaler than a retailer you should have fewer financial worries.

Wholesalers can be either general dealers, as in food or hardware, or specialists dealing in a narrow engineering field, such as fasteners or adhesives. While 'middleman' has tended to become a term of general abuse, for the small man, wholesalers can perform a valuable role.

BUT NOW FOR THE DISADVANTAGES

Wholesalers are sometimes accused of carrying too many lines and of failing to give sufficient weight to a firm's products. Because they have been in the trade for generations, some have failed to move with the times and have been caught by the changing patterns of distribution.

Since the abolition of resale price maintenance some manufacturers have regretted the loss of ability to control the *price* at which goods are sold.

Another body in the way also reduces the *selection* of outlets where consumers can view the merchandise. Links with a dealer network are weakened.

Mark-ups are rarely less than 30 per cent and can be more, depending on the trade you are in. It is this distaste of paying any margin that probably offends new small firms. What they fail to realise is the cost of going direct. The wholesaler should know his market and be employing a sales force to best advantage.

CHANGING ROLES

Established patterns are being eroded by the great buying power of multiple chains and big manufacturers who increasingly negotiate their own deals direct. Hypermarkets are exerting their own pressures on the retail trade forcing the shops to group together (Vivo, Spar etc). Buying groups in industry and even educational suppliers are squeezing out wholesalers. In the south west a buying group of more than a dozen counties have formed their own consortium to purchase supplies in millions. Increasingly direct marketing is the thrust. Only 10 years ago selling by post was reserved for the kitchen gadget in the Sunday small-ads. Clive Sinclair bases his revolutionary computer operation on attacking the consumer market direct. I strongly suspect that he mistrusted the High Street's ability to understand and sell his innovatory products.

DELIVERING SMALL ORDERS

The real cost of distributing your goods or making service calls is frequently under-estimated. You may well be consistently undercharging for low value drops in the belief that others along the way will make up for it, but you can carry service too far. The first priority is to make out schedules for each type of vehicle you use and get the cost down to a mileage basis. Don't forget depreciation. For example, for the average light van, the magazine *Motor Transport* says you should charge 51p a mile, including the driver's wages. If, as so often happens in small firms, the owner delivers as well then the loss of productive time must be accounted for.

Having got a basic costing for delivery the next logical step is to compare this method with using an outside carrier, either the Post Office, Roadline or one of the many national carriers. Most towns can produce a reliable, independent carrier as well.

For urgent deliveries Red Star is convenient if you're near a main line station: same day delivery is possible for most areas of the country. You simply advise the recipient which station the goods arrive at. For next day delivery try the many national carriers, Securicor for one, that do a door-to-door service.

The usual argument against contracting out is, 'While I'm there I can often pick up another order.' Whatever happened to the telephone?

The ultimate extension of this exercise is to cost out each *customer* on a profit basis taking into account the selling costs, discounts allowed and distribution costs. You may find that delivering every other week, raising the minimum order value or reducing the quantity discount restores a marginal customer to one of profit.

How to get the best out of an agent

Wholesalers/distributors purchase the goods and sell on. In return they expect a minimum of 30 per cent mark-up. To reduce the distribution cost an agent can be used.

- Agents usually work for a direct commission on volume only.
- Commission varies but is rarely less than 7½ per cent and 15 per cent is not unknown.
- The goods are not sold to the agent but invoiced direct to the stockist.
- The agent may not see the goods at all, apart from sales samples, as they are delivered direct to the buyer.

Few small firms can afford their own sales force and perhaps fewer still enjoy selling as a pastime. But someone has to do it! It is supposed to cost around £20,000 a year (1985) to keep a good salesman on the road, including all his car and general travelling expenses. Inevitably there is a running-in period where the investment is awaiting some return. And you run the risk of picking the wrong guy.

The logical sales route is via agents. A good agent will have *contacts* in your field, buyers personally known to him, with perhaps many years of detailed product knowledge. The important thing to remember all the time is that, like you, he is in business on his *own account* and he stands or falls by his own efforts. If he doesn't sell he won't earn.

Agents are paid purely on commission. You as principal pay out directly on results. It is obviously in both your interests to develop a close working relationship and is not a situation where you can shovel all the responsibility for sales on to someone else and forget about it. That will quickly lead to disillusionment. You will join the throng of firms who say, 'Agents don't work.'

HOW TO FIND AN AGENT
There are two national bodies that look after agents — the British Agents Register (24 Mount Parade, Harrogate HG1 1BP; 0423 60608) and the Manufacturer's Agents Association (13a West Street, Reigate, Surrey; RH2 9BL; 07372 43492). Contact can be made through them, although not every agent belongs, of course.

The most successful way, I believe, is by asking at stockists where your product should be sold. Ask them who their best agents are as they know the bright and professional characters. Then draw up a short list and contact them. You can also place ads in relevant trade journals, or hang a sign on your exhibition stand. The *Daily Telegraph* is also widely studied for the classified ads — 'Agents Wanted'. As always, the most reliable guide should be personal recommendation. Good agents are hard to find, and just as hard to retain.

HOW TO CHOOSE AN AGENT
Most agents work on their own, though partnerships of several individuals, or even limited companies, are not unknown. You should find out:

1. What other agencies he already has. Most carry at least three, with occasionally as many as eight. Too many, and

149

a one-man band won't have the time to devote to your product line.

The agent should not accept *competing* products. Related, but not competitive. For example, if he is calling on engineering firms he should not carry two types of ear muffs (from different principals) but it would be quite legitimate to sell, say, cutting fluid. There must be no conflict, otherwise he will be in an impossible situation.

2. Ask about his proven selling record. An efficient agent will be glad to show evidence (without breaking confidences) of his turnover and commissions.
3. He should obviously have a telephone, a reasonable car, stable home life and a generally businesslike approach.
4. Probe his connections. Drop a few names and see if he really has the in-depth knowledge he claims. *Contacts* are the agent's most vital asset — without them he will not sell for you.
5. What territory does he already cover? He is unlikely to stretch beyond his other clients just for you.
6. The crunch question. Would you wish this man (or woman) to represent your business? Does he appear honest, reliable, professional, engaging?

At the interview, and you *will* of course interview him, you will be able to form an opinion of his professionalism more from the probing questions he should be asking *you*. Agencies are really a partnership, certainly not an employer-employee relationship where you can discipline for omissions. It is in his interests to sell good products at the right price with sufficient profit, just as much as it is in yours. He will want a lasting relationship to develop his contacts and market. A good agent will spend a considerable amount of time and effort investing in a new product range.

For your part you must be prepared to back him up, make visits in the field, give and take on discounts where necessary, support at trade fairs, and provide advertising and literature as appropriate. As the man at the sharp end your agent should be feeding you with customer reaction and market trends to keep you up to date. The alert agent will have done some canvassing among your customers before he sees you, to gauge whether you and your products are worth his allegiance. The questions he should ask are:

1. How do you promote the product range? Trade fairs, advertising, and if so is the budget increasing or static?
2. Can you meet increased orders? There is little point in going out for more business if production is not sorted out.
3. Is it a new product that has yet to find acceptance? It is always easier to sell a tried and proven line.
4. What are the existing sales for the territory offered? The agent will want to know his potential commission which is based on this figure.
5. Are any price adjustments on the way?
6. What other agents do you use and am I taking over from another? He will probably ask for the name and it is hard for the honest firm to think of a good enough reason to refuse.
7. What sales aids do you supply? These can include slides, sample books, models and point of sale (POS) material.
8. What technical training can you provide?

The agent will want to be convinced that both you and the product have a future.

THE AGENCY AGREEMENT

It is vital that a written agreement is made between you both setting out the terms of the relationship. It has to be fair to both parties otherwise you'll get off to a bad start from the beginning.

If things proceed smoothly you will never refer to it but misunderstandings are the most common cause of a break-up. There are special books devoted to legal agency agreements but for simplicity the clauses below should be covered. It is not essential for a solicitor to be involved as long as the letter is clear.

1. The *territory* in which the agent operates. It must be exclusive.
2. The *products* he is to promote. This is not as simple as you think. You as manufacturer may well produce lines other than that which you put out on agency. Make it clear that if he sells non-agreement products he will be specifically rewarded. Vague guidelines are a common cause of friction.
3. The *categories* of customer he will call on. The principal may ask the agent to widen his existing contacts by calling

on a fresh range of outlets. A definition of 'house accounts' must be made. It often happens that the principal retains several large accounts for himself, ie without paying agency commission even though the client is within his territory. It should be made clear that the agent will not service any account for which he gains no reward. It is better for both sides if house accounts are kept to a minimum.

4. *Commission terms*. You must spell out the rates, dates and frequency of payment. It is usual to pay commission on all orders (net) in the month following the date of invoice — not when the client pays the bill! The actual rates vary enormously from 1 per cent on high value capital goods to over 20 per cent in some of the gift trades. The average is around 10 per cent. Rates are normally lower on larger volume customers such as wholesalers and department stores and should really reflect the amount and difficulty of work involved. Commission should be paid on *all* orders received regardless of whether they came direct from the customer or via the agent.

5. *Agent's authority*. It should be spelled out what discretion the agent has to vary the pricing to secure an order. It is often sensible to allow some variation to the man on the spot but how much should be detailed.

6. *Period* of agreement. It must be clear on what terms the agent will be working. It is sensible and usual to split the agreement into *two* parts. The first period — the honeymoon — will give both parties a reasonable time to decide whether they are suited. Anything less than three months is too short for the agent to familiarise himself with the product and settle into the market. The principal will want to know in practice what his agent is like in the field.

Notice of *termination* on either side can be one month for the first year and six months thereafter. This seems to work reasonably well. Both sides have security. The principal has representation out in the field and the agent should feel that his income will not be cut off at short notice.

7. Other clauses should cover out-of-pocket expenses, attendance at trade shows, visits to the factory, training courses, advertising support, stock to be carried and after-sales service. It is rare for agents to collect debts.

But I stress again — an agreement will not rescue a sour relationship. Like a marriage, you have to work at it to keep it on the rails. The national average for agencies' survival is three years. Try and beat it!

Complaints

Everyone gets them at some time or another even in the best run firm, but it does present an *opportunity*. A complaining customer who is turned round to a satisfied one is a buyer for life. It helps if one specific person in a senior position is trained and kept for dealing with complainers. Call him the 'Customer Relations Manager' or even Director: people love to deal with status.

The procedure is straightforward.

1. Thank the customer for bringing the matter to your attention. 'We are very mindful of our good name and if rarely something falls short of our high standards — we want to know about it.'
2. Apologise for his being upset, but at this stage don't admit to specific blame.
3. Make sure you get the *facts*; there are always two sides to every argument. Record the dates, quantity, delivery, invoice etc.
4. Listen patiently and never interrupt or justify. Let the customer run out of steam and get it off his chest. Butting in while he's in full flow will only spark him off to new heights of fury.
5. Then tell the customer what *action* you'll be taking and keep him informed, obviously the more promptly the better. If there is any doubt, replace the goods without question. The business you will derive from a no-quibble guarantee will stand you in good stead. A nice touch is to refer the matter to the 'Executive Complaints Board' which doesn't exist. A soothing letter from the 'chairman' will impress most people no end.

Having said all that, once in a blue moon you will come across a professional complainer. Having satisfied him as fairly as you can — don't prolong the argument. Life is too short and there are more people out there who can do you some good.

Retail mark-ups

It often comes as a great shock to the new firm owner to find the goods he has so painstakingly produced boldly displayed in the High Street at twice the price he has sold them for.

The lowest mark-up is probably in newsagents who average 17 per cent on confectionery. They have to rely on volume and a fast-moving turnover to make a living, which is why location is so important for these shops. At the other end of the scale are jewellers, furriers and the gift trade who rarely drop below 100 per cent. Many of the better class London stores add on 200 per cent or more.

This is why it is so important to study your markets and learn the pattern of trade and add-ons before fixing a price structure. If the margin just isn't there you will have to re-think your marketing strategy and look at different ways of reaching the consumer. Don't confuse margins with mark-ups: an item bought in at £10 can be marked up 50 per cent to sell at £15, but the margin, ie profit, will be $33\frac{1}{3}$ per cent — £5 as a percentage of the £15 selling price.

The following table may help to remind you what mark-up you need to add on to retain your gross margin.

Mark-up per cent	Margin per cent
5.3	5
8.11	7.5
11.11	10
14.3	12.5
17.65	15
25	20
33.33	25
42.9	30
50	33.33

Do not forget that to find the VAT element of the selling price, you *deduct* 13.043 per cent *not* 15 per cent although the VAT man prefers you to multiply by 3 and divide by 23.

Whichever pattern of distribution is used never lose touch with the people who buy — your consumers.

To conclude this chapter on selling here is an old salesman's joke that is worth a wider audience. Grocer Goldberg was showing his new junior round the stock room.

'My, what a lot of cheese you must sell!'

'Not me,' said Goldberg, 'But you should meet the man who sells *me* cheese!'

Chapter 6

Franchise to Expand

The concept of franchising has a place here because of its potential for growth from a limited base in a marketing context.

Franchising has been around since the last century and has enjoyed spectacular growth in the United States. The first UK franchises were simple licences to operate a distributorship — Shell garages or Austin cars. Some franchises today are still no more than that — a cloak for distributors as a means of securing more outlets.

The business format franchise

Of more interest is a complete business package bought 'off the peg' and known as the *business format* franchise. The basis of the scheme is a novel idea, a process or service, or a patented piece of machinery, that is often trade marked. Around it has been developed a blueprint for success — a manner of doing business where all the pitfalls have been ironed out, supplies, premises, layout and merchandising brought down to a cohesive package that can be marketed and replicated. Implicit in the package is thorough training before and during the life of the franchise, as required.

The *franchisor* is the originator and guardian of the format who licenses it to the *franchisee*. There is considerable responsibility on the part of the franchisor to choose carefully those to whom he sells the rights. To the consumer it is immaterial whether the service is provided by a franchised chain or an individual business, but the image of all franchisees can be tarnished by one indifferent member. They are all supporting one another. Ethics, goodwill and trust are needed in large quantities. At the root of franchising is the belief that people (the franchisees) tend to work harder when they have their own business. As many franchisees are completely new to business, it is worth recording that their failure rate is considerably lower than for the general run of small firms. In the States around 10 per cent of franchises fail after five years, while the figure is 90 per cent for other new businesses. It is thought that the situation is similar in the UK. It is noteworthy that British banks seem quite happy to advance purchase fees for franchises: if our banks are willing to back them there can't be much wrong with the idea.

Franchising in this country really started with Joe Lyons and the decline of the traditional Corner House tea shops. One bright J Lyons executive saw what was happening in the States and introduced the concept of franchising identical fast food outlets. They make their money by charging an initial setting-up fee and by restricting the purchases of the raw material (Wimpys etc) to their own warehouse.

After a slow start there are now reckoned to be about 10,000 franchised outlets in this country supplying everything from wedding dresses to drain cleaning, printing to kebabs. Sales turnover is hard to estimate but is probably now over £1 billion. In the USA franchising probably accounts for one-third of all retail sales − a staggering proportion − and an actual figure of possibly £500 billion. We therefore have a long way to go.

Franchising is above all a *marketing* concept. The attractions to a supplier are:

1. Expansion using someone else's capital and enthusiasm.
2. Improved penetration of the market.
3. Creation of a tied market for his increased production.
4. The generation of some cash up front and further regular, hopefully increasing, income as the network expands.
5. Reaching areas, even overseas, which might be difficult to tackle economically from base.
6. Fewer staff management problems than in expansion by conventional means.
7. Once the network has expanded he then has the ability to negotiate bulk rates, deal with national companies and have more clout in the market.

So how do you set about franchising your operation to others? You must first have completely ironed out the bugs in your own operation. It is no use marketing an unproven idea using the first prospect's money, hopes and dreams as a test bed. That is what gets franchising a bad name. Get the British Franchise Association's Code of Ethics and other literature. Their address is Franchise Chambers, 75a Bell Street, Henley-on-Thames, Oxfordshire RG9 2BD: 0491 578049. You will not be eligible for full membership until you have been running for a while. That need not bar you from asking them for advice as they are always helpful to genuine enquirers. Several seminars are held every year to outline the profitable way to market franchising. Martin Mendelsohn's *Guide to Franchising* is also an invaluable work. To whet your appetite it might be illuminating to list some of the businesses that have been successfully franchised. In this country food outlets have been the most popular.

1. *Bath renovation:* Bathcare
2. *Car hire:* Budget Rent A Car
3. *Car maintenance:* Midas, Home Tune and Snap-On-Tools
4. *Cosmetics:* Yves Rocher
5. *Drain cleaning:* Dyno-Rod
6. *Food:* Kentucky Fried Chicken, Spud-U-Like, Pizza Express, Cookie Coach Company, Wimpy and Little Chef
7. *Hotels:* Holiday Inn
8. *Ice cream:* Lyons Maid, Baskin Robbins
9. *Office cleaning:* ServiceMaster
10. *Print shops:* Prontaprint, PDC Copyprint
11. *Travel agents:* Exchange Travel
12. *Wedding dresses:* Pronuptia

It can be seen that the essence of a franchise operation is a successful business idea that is proven, profitable for both parties, capable of replication, able to be assimilated with reasonable training and one that is helped by a continuing relationship. The successful franchises are also continually developing and innovating. The market doesn't remain static and neither should the franchisor.

Developing a franchise scheme

We have seen the scope for this type of activity and you must decide whether your operation is ripe for expansion along these lines. It would be foolish to embark until you are completely in control of your own business and making steady profits. To a large extent franchisees will want to be satisfied that all the problems have been removed by looking hard at what you have already achieved. You will be the expert in all things to do with the operation. You will have to train the new franchisees in every aspect of the business, imparting trade know-how and secrets, perhaps hard won. The most efficient method of production will have been decided, the correct machines, layout, costing, stock levels, materials, premises, promotion and advertising package. The marketing potential of the operation will have been tested by varying the location, opening hours, advertising message and appeal to different segments of the market.

Experience from other franchisors shows that you may not have to train the franchisees in your operation only but in basic business methods as well. It is vital, therefore, that you arrive at a simple system of paperwork that covers recording sales, stock levels and re-ordering in a single operation. It is simplest to encompass all the knowledge and detail in an *operations manual* that will be commonly referred to at every stage. This will set down in great detail such matters as staff training and the explicit duties of each member of the production team. It will lay down standards to be observed, because one poor outlet can lower the image of the whole chain.

The franchise contract

This legal agreement binds the parties and sets out the rights and obligations expected of each. As franchising is a specialist field you would be wise to consult a commercial solicitor well versed in this area and to draw heavily on the experience of the BFA and its Code of Ethics.

The document will set out:

1. The nature and name of the activity being franchised (the package to be licensed, the trade marks, methods, recipes, specifications, know-how required to run a successful outlet). Although each individual is running his own business all the outlets must conform to the same range and quality of goods and service.
2. The franchise territory.
3. The term of the franchise.
4. The franchise fee and royalty.
5. What the franchisor agrees to do (what is being provided by way of assistance, training, shop fittings, equipment, stock, promotional material, advertising etc).
6. What the franchisee undertakes to do.
7. The conditions under which the franchisee may sell or assign the business.
8. The conditions under which the franchisee may terminate the franchise and what his obligations are in that case.
9. The terms and obligations of the franchisor in similar circumstances.

There are a hundred and one points that demand explicit coverage and unless they are in the contract disputes are sure to arise.

Some of the banks have also appointed franchising specialists who should be approached. The big four are:

Barclays Bank plc, Marketing Department, Juxon House, 6th floor, 94 St Paul's Churchyard, London EC4M 8EH; tel 01-248 9155, contact Franchise Marketing Manager.

Lloyds Bank plc, 71 Lombard Street, London EC3P 3BG; tel 01-626 1500.

Midland Bank plc, Business Sector Marketing Unit, Poultry, London EC2P 2BX; tel 01-606 9911.

National Westminster Bank plc, Small Business Section, Domestic Banking Division, 3rd floor, 116 Fenchurch Street, London EC3M 5AN; tel 01-726 1875, contact Franchise Marketing Manager.

How do you make your money?

You will have realised by now that franchising is not for the unskilled or timid. It demands a high degree of professionalism in marketing, finance, business management in general and, perhaps most important of all, an ability to pick and nurture the right franchisees. There is a long period when you have to perfect your own business, make it into a marketable commodity, recruit and train staff to be your own management team, and consult a whole range of experts — legal and financial — before launching the franchise package. It is not a way of making money *quickly*.

There may be a variety of ways in which the franchisor will make his income. The main ones are:

1. The initial fee to set up in business. Where this is large the payment can be spread over a period. This could include a fee for the right to use the brand name plus the general sum to cover training, supplies, equipment and promotion to open the premises.
2. There is usually a consumable product that must be continually purchased to make sales. The franchisor will invariably stipulate that these purchases must be made through him. He will build a profit margin into the price.
3. The operating premises which are leased to the franchisee may be owned by the franchisor. Large franchise chains

    are sometimes able to negotiate very favourable terms and make a profit by loading the rental.

4. Vital equipment can be purchased by the franchisor and leased out to the users.

5. The most popular way of generating an income is to charge a simple royalty fee on the sales turnover. This way both parties know what is being charged. It does not arouse the suspicion in the franchisee's mind that the cost of supplies is being loaded.

Selling the package

You must resist the temptation to sign up any franchisees who have the money in their hands. The whole operation will stand or fall by the quality of your new colleagues, for this in effect is what they are. The image of the chain is totally reliant on whom you pick to bear your brand and it would be most unfortunate if the first few turned out to be duds. Any later franchisee would probe the merits of the offer hard and would be strongly influenced by existing outlets.

The cheapest way of promoting the franchise is undoubtedly to write a story for the ever increasing number of business magazines setting out what is on offer. There is even a magazine called *Franchise World* (James House, 37 Nottingham Road, London SW17 7EA; 01-767 1371) that specialises in this sector. If your proposed franchise is a specialist service don't neglect the relevant trade journals. Advertising can be aimed at the numerous 'Business Opportunities' columns of the national papers. Write to those clearing banks that have franchise departments (listed above).

As you will want to present the format in the best light make sure that your promotional literature is first class and *factual*. Too many franchises have promised rich pickings for little effort. Financial forecasts must not be over-optimistic. Don't forget to say what profits, not just turnover, can be expected and how your income or continuing fees will be derived.

Interviewing the franchisee

With the size of redundancy payments now being offered and officers in the services retiring at an early age, there is normally no lack of applicants able to find the initial fee. It is vital that a very thorough examination is conducted to satisfy both parties that a working relationship can be established. After all, next to the house purchase this is probably the biggest commitment anyone will take on.

In many ways the successful franchisees follow new publicans. They tend to be energetic and middle aged, with the wife wholeheartedly behind the man. The hours are similarly demanding and they both like meeting people. The husband tends to be frustrated working for big companies and has a burning desire to be his own boss. The franchise concept suits him because he probably has not run a small business before. The attraction is a proven vehicle combined with training and back-up.

Having interviewed and shown the prospects your pilot operation it is important to visit their home. A large part of the success of franchising relies on organisation and portraying a fresh image. If their house lacks these essential ingredients they are unlikely to change in business.

Setting up the franchise

This is the time to prove that all your promises in selling the format carry weight. The new franchisee is at his most vulnerable and it is vital that full training before, and nursing during, the opening stages is offered. Your team must be prepared to set aside weeks if necessary for working in the new premises guiding the embryo operation. After this initial nervous period you must be ready to provide instant back-up whenever required. Only in this way can trust and a bond be established to expand the business.

After a while you may have to encourage the franchisee to solve his own problems to a greater extent — it is his business after all.

Improvements and innovations

It is important that the franchise continues to develop new products, services, merchandising and image. Like any other chain the offers must continue to meet consumer preferences. You should encourage your franchisees to bring forward ideas and share them through the network. The franchisor should retain several 'company stores' in which to try out ideas and keep ahead of the other outlets. It is easy to lose the initial respect and impetus by resting on your laurels. You must still be the one who leads by example.

And now the drawbacks

Having painted all the good points of franchising as a marketing tool to expansion it would be unrealistic not to lay out the problems. Franchising is still in its infancy and has attracted too many wide boys for comfort. The press has latched on to some overblown operations that promised riches for little effort. In some minds it is associated with pyramid selling, now outlawed.

The BFA is making a good attempt to lay down standards but only about a third of franchisors belong. As with all such associations they can only dismiss members for transgression — there is no legal redress to the BFA. From the franchisor's point of view there are the following disadvantages:

1. You may well appoint the wrong franchisees. They may not maintain standards, reflecting a poor image to the consumer and damaging the goodwill of the operation.
2. Once installed the franchisees may become complacent and fail to innovate or pick · up suggestions for continual improvement.
3. Friction may arise on a number of matters. As it is the franchisees' own business and money at risk, it is impossible for you to lay down the law as if it were merely a branch operation. They have to be coaxed, educated and shown by example.
4. The successful franchisee may feel that once established he owes nothing to the franchisor and will resent having to pay a continual royalty on sales. He is the one putting in all the hard work and there may be resentment at the contractual relationship. In some cases the franchisee may indeed outgrow the expertise of the franchisor and develop beyond the original concept. There can be little regard for the franchisor in these circumstances.
5. There must be a large element of trust and respect between the parties brought about by an understanding of their respective roles. At the root of the relationship must be excellent communication to remove any suspicion and misunderstandings.

From the franchisee's point of view the drawbacks, in addition to those allied to points 1 to 5 listed above, are:

1. The concept may be unproven. The franchisor is using the franchisee's money and enthusiasm to test the idea. Expected turnover and profits may be grossly exaggerated.

2. Training and back-up may be inadequate. Once a contract has been signed and money has changed hands it is virtually impossible to force the franchisor to carry out his promises if he is so minded to avoid them. It is so important to investigate the franchise thoroughly first.

3. What has been promised verbally may either not appear in the contract or fail to materialise after. So much of franchising is concerned with intangibles such as know-how, training and service that it is wide open to fraud.

4. The franchise really has to make *two* profits — one for each party — and there are not many new businesses making margins of that order. Most disappointment arises from this fact. To be successful the business has to be quite exceptional, and in today's economic climate with high borrowing costs, it is asking a lot.

5. Disposal value is usually most uncertain, and the franchisee may not benefit from his own hard work. There are invariably close restrictions on how the licence may be assigned. This runs counter to the genuine independent businessman who can sell to whomsoever he likes.

6. The contract may be too restrictive, stopping the successful franchisee developing in new directions.

7. The best areas will be taken first and will tend to be cheaper. Once the franchise is seen to be successful the initial fees are bound to rise. It is always difficult to evaluate a new enterprise from few outlets.

Chapter 7
Direct Response Marketing

The marketing we've looked at till now has tended to be geared to developing sales through intermediaries and third parties: wholesalers, agents and conventional stockists. This chapter is devoted to the possibilities of direct selling, and showing that the development of a *direct* relationship with the client is not only logical but profitable. My definition of direct response marketing is any situation where you make the offer straight to the purchaser. For the small firm this has obvious advantages: flexible hours can be worked; part-time staff can be pulled in for rush jobs; cash flow can be improved and, potentially, sales can be made more immediately profitable. Direct mail and mail order do not need lavish premises in the High Street. Sometimes it is a positive advantage not to be there. More people, I suspect, will happily send for Fair Isle jumpers to the remoteness of Scotland than to an address in Slough.

The biggest advantage of promotion by direct mail over other methods is surely the ability to *test*. So much of advertising is hard to quantify that this feature should come as a godsend to small firms. Any aspect of the mailing can be changed (offer, brochure, sales letter) and the response directly measured. Not only can the effect of changes be accurately recorded but the result is quickly known. There are no long waits for agents or distributors to react. The most profitable way of expanding sales is by selling more products to your existing customers, not by continually hunting for fresh clients. We are all creatures of habit. Providing we've had good service we tend to go back to the same supplier. All the motor manufacturers, for example, like to cover the range, from cheap mini car to luxury saloon, in the hope that the purchase of one model will lead to another.

It takes money to keep hunting for more names to influence through promotion and advertising. How much simpler to mail out fresh opportunities to contented known customers who will come back and buy more of the same or some of a similar product.

The openings are there but how many take them? Think of all those firms sending out monthly invoices and never using the same stamp to push more products. All it takes is a handbill and an order form. I have a monthly account with an oil company and their statement arrives every six months. I happen to know that they also own a hardware store, garage and gift shop but they are very shy about letting me know what bargains are on offer.

There are a number of areas where businesses could exploit their existing direct links and make more money:

1. Technical reps doing service or repair work. Are they trained to sell? Frequently they are in the best position of all to generate further business. I am often amazed to see businesses firmly divided between sales and service staff. Is there not common ground here?

2. Always look for add-on products to sell. Those that do it well are perhaps Action Man and Lego, two toys that grow and grow. The electric drill ushered in a range of labour-saving devices from sanders to polishers, lathes and circular saws: it's the attachments that make the money. Make the first purchase — the drill — and you will be hooked on all the accessories till you have a complete home workshop. I'm waiting for Kodak to give every child a camera. The films are where the money is.

3. Anything related to return coupons or guarantee cards gives a ready-made bank of names. Mail out something that will harmonise with the original product.

4. Any business that regularly mails out statements or newsletters. If you are really stumped for offers sell the facility to others.

Making the most of mail order

The mail order industry is dominated by the catalogue companies, GUS, Littlewoods, Freemans etc. Around 90 per cent of the market is cornered by these lavish producers of home catalogues and something over 80 per cent of the sales are on credit. There is room for the small specialist catalogue — hobbies, sports goods, gardening etc — but nothing remotely on the scale of the big boys.

The small firm concentrates on selling 'off the page' — small space ads placed in special interest magazines or the more general *Exchange & Mart*. The national press have their own truncated version in their 'Postal Bargains' slot. They present the chance to reach millions of readers at a moderate cost. But whether they *pull* or not is up to you. To summarise the drawbacks first:

1. Black and white newsprint gives limited scope for creative ability.
2. The space allowed in many of the slots is not sufficient for products that require a lengthy explanation.
3. Space is often booked well in advance, particularly near Christmas.
4. Quite rightly, you have to abide by the codes of practice that cover mail order advertising, but practices seem to differ between papers.

THE MAIL ORDER PROTECTION SCHEME
All adverts that ask for *money in advance of the goods*, with the exception of classified ads, must conform to the Mail Order Protection Scheme. It is there to protect the customers' money in the event of the advertiser's failure. The details to be submitted are:

1. Latest accounts.
2. Bank reference.
3. Stock levels — to convince them you will not forward sell.
4. Advertising agents.
5. Details of the advert and product.

It should take no longer than a month to gain clearance. You will then have to pay a fee to the common fund based on the advertising costs.

Full details of the scheme are available by sending a stamped and addressed envelope to Mail Order Protection Scheme, Newspaper Publishers Association Ltd, 16 Took's Court, London EC4A 1LB.

HOW TO INCREASE YOUR SALES FROM SMALL ADS
Small ads are a popular medium for new small firms but so many expect too much from a modest expenditure. A national paper will charge around £40 for a space not much bigger than a large postage stamp. Strangely enough I haven't yet found a paper that has researched the response to its own columns. My own small sample suggests that you can expect at best 30 enquiries for each insertion, and this is from a Sunday paper

with a circulation of over a million copies. It is therefore vital that your sales forecast is realistic. As you are required to deliver the goods within 28 days of receiving the order it is obviously important that supplies are to hand. Some golden rules for successful small ads are:

1. Don't cram too much into your copy. Go for one *headline* that proclaims your main selling benefit.
2. Use a good *illustration*. Invariably a line drawing is better for a small ad than a photo.
3. Give clear *instructions* on how to order.
4. Always give a cast-iron *guarantee* — 'Money back if not delighted.'
5. *Timing* is very important. Most small ad sales are impulse purchases, so take account of seasonal influences, weather, holidays etc.
6. Always state the *price* and keep postage as a separate item.
7. Quote the *delivery time*.
8. *Avoid box numbers* — response is poor.
9. *Key* your ads so you know where the response is coming from (see page 168).
10. *Avoid fragile items* and ones that require elaborate packing.
11. Make a good *offer* — 'Buy three, get one free.'
12. Sell one of a series. *Avoid isolated products* that do not lead to further desirable items.
13. Refund the cost of a *catalogue* by knocking it off the price of the first order.
14. Don't be too ambitious in going for high-priced items. Keep your promotion in the lower range. Once you've got your prospects hooked tempt them with your de luxe items.
15. Advertise in papers and magazines that carry a lot of small ads with, of course, similar products to your own. Don't be a trail-blazer.
16. Allow for the use of *plastic money* — Barclaycard, Access etc; 60 per cent of the eligible UK population now hold a credit card.
17. Handle all *returns and complaints* promptly. Dissatisfied customers can quickly get you into bad odour with the journals, apart from being bad business ethically and commercially.
18. If space permits, always use a *coupon*.

There is always the problem of 'Do I ask them to write for a brochure or do I ask for cash with order?' The decision will depend on the nature of the goods, their price and the space you have booked. Many people are reluctant to send cash to new unknown firms.

Only small ads are exempt from the Mail Order Protection Scheme. Display ads that ask for money direct with the order are subject to contributions to the fund. All but cheap, simple items will have to be fully described by means of an illustrated brochure. Colour can then add impact.

LEARN WHERE YOUR RESPONSE COMES FROM

Before you start you rarely know the perfect place to advertise. All successful mail order operators *key* their ads. Place a code in your coupon or ad and monitor the replies. The address can be slightly varied, even misspelt to indicate the source, as long as the post office can deliver. People tend to copy exactly what is printed. For example, if your address is 14 Castleton Street, use Castletown instead. Invent a mythical person. Miss North for *Guardian* readers or Miss Moon for readers of the *Sun*. The clumsy way of doing it is to use 'Dept ST1' for *Sunday Times* or 'RT' for *Radio Times* etc.

If your enquiries are coming in by coupon then either put a serial number in the corner or rely on looking on the reverse where a different printing will show which issue it came from. Make sure you get a copy!

TEST YOUR PACKAGING

Packaging can be an expensive item in mail order. Ask your packaging wholesaler to call and try out various materials, posting them back to yourself. Experiment with corrugated, tri-wall, bubble pack, polystyrene, polyurethane foam and all the other materials now available. For small packs and fairly low volumes you may find a trip to your local box maker fruitful. You can probably pick up 'offcuts' and make up wrap-rounds yourself. You can waste a lot of time on inefficient packing, so gear up properly for it. Set aside a separate packing area with plenty of clear flat space. Suspend your rolls of paper and card in position over the bench and use dispensers for parcel tape and string. It's still hard to beat rolled newspaper to fill up corners in packs.

DREAM UP AN ENTICEMENT

Mail order definitely works better if you put in a good offer. In the ad-man's phrase, always work for 'perceived value'. Your offers can come in many forms:

'Buy the set and get a free travelling case.'
'Buy two sheets and we will include an extra pillowcase — free.'
'Bring your film to us and get your next one free.'

The attraction for the supplier is higher value per sale, probably no more packaging and paperwork, and continuity.

THE REAL SECRET
Don't expect to make money from your first promotion. The hard part is landing your first fish, finding customers from all those prospects. Once you have isolated what may well be under 1 per cent of the readership go on and sell them something else. Your conversion rate to this second mailing has to be significantly higher. If it isn't then you haven't chosen your sequence of products carefully enough.

Aim at least to break even on the first sale: profits will follow on.

HOW TO CHOOSE THE RIGHT PRODUCT
The national mail order catalogue companies can sell virtually anything, from coats to cookers. Without having the name, credit terms or advertising muscle small firms are necessarily restricted. The most successful items for those with limited resources tend to have the following attributes:

1. *Uniqueness* or at least rarity; an item which is not generally available in the High Street. This attribute could be either because it is a minority interest (cigarette cards) and sold only through a few specialist shops, or it is custom made to order. Its scarcity makes it desirable.
2. The price asked could be more attractive than the High Street offering. Usually it is not a wise move to rely on low margins to shift mail order items.
3. Easily packaged and transportable.
4. Does not need to be *demonstrated*.
5. The attraction can be described within the limitations of a small space ad.
6. Fulfils a genuine consumer *need*. There is a ready-made market for the product. The reader should be saying, 'Yes, I could do with one of those.'

7. It is a *proven* product. You won't be troubled with unreliability and consequent returns, replacements and refunds.
8. A large demand (if you're lucky) can be met quickly. Sinclair was caught out with the demand for Spectrums after launching, with some people waiting up to six months. Fortunately, it was such a good offer that customers were, albeit reluctantly, prepared to wait.

Beware of components that have to be imported. When does the next boat load get in? Some are also subject to import restrictions — cotton goods for example — at the time of writing.

Why direct mail is so cost effective

Direct mail's major and unique advantage is the ability to pinpoint your prospect exactly. It's the rifle rather than the shotgun approach. If you can draw up a list of all the people who might be users of your product and send them a *letter* explaining what it is, then you have eliminated much of the waste of space advertising.

However, life or selling is not that simple. Direct mail is becoming an abused medium and many firms who should know better pump out more and more letters in the belief that the sheer weight of mail will convince people to buy.

I recently asked an architect friend to save all his post that fell into the direct mail category over a three-week period. I reckon that architects and doctors probably get as much as anybody. It came to about 10 pounds in weight (it is only a small practice!). Around 70 per cent was of no relevance at all as it was directed at surveyors, structural engineers and other professions. The senders had not even tried to understand what architects were responsible for. There were several instances of duplication and, in one case, triplication of the same promotional material. If that pattern were to be repeated across every firm then the wastage would be immense.

Two examples from this selection are worth spelling out:

- The international contractors John Mowlem sent out a 24-page illustrated newsletter on their global activities. But who really wants such information as who won the darts match in Abu Dhabi? What architect has a spare hour to read it anyway?
- British Rail sent out a nicely presented 'Executive Timetable' — a guide to inter-city travel. Unfortunately, the nearest major station to his office was not mentioned.

These are two simple examples of expensive print sent to the wrong audience.

SUCCESS SPRINGS FROM YOUR LIST

The first rule of marketing is to identify the target audience. Spend as much time on compiling your *list* of prospects as thinking about what you want to say to them. It is *that* import ant because the right message to the wrong people is money down the pillar box. That list, once you have struck the right profile, is your most valuable commodity. Hoard and gloat over every name.

Lists are by definition collections of names, of real *people*, with a common interest. If you always think of them as people and not just addresses then all your promotions will be human. They may be stamp collectors, vintage car enthusiasts, chemists or timber importers.

Direct mail is now a huge and expanding industry in its own right and there is a very good chance that someone already holds the list that you want. But there are pitfalls in using existing lists. We live in a fluid world. The national average for moving house is once every eight years, with regional variations. Putting it another way, a list of householders will be 12 per cent *inaccurate* in a year's time. The commercial world is not much better: around 10,000 businesses a month close their doors — either through liquidation, merger or because their owners have had enough.

You can build your list from a variety of sources:

1. From your own internal records.
2. Compiled from publicly available lists in year-books, directories, *Yellow Pages* etc.
3. List brokers. These are specialist agencies who deal solely in tracking down and renting out mailing lists. To track *them* down contact the British Direct Marketing Association (BDMA) (see page 191).

The most productive list will be your *own*. You are sending out a proposition to customers who already know you and have dealt with your staff and products before. Concentrate on these first. Work through your sales ledger, exhibition visitors' book, reps' leads, enquiries to ads, guarantee cards — any source that will yield names and contacts of relevance. Never throw away a name.

If your own list is not big enough or you want to expand then there are several directions to pursue. Look in the *Direct-*

ory of British Associations and *Current British Directories* (see Chapter 2) for leads. Some association secretaries will rent out their list of members or you can, somewhat laboriously, copy out the list you want from a library copy. Most of the lists will probably already be held on a computer file somewhere. Your list broker will find out the details. The *Direct Mail Data Book* (Benn) details many list holders but inevitably it is out of date. The magazine *Direct Response* will give further clues. The *Yellow Pages* data bank for the *country* is available for trades and industry in 2000-odd categories. You need not order names for the whole country but can split down precisely to postal code districts. Write to Commercial Names and Numbers, 107 Powis Street, London SE18; 01-855 7821. Many journals will rent out their circulation listings. This is usually a very reliable source as readers tend to keep the publisher advised of changes of address.

Compiled lists can cover literally everything. If you are a fur coat manufacturer you can even rent a list of wealthy people. Consumer and industrial lists are built up from a variety of sources. A consumers list could be nothing more refined than the electoral roll split up into districts. Some are often replies to adverts — enquirers rather than purchasers — though you can get access to these as well.

Another way of acquiring names is to exchange an agreed number of yours with a similar product category held by another.

QUESTIONS TO ASK OF A BOUGHT-IN LIST
1. For what purpose was the list compiled? It will be helpful to find out the source of names, when they were last mailed and how up to date the information is. For example, a list of rose growers could be taken from the circulation list of a gardening magazine, the enquiry list to a rose advert or postal buyers from a specialist nursery.
2. You want to be reasonably happy that 'gone-aways' have been removed. One major problem is that the post office will not guarantee to return gone-aways if posted second class. If any user mails first class then the subsequent returns could dramatically clean the list.

    You can try printing the return address on the envelope but this can deter people from opening it: 'It's only a circular.' Check that you will get a refund from the list owner for any returns.

    Duplications are sometimes rife. Apart from the waste

of money many people are so irritated to receive several requests from the same source that they won't buy even if they like the offer!

3. Can you *rent* or *buy*? Many rented lists are for a once-only use. To prevent abuse there will be hidden 'sleepers' tucked in the addresses as a check on your mailings. This device is also known as 'seeding'. The cost of a list will vary between £25 and over £100 per 1000 names.

4. What size *sample* can you test? There's no point in sending out thousands of your expensive mailings to a bought-in list till you know that the profile is *your* target. Test response by sampling a smaller number first. List holders will stipulate differing lower limits: under 1000 names is statistically unreliable. Many would go for 5000 if you are aiming for say 50,000 and above. As the national response is between 1 and 2 per cent you have little to judge on if few reply: you could easily jump to the wrong conclusions when you come to roll out the remainder.

5. Find the *price bracket* that previous prospects were mailed. Response will have differed if it was a £10 or a £100 offer.

6. Is the list by firm, job title, or named individuals? Response is always better if the mailing is to a specific person. The more personal the communication the less it looks like a dreaded soap coupon.

7. The mechanics must be investigated. Many lists nowadays are held on computer tape and can be run through a printer to produce self-adhesive labels. Better if the list can be produced by a word processor, each address individually matched to an envelope. A mailing house can do this for you amazingly quickly on some lovely expensive machines.

8. Find out the total costs and whether there are extras for label or tape production. There might also be a minimum charge for small runs.

9. Ask for a sample of their printed label. One of the biggest list managers in the business has a wretched all-caps printer that is a dead give-away for circular haters.

10. Some lists are not available to competitors. Find out the restrictions before you get too excited.

11. It is more important to find out the success rates of previous mailings. Take into consideration what was offered, for comparison.

12. The world can be divided into those who buy by mail order and those who don't. You will get a better response

from a list of actual *buyers* than coupon redeemers or competition entrants. It's a case of finding the most potentially responsive audience and, by extension, lists that are mailed frequently generate more response than those that are left to slumber.

13. Finally, you will want to know how long it will take to get your list after ordering so you can prepare your brochures and sales letters in readiness.

MERGE AND PURGE

This is not a variety act but an essential operation if you are combining several lists, one of which is perhaps your own. If they are all on computer run them through to remove duplications.

As the lists are the basis of all mailings it is worth devoting some thought to how you are going to store all that data. Don't wait till you have shoe boxes full of information before you start sorting out a system. Computers have greatly simplified the task of cross-referencing and several interesting facets can be pulled out. You will find it useful to record:

1. Name, address and post code. Although the post code has been a nuisance to everybody else it has been a boon to direct mailers. Millions of names can be segmented purely by those vital letters.
2. Your coding for the ad or coupon. You must measure the response from each source.
3. The date of putting the new customer on the list.
4. Other details such as age group, sex, type of purchase etc can be useful, not only for future sales but for renting out to other mailers. Don't forget you can make *money* renting out your list.

When you are test sampling it is more realistic to order every *tenth* name rather than, say, the first 5000. These could be very unrepresentative of the whole list. The trade jargon for this is '1 in nth selection'.

WHAT'S IN A NAME?

Most consumer mailings are now addressed by *name* rather than to 'The Occupier' for obvious reasons. There are so many sources for finding the named individual — electoral and club membership lists, professional subscriptions; even *Which?* rent out their list of members now; some 600,000 of them.

Industry is not so well covered. Where you have the name include it, but always put the *job title* as well. People move on and their successors may well open the mail.

There is another rather more subtle reason for including the person's name. His (or her) secretary may be less inclined to open or destroy mail personally addressed. Research has shown that most executives still open their own mail.

What do you send?

You should send a prospect *at least* four items:

1. Your sales letter
2. An illustrated brochure or specification sheet
3. Order form
4. Return envelope.

Depending on your product and purse this list can grow to include a sample, catalogue, testimonials, competition or give-away. If you have a fertile mind direct mail is where you come into your own. Your fancy can take flight.

I have come across plenty of firms who go to some trouble to design a nice brochure and believe all they need do is to mail it out, the 'If they want to buy they'll contact me' approach. It doesn't work like that. People need persuading and to get results you have to make it convenient for them to order.

The most important of the four essential items is your *letter*. It is perhaps no more than convention that we communicate by writing a letter but if it works why pioneer? Each part of your mailing package requires careful thought and planning as every piece can contribute to the response. But in turn it can also provide traps for the unwary.

PRESENTATION

It is essential that your readers form a good impression of you. Photocopy letters are therefore *out*.

Poorly printed letter-headings, indifferent paper and spelling are really unforgivable: most important is to spell the prospect's name, firm and address correctly. We all get a little irritated when we receive letters incorrectly addressed: it's that old word 'courtesy'. Forget that you may be sending out 5000 letters. To the recipient it is a single communication, so get your printer to use a *typewriter letter style* as though it emanated from you direct. For small runs you can type in the addressee yourself, so use your own typewriter (with a carbon ribbon) to produce the original letter from which your printer will make up the plate. For more lengthy operations you will need to go to a mailing house with the sophisticated machines necessary to match in the letter and envelope. The more personal your communication looks the more chance you have that it will be acted upon.

I know of one very successful firm that actually hand writes all its direct mail envelopes — all 20,000 of them. They have actually had complimentary letters back: 'How nice to get a personal letter.' But that is for the consumer market.

Avoid brown manilla envelopes, at least for the outer pack. They look cheap and nasty. Self-seal envelopes, although dearer, save time if you are sticking by hand. Window envelopes save typing the address twice and are finding favour: as everything from phone bills to invoices are now sent out in one of these, the old argument that direct mail has to use plain white envelopes is dying.

HOW TO WRITE EFFECTIVE SALES LETTERS

The major drawback to using direct mail is that many others use it too. It has lost its novelty. Although it is true to say that most mail is opened (over 95 per cent, research suggests) you have only a few *seconds* to make an impact. That is the decision time. It is that *first glance* which will determine whether the reader is hooked enough to carry on and absorb your proposition or it finds the waste-paper basket.

Your headline or opening sentence must spell out a major benefit and answer the reader's question, *'What's in it for me?'* This really is the key to successful direct mail and is why the national average for response remains obstinately at 2 per cent. Not enough thought is given to spelling out the user benefits early in the letter.

Think about the objective

You must be clear in your mind what you are trying to do. Are you trying to get direct orders or simply elicit enquiries for personal visits? Are you announcing the opening of a new shop, inviting competition entries or magazine subscriptions? The style of your letter must reflect the task in hand. Don't ask too much of one letter: you may need to do it in two parts.

JOHNSTON EDUCATIONAL SERVICE

Director: T. V. W. Johnston

25 MIDDLETON ROAD, HORSHAM, WEST SUSSEX RH12 1JS

Horsham 53382

Date as postmarked

The Promotions and Sales Manager.

Dear Sir,

      May I take a brief moment of your time in these cost conscious days to mention my promotional service to the Technical, and Further Education college market.

      My mobile exhibition service provides a method of having material brought to the notice of the many lecturers and college librarians, at a very small outlay in comparison with one's own representatives. With the present restraint on college funds they are having to be more selective in what they can buy and there is no doubt that books and publications actually seen by the staff, are far more likely to be ordered than those only known about by catalogue and mailed information.

      As my exhibitions are held in a great many Technical Colleges, Polytechnics, Colleges of Technology, and colleges of Higher and Further Education, any titles on display do get a wide audience and this might be worth bearing in mind in the structure of your existing sales methods. I am well aware that many publishers of suitable material will have existing forms of representation, but it might well assist sales, to perhaps have several leading titles on display in addition to your present coverage. Even clients with only one suitable title aimed at this market find my service ideal.

Sales letter

JOHNSTON EDUCATIONAL SERVICE

Director: T. V. W. Johnston

25 MIDDLETON ROAD, HORSHAM, WEST SUSSEX RH12 1JS

Horsham 53382

Cont.

The cost to you of this service is very reasonable, a mere 55 pence per title per exhibition, with some one hundred and forty college exhibitions in a full year.

This is a huge market and there is still a great demand for the right type of book, particularly of course the new T.E.C. and B.E.C. courses with other areas as well, particularly craft subjects, Motor Vehicle, Electronics, Microelectronics, Word Processors, Computing and Catering, and indeed any suitable material of interest to the many relevant college courses.

I have a small amount of space on my display stands at present, and if there is any way in which you feel I might be able to assist you with your sales promotion, I do hope you will not hesitate to contact me.

Yours sincerely,

T.V.W. Johnston

T.V.W. Johnston
Director

Sales letter (continued)

Long letter or short?

Two factors determine this question: your audience and the product. On the assumption that few businessmen have time to read a two-page letter it seems folly to deter them with a thousand words of type. It is far better to use the letter as a prelude to a personal visit or to back up an illustrated brochure or sample. Let pictures tell the story.

Mailings to the household tend to be longer as your audience has more time to digest your pearls of wisdom. Never write more than you need to, however. Padding is a turn-off and people will only read as long as their interest is held.

What do you say?

Think of your audience and write as if you were speaking face to face. This must be the essence of all good communications. Leave your high-blown phrases and contrived jargon behind and use simple direct English. The letter must flow and lead the reader along. The techniques to use are not particularly subtle or devious. Avoid long sentences and keep to one theme per paragraph. To keep the reader hooked carry on one idea to the next paragraph by using open-ended questions or statements, for example, 'Why do you think Rolls Royce used Connolly leather?' and then answer it in the next sentence.

Be *factual*. Opinions are always suspect. State what the product will do in terms of performance and translate this into user benefits. Always write looking through the user's eyes, as though he already has possession. If you stick to the facts you must carry *conviction* which is the most important quality that can shine through.

As with all advertising the misuse of overworked words like 'unique', 'fabulous' and 'extraordinary' will produce the opposite reaction in the reader's mind. Legitimate buzz words like 'new', 'free trial', 'money back' should certainly be employed in their proper context.

Always be *sincere*. I have never believed that the American style of salesmanship — 'Have a nice day' — can cross the Atlantic, with all its overblown bonhomie.

We all believe the BBC news because of the simple, direct way of broadcasting. There is no arm waving or histrionics. Contrast that with some of the tabloids' methods of presentation.

Give a reason to act

Having aroused interest and desire you must then give a *reason* for action. The hardest thing to achieve is an immediate response. Unless it is done *then* it won't be done at all. The most telling way to open your letter is to make the reason your offer: 'limited stocks', 'pre-budget', 'end of range' etc. Remind the readers again at the close and give them a strong reason for making contact.

Don't forget the PS

I don't pretend to understand why, but everyone reads the PS. Maybe because it stands alone. Surely no one really believes that you rushed back to the printer and asked him to squeeze an extra vital point before he went to tea? No, but the PS can work for you as well as the opening benefit.

Drayton Bird in his excellent book *Commonsense Direct Marketing* quotes a lovely example of the value of the PS.

On his first mail shot to Bullworker prospects he received a 10 per cent response. An American, Bernie Silver, showed him how to pull more:

'*How many units have you got in the warehouse?*'
About 300 was Bird's estimate.
'*Great. Write a PS and tell them that's all you've got, so they should reply now.*'
He did and the response doubled.

WHAT ELSE CAN YOU SEND?

The more pieces of literature you can send the more chances you will have to make a sale. But watch the postal steps. Most people will pick each piece up and scan it, no matter how briefly, which gives a further 'opportunity to see'.

Unless you are launching a brand new product you should be able to include some testimonials from satisfied customers. Reprint their actual letters exactly as received — spelling and all. It carries more conviction. (You must get their permission first, of course.) An endorsement from someone else means much more than if *you* are saying it.

Direct mail lends itself to imaginative treatment. An American fire insurance firm mails letters looking as though they've been scorched.

A stain-proof contract carpet has been sold to architects by sending a 4-inch square sample with a sachet of tomato sauce.

They are invited to spread it (spatula provided) on the carpet and then wash it off under a tap.

Two-part mailings can be done in the same way. I'm hoping a local sedimentation expert I know will be mailing consulting engineers with a small plastic bag of sea sand, asking them to identify it. The second posting will bring the answer and offer his services for pollution and scour prediction.

One of the more imaginative uses of direct mail has gone down in history as the Ida Clackett letter. The letter was written in a childish hand and said:

> Dear Mr Manager,
>
> I am writing to you because I'm your cleaner. I was in your office and saw a lot of papers on your desk and they meant nothing to me but when I was in the pub last night a man said to me I'll give you £500 to borrow your keys and go in. I don't want to do that, I don't think that's right but five hundred pounds is a lot of money.
>
> (Signed) *Ida Clackett*

A few days later a rep called from Ofrex, a shredding machine company!

You can use direct mail to send out keys, only one of which will open a safe on your premises at an open day, or start a new car, etc.

OTHER TECHNIQUES

1. Provide emphases by printing in two or three colours and underlining to bring out the main points.
2. Start saying 'I', move to 'we', finish with 'you'. Build a partnership. Change from the general to the particular.
3. Handwritten marginal notes, used sparingly, bring personalisation a bit closer. By handwritten I mean you should add a few words on to the original before printing.
4. Never put 'Dear Sir/Madam' or 'The Occupier'. Avoid the salutation altogether by starting off, 'Good Morning'.
5. If you are writing to a female audience try a tinted paper. Pink is supposed to be most effective. Or scented.
6. I don't believe it is so important to reply pay the envelope if you are mailing business users. All mail will tend to go through the franking machine anyway, but if you are only mailing small firms then many will not have the luxury of such a machine and will be counting the cost and convenience.

7. The return envelope can be cheap manilla. There is no point in wasting money on incoming mail.

8. The outer envelope can work as well, arousing curiosity without divulging the contents. If you include a free gift or sample, say so on the outside. In effect it should be saying, 'Open me'.

9. Print a row of alternatives with little boxes to tick and make it easy for people to respond.

   Please send further details ☐
   Please make an appointment ☐
   I would like to see more of your range ☐
   Send me the de luxe version ☐
   Please send me ☐ items
   Have you a home telephone? Yes ☐ No ☐

10. Use a separate order form. It should be just as nicely designed as the sales letter — after all, it is asking for a commitment from the prospects. Leave them in no doubt what to do, and when to use BLOCK CAPITALS. Design the form with plenty of space so that it gives you minimum trouble in taking off quantities and checking. Print your address on this as well as on the sales letter. The order form should be coded so that you know from which mailing it was generated. There is sometimes a considerable time lag between mailing and response.

    The order form is a good place to ask, 'Who else might be interested in this offer?' Recommendations to friends enjoy a much higher response than your original mailings.

11. Always keep a record of what you have sent. How can you learn and improve if you don't record your mailings? When it comes to testing different ideas you will have lost the comparison.

12. Tie up with the main credit card companies. Offering credit increases results.

Testing, testing

The great advantage of direct response advertising over other forms of promotion is the ability to measure results quickly and directly. Change your offer and, provided your mailing isn't too small, you would expect the response to vary — all things being equal. You can test more than the offer.

Let John Roland show you how to save money on your next production

☐ **YES,** we would like to know how to make better use of resources and save money on our next programme. We are planning a:

☐ **Video**   ☐ **Film**   ☐ **Slide/Tape show**   ☐ **Combivision show**

The general purpose is (sales, training, etc):

_____

Company Name:_____

The person to contact in my company is:_____

Telephone number and extension:_____

☐ **NO,** we are not planning any audio visual shows at present, but please contact us again in ☐ 3 months ☐ 6 months.

Reply card

1. Change the layout, headline, picture, position — anything of importance — to see whether you can pull in more punters, but only change one thing at a time, otherwise you won't know which one was the attraction.
2. Split your mailings in half and vary the theme to see which is the more attractive. Repeat with a large mailing. If you're aiming for a very big posting then it is safer to do a test sample again.

As I've said before small mailings are statistically vulnerable. When you are working on very low response rates a few either way can upset a large number of percentage points. (The post office put out some very good free booklets on regression analysis and multivariate testing that are beyond my ken but perhaps not yours.)

Test sampling with industrial users has to be more sophisticated to produce reliable results, as one user or specifier could be responsible for bulk purchases whereas there are more private consumers but each buys less. All I would suggest to a new small firm is to beware of jumping to hopeful conclusions on one small mailing. If in doubt test again. There is plenty of skilled advice now within the industry to advise you on predictions and probabilities.

WHY YOU SHOULD TEST

Much of advertising is hard to quantify. Exhibitions can be very expensive and often it is impossible to say what business has resulted directly from them. Display ads, unless you put in a coupon, will not let you know what has been achieved. The same goes for all the rest — posters, programmes, give-aways, diaries and the like. Direct response advertising allows you to form a judgement on the expenditure.

Testing, with its quick response, allows scope for adjustment to give you better value for money. Testing can prove your ideas. The most skilled agency in the country does not *know* what the public will buy until the offer is made. You are committed by then.

The big companies use what is termed an A/B split. Large circulation papers and magazines are printed on rotary cylinders that print more than one copy of a page at a time. This means you can run variations of your ad that will be bound up in the *same* edition. As they are printed alternately, newsagents in the same town will get an equal mix of the two versions of your ad providing the perfect test medium. Not all magazines are able to offer this facility but it is worth bearing in mind. You can also provide your own copy in the form of a loose insert (see page 187). Prepare alternative versions merged into one pile so that you get a true comparison.

TEST AGAINST A BOUGHT-IN LIST

When you are in the mood for expansion and thinking of renting a new list of prospects, test a sample against the same number of your own. Your own list should give a better response for the reasons given before, but it will be a good yardstick for comparison. Make sure that the identical offer is made to both listings and at the same time, of course.

HOW TO TEST SMALL ADS

If the readership profile for two magazines is identical then you can run two ads on the same day. Make an adjustment for circulation, of course. There must be several fields of interest that are in direct competition, such as the present welter of computer, hi-fi and motoring magazines that are aimed at the same market segment. Probably the more trustworthy way is to alternate your ad in successive issues.

Instead of one big ad, try two smaller ones in the same issue.

The great fascination about all advertising is that there is never one answer. We all think we know what makes a good ad, but the only measure of acceptability is whether it *sells*. And the only way to find out is to *test*.

THE RESPONSE YOU CAN EXPECT

I've talked glibly through this chapter about the magic national average of a 2 per cent enquiry rate as if that were immutable. Every promotion is different. Even a ½ per cent actual order rate could be quite acceptable. In a humble way I have been involved in a mailing that generated a 10 per cent enquiry rate and there are many cases on record that have exceeded 15 per cent. You have to cover your costs and meet your objectives. The main point to bear in mind is that the results of your first mailing to a strange list will probably be marginal. Your second effort to the converts should be very much better. If it isn't, there is something very wrong.

MEMBER GET A MEMBER

MGM campaigns can be very fruitful. We all recognise that the best advertising is by personal recommendation and it's the same with direct response. It sometimes helps to offer a premium to the introducing friend when the new member places the first order. Your order forms should have a space for 'further addresses'. When sending on these requests always do a fresh personal letter: 'Mrs Jones suggested I send you our new catalogue . . .'. The response from this added touch has proved to be the greatest of all. First, because the friend knows the likes of the prospect, eliminating most of the wastage inherent in all direct mail. Second, perhaps the new member 'doesn't want to let her down'.

It all costs money

The costs of mail order and direct mail operations are more easily predictable and measurable than other ways of drumming up business. Printing, list buying, postage and handling can all be computed in advance. By testing against a representative sample a scientific decision can be made on profitability if a large list is then rolled out. But distinctions should be made between the different areas where costs are incurred.

The *enquiry* cost is the cost of just getting a prospect to reply and ask for information. This is made up of a mailing list rental (if bought in) or what you have spent to compile your own. It is the costs of getting the names on to labels, envelopes, all your printing bills, stationery and postage, plus the cost of adverts if you've derived enquiries from that source. Divide your total expenditure by the number of replies to arrive at a unit figure.

The *reply* cost is the total amount spent to satisfy enquirers: more leaflets, stationery and postage.

The *order* cost is the grand total divided by the number of actual orders received. You are then in a position to work out your break-even position for each article. A critical figure is always your *conversion ratio*. Are you getting a lot of casual enquiries that fail to materialise into orders? Should you make the ad more explicit to deter these time wasters or make the reply mechanism harder by cutting out freepost? Or is there something wrong with your sales literature or follow-up procedure? Telephone research will probably reveal the answer in short order.

These are some of the direct costs involved. Hopefully, you will not be launching an unproven product. The upset could be *returns*.

Door to door

An alternative to selling off the page and direct mail is door-to-door distribution.

There are four main ways of arranging this. The post office themselves can distribute your message along with the morning post. You can pick as small an area as a postman's 'walk'. This is the most expensive way. There are also a number of national distribution organisations from the pools promoters downwards. Your local newsagent (or I have heard of the milkman doing deliveries) may include a handbill in every *Daily Mirror* or *Times* according to your audience. Lastly, the local Cub pack is always looking for ways of fund raising.

While you do have the advantage of being able to pick your precise area, traditionally the response is very low and much worse than for direct mail.

Inserts can be the most effective of all

An increasingly popular way of reaching your target audience is by means of a magazine insert. This is a separate card or brochure supplied by you to a carrier journal or customer mailing. Technically, an insert is a loose copy — an inset is one which is bound in. The advantages are obvious:

1. No envelope addressing or list compiling.
2. You have great freedom to design your promotional message.
3. A reply card can be easily designed in.
4. It is generally the first thing people see when they open the magazine.
5. A decision must be made. Is it read or discarded? A very high proportion are read, unlike ads buried in a back page which may never get seen.

As against that the *drawbacks* are:

1. Only the first reader tends to see the insert. They are rarely retained. Base your costings on circulation not readership.
2. You are sunk if the reader opens the magazine over the waste-paper basket.
3. The reply mechanism needs some thought. If you're printing on card then make sure it is substantial enough to come back through the post. The business reply card must

187

conform to post office preferred sizes. Perforating the card improves response. This is much more expensive than printing on paper, which requires a fold-up return and from which response is much poorer.

Compared with direct mail, inserts enjoy a much better response. The same rules for design still apply: use a good headline, eye-catching illustrations and colour.

The costs vary between magazines, of course, but tend to be based around the page cost mark. There are, however, bargains to be had among the specialist journals of restricted circulation that often carry little or no advertising anyway. The return rate for these can be very high.

You may have to book up some issues ahead. Periodicals have to ration the number of inserts they will take because of the postal steps. *British Rate and Data* will tell you which magazines take an insert.

FOOD FOR THOUGHT
The market is expanding fast. Everyone from the electricity boards to your local authority is waking up to the fact that their envelope can carry a commercial fee-paying leaflet. Look around your locality and grab what's going.

Form a club

A lovely way of retaining old customers and making them feel special is to form a club that offers benefits worth having. It has many applications.

1. Garages can offer 10 per cent off future services or accessories on all cars sold over a certain price. It keeps the customers coming back and gives the sales department further opportunities to retain their custom.
2. Tour operators can give priority booking to members who have had holidays with them before: a very valued offer with areas much in demand, eg *gîtes* in France.
3. Advance notice or special days on sales.
4. Book clubs enjoy reductions on publishers' prices providing they buy so many books a year.
5. Hold regular get-togethers and social events, invite expert speakers or organise trips related to your club's interest.
6. Produce a regular newsletter and invite contributions from the members. Highlight any new products or services that

you are bringing in, making an introductory offer to members.

7. Once the membership has built up you should be able to negotiate bulk buys for commodities, discounts for patronising certain establishments and other goodies like insurance and finance, depending on what your members' interests are.

8. Run an advice service.

9. If you really want to push the boat out you can go in for club ties, badges and car stickers.

Party plan

This is the home sales method pioneered by Tupperware and now used by countless others. It has great appeal to small firms because you can reach the public quickly and the profit margins should be good. It is particularly suitable for items in the craft field that need to be seen and handled.

The organisers tend to be self-employed and arrange their own parties. They make their commission on the difference between the price at which they purchase the goods and the price for which the goods sell at the party.

A gift is normally made to the hostess at whose house the affair is arranged, rising in value if targets are met.

Party plan can work very well *if* you are good at organising and motivating your lasses on the road. Best to leave that side to a capable lady, leaving you to concentrate on production.

The *advantages* are:

1. The method is well proven. There are many experienced party-plan organisers out there looking for new lines.

2. The discount structure, although some variation is around, seems to be of the order of one-third off gross sales to the organiser.

3. Production can in many cases be geared to orders.

4. It's a method of selling that lends itself to test sampling.

5. It can work very well if your product is linked to the ladies. Some products — sex aids or exotic lingerie — possibly work better at a party than with other forms of promotion. There is an air of daring (I am told).

The *disadvantages* could be seen in motivating your sales force, especially if you are reliant on some keen but possibly untrained staff. The weather could be bad, or the television more attractive. You have to coordinate all the orders, deliver the goods and collect the money. Invitation cards and order forms have to be supplied.

The big firms set up their party organisers as agents. They buy their sample range, from which they take orders, and all the necessary promotional material.

When you get bigger

The direct response industry can take all the practical worries from you. There are many automated mailing houses or 'letter shops' that will stuff millions of envelopes from computer-prepared lists based on ACORN. This is the latest number-crunching development that covers the country, working from electoral rolls and the division of the population into 36 neighbourhood types. This method predicts that the bourgeoisie of Surbiton will buy the same goods as those of Harrogate, and their *individual* addresses will be on tape. Frightening!

Fulfilment houses will look after the whole shebang of response to orders, and post and pack from their warehouse. All you have to do is count the money (going in or out, I'll leave to you).

The post office

This chapter would not be complete without a word about your friendly post office. Direct response marketing couldn't exist without it. They are now much more marketing conscious and have a number of 'money off' schemes to help new starters and bulk users.

Go along and see your local postal services representative (the address is in the phone book under Post Office). He will tell you about the 1000 free offer where you can have at least the first 1000 mailings *free* if you haven't used direct mail before. That's worth £130 at 1985 prices. It's on a sliding scale so if you mail 5000 you could get 2500 posted free. From then on there are rebates for bulk postings. Other offers include business reply and freepost (first 300 back free). Ask about parcel contracts as well.

On a more mundane level, if you take more than 120 letters all the same size and weight along to your Crown PO they will run them through their franking machine. Sort them the right way round and in bundles of 50.

Sources

Direct Mail Producers Association (DMPA), 34 Grand Avenue, London N10 3BP; 01-883 7229

British Direct Marketing Association (BDMA), 1 New Oxford Street, London WC1A 1HQ; 01-242 2254

Direct Response, Macro Publishing Ltd, 41b High Street, Hoddesdon, Hertfordshire EN11 8TA; 09924 69556

Direct Marketing Services (year-book) Benn Publications, Sovereign Way, Tonbridge, Kent TN9 1RW; 0732 364422.

Buying by Post, Office of Fair Trading (useful free leaflet).

Chapter 8

Sales Promotion

Twice as much money is now spent on sales promotion (SP) techniques as agency advertising. And that's a lot of money. The growth has been recent and dramatic, yet small firms have almost ignored the possibilities. Many of the promotion methods are only applicable to the mass consumer market but you may glean some ideas by understanding the principles.

Advertising campaigns tend to be aimed at a long-term build-up, while SP can be slotted in to create a quick demand. Both activities must work in harmony.

Sales promotion discounts are short-term offers made at the point of sale to induce customers to buy on impulse away from the competition. They must be short term, otherwise a permanent discount could then become part of the basic pricing structure. A 10 per cent cut in the price of sunglasses in September is specifically aimed at clearing stocks after the season. A coupon on Tide giving money off the next packet is to increase brand loyalty. But if such promotion is pursued permanently all the manufacturer has done is to *bring forward* future sales, leaving a subsequent drop until housewives have depleted their shelves. Sales promotion should ideally smooth out cycles of demand not create them.

You will quickly grasp that the big SP spenders mainly centre on mass-marketed consumer products where the market tends to be stable, if not saturated, and differences between brands are minute, if not illusory. Many of the key differentials are achieved in SP by clever packaging and merchandising. Large companies tend to regard exhibitions as part of the SP budget as well.

The search is always on for originality too, but there are not many areas left untapped. You can't get much lower than plastic daffodils to sell detergents or bingo to sell newspapers.

For those with limited advertising appropriations it should still be recognised that some SP is a perfectly valid marketing weapon, as long as the objectives are clearly recognised.

The problems of increasing sales often revolve around getting the wholesaler and/or retailer to take more stock. A competition aimed at the wholesalers' reps may increase demand but this could cause bottlenecks in the shops, requiring a different promotion to pull stocks through at the other end. What trade you are in will largely govern the pattern of distribution and, by extension, which part of the chain needs to be tempted.

Suggested SP techniques to meet different marketing objectives

1. The manufacturer needs year-round production to keep his work-force but the demand is seasonal.

    Try discounts in the off-season to encourage early purchase, delayed invoicing or giving longer credit. Backed up by a good forward contract, the manufacturer can often approach his suppliers or subcontractors and negotiate more favourable terms or arrange bank backing. Obviously, cash flow needs watching. Factoring is sometimes used in these cases.

    Factoring improves cash flow and is possible where turnover exceeds £50,000 per annum, but many factors look for £200,000 or more. The factoring company 'buys' your trade debts and takes over the day-to-day invoicing and debt collecting for your business. You can get up to 80 per cent of the invoice value in advance, with the balance coming when the customer pays up. There is a factoring charge for running the sales ledger plus a finance charge for receiving money in advance. See page 224.

2. Launching a new, untried product.

    Sell samples, offer free trials, guarantee buy-back, introduce sale or return, give the option of delayed payment (a post-dated bankers' order is a popular method with magazines).

3. The new product is marginally better than the one it replaces.

    For the launch only, try discounts for bulk orders (buy 12 get 1 free), coupons either on the packet or cut out of a newspaper or handbill (bring this with you and we'll knock 50p off each item). Competitions.

4. The price is too high for the perceived value.

    Offer Access, Barclaycard etc facility. Tie up with a finance house to give instant credit or run your own hire purchase agreements (get a credit licence) and block discount them. This involves assigning the agreements to a finance house and batching them up at intervals to receive probably two-thirds of the value. It is a good method of unlocking value.

5. To encourage more stockists.

SP techniques to employ could be good point of sale material, dispensers etc, bonuses for targets, staff training if it is a technical product, back-up advertising or PR to encourage enquiries.

Price cutting

This is the most easily recognised and abused SP technique to make your product more competitive. Price reductions are made for a variety of reasons:

1. To clear stocks before a new line is introduced.
2. To generate more cash quickly — perhaps to stay in business!
3. To embarrass a competitor.
4. To get a new product on the market quickly.
5. To improve penetration of a saturated market.
6. As a loss leader, to draw people on to the premises and sell them more profitable lines.
7. To defeat the launch of a rival's product.
8. As a deliberate change in marketing strategy. Some firms are known to be fast turnover, low-margin operators.
9. To correct a buying fault and clear dead stock.
10. To dress up the balance sheet. Cash can replace a high stock figure.
11. To reduce the chore of stocktaking, which can also be a heavy cost in many multi-component industries.
12. To clear retailers' stocks and pull more through the wholesale chain.
13. To get publicity! A new pub can offer beer at pre-war prices — for the first 100 customers. Petrol has been similarly promoted.

You can probably think of more. How much to reduce by is always the problem: too little and the demand may not be there, too much and you're giving away your profit. You must always be careful not to upset the stockists who may have full-price goods on their shelves. If goods are too cheap, people will regard them as seconds. They can, of course, be under-priced in the first place: there are many tales of items sticking, which have sold well after a price *rise*. Undervalued items − 'There must be something wrong with it.' Back to *perceived* value again.

Try repacking or re-labelling and selling the goods in a different way if the cost is not prohibitive.

When to shout 'Sale'

Some traders are always having a sale and the promotion loses any relevance. The alleged price cut becomes the normal trading level. In SP terms, for a price cut to be successful it must meet the objectives. If the object is permanently to increase demand, then the item must be one that is continually bought and one which has several competing brands. The differences between the brands should not be so minute that retaliation switches customers back and forth in response to price cutting. No one wins there (except the consumer) and one of you will go out of business or drop that line.

If your price reduction results in increased sales but is followed by a 'starvation' period while consumers use up stocks, little will have been gained, unless the object was to solve a production problem. The idea of a price offer is to encourage that elusive phenomenon, brand loyalty, and this should take over to make up the profit lost during the offer period. All too often price cuts are made without planning ahead. Turnover is useless without profit.

Money-off coupons

These are endemic among the detergent manufacturers, so much so that the phrase 'soap coupons' has passed into the language as a term of derision, along with 'the pound in your pocket'. But there are ways in which a small firm can use the idea to good effect. For instance, coupons in newspaper ads, handbills, show catalogues etc make people read the ad and encourage custom through the door.

Research has shown that the 'money off' must be of the order of 15 per cent to be effective.

Competitions

From Spot the Ball to writing a slogan, the field for competitions is immense. Prizes can range from two weeks in Skegness to as many items as you can stack in a supermarket trolley in two minutes. (Entries are usually conditional on showing a proof of purchase, by sending in part of the packet.) To get maximum impact the competition needs to be widely promoted, which usually cuts out the small firm unless you can dream up an unusually novel contest which attracts publicity on its own merits.

On a restricted budget, competitions can be held within an exhibition or the local show. The problem at exhibitions is always to attract stand visitors, and a bright snappy contest usually succeeds. Prizes need not be grand — bottles of whisky or give-aways associated with your firm can be very successful. Make sure that the business card is extracted as part of the entry procedure.

If your product does not lend itself to being given away, tie in with another promoter who may give you a bargain offer. Scratch each other's backs. The motor trade, for example, is adept at showroom contests to draw old customers back for new car launches. See page 198 on business gifts.

The *law* on competitions is complex. Some element of skill must be present to distinguish a competition from a *lottery* which offers prizes by chance. Certain kinds of chance competitions are permitted but as the regulations (Lotteries and Amusements Act 1976) are strictly enforced this is not an area for the amateur. Several decisions (Spot the Ball) have even reached the House of Lords. There is a *code of practice* (The British Code of Sales Promotion Practice) which sets out detailed guidelines. Major points are:

1. Legal advice should be taken first.
2. Rules should be carefully worded and easy to understand.
3. Proof of posting is not proof of delivery.
4. The closing date must be clearly shown.
5. The number and size of prizes must be stated.
6. You must say whether there are any geographical limitations, or restrictions on the number of entries from each person or family.
7. If there are requirements to buy this or any other product.

The code is set out in John Williams' book *The Manual of Sales Promotion* published by Innovation Ltd, 39 Charing Cross Road, London WC2H 0AR; 01-434 1533.

Container premiums

Beloved of the gift trade, for example, where Cornish honey is sold in 6 oz pottery jars at a premium price, this is a field worth exploring as there is plenty of scope for the adventurous mind. The packaging industry covers a multitude of materials and I suggest you take one of the trade magazines — *Packaging*, for example — or visit PAKEX, the big trade show, when it comes along.

I heard a while ago of a small match firm producing matches in a plastic box on the theory that a reusable container would have a hundred uses afterwards.

When I was rearing puppies I fed them an orphan lamb food that came in an excellent plastic bucket. The milk food was good and the bucket came in handy later as well.

Get them hooked on series

A favourite SP method is to produce a series. Give away the second item on purchase of the first. Promotions for record clubs, book and magazine parts, medallions and plates all use this method. If the products are good then many will buy the whole lot over a period. It all started, I suspect, with cigarette cards. It can be looked on as a method of extended credit which few small firms can afford to carry.

Limited editions of collectables (limited to those who send in £30 by a certain date worldwide!) seem to be enjoying a long vogue.

Self-liquidators (or bargain offers)

A thoroughly confusing term that has little to do with buoyancy. A self-liquidating premium is a special offer that is available only to purchasers of a particular product — a bought-in line that is cheaper (or seen to be) than that obtainable elsewhere. You have only to look at your cornflakes packet to get the message. It can be a very successful promotion and has more appeal if there is some link between your product and the bargain offer.

Multi-packs

This is the 'buy two get one free' offer where two packs are taped together. Variations of this are *banded* offers where two different products are sold together, such as a paint brush sold with 5 litres of paint. This is usually successful only when the first product has a ready market and is often used to sample the response.

Business gifts

Gifts or bribery? My first experience of the shady world of business was, as the newest recruit to a local builders, to take bottles of amber liquid to the local planning office. All open and above board. Well, it was Christmas. But one of the trips was to deliver an anonymous crate to the *home* of the Chief Planning Officer! (Record players were much sought after 20 years ago.)

There are, however, quite legitimate ways of keeping your name in front of the buyer without resorting to such methods. The field is vast: calendars, diaries, telephone pads, pen sets, key rings, paper openers, wall clocks, maps — anything that will take *your* name and be kept in the office as a reminder. A good source for tracking down specialist suppliers is the magazine, *Incentive Marketing & Sales Promotion*.

That supremo of sales training, John Fenton (the man in the white suit) doesn't believe in calendars or diaries as most buyers get deluged with them, although looking at the array of thriving calendar printers it is difficult to believe they're not doing someone any good.

His idea is to find the buyer's interest. It could be vintage cars, steam locomotives, butterflies or Marilyn Monroe. You say to the buyer: 'If I could get a nice framed print of . . . would you accept it?' Of course he would. There are plenty of prints or photos to choose from. Get it well framed (which need not be expensive) and leave room for an engraved plaque — 'Presented in appreciation — by the Widget Co Ltd'.

It will stay on the wall longer than any ephemeral calendar and infuriate visiting reps.

In the same vein *entertain* only to say 'thank you', never to say 'please'. The latter approach will never get you worthwhile business.

Chapter 9
Packaging and Point of Sale

The average UK family buys 40 packages a week, 2000 a year, or – in cash terms – the industry generates £4000 million a year. Yet for many small firms packaging is a neglected field. We all accept that goods have to be protected simply to be transported from workshop to showroom, but most goods have to compete on a shelf with neighbouring products. This is where the battle is often lost.

A well designed pack will attract attention, inform the customer, display the contents in some cases, protect, maintain the freshness and quality, and sometimes even be useful in its own right afterwards. It must therefore be functional, protective, informative, convenient and *sell* the product, and all at a minimum cost.

Packaging can be divided into two functions: the immediate enclosure around the product and a stouter transportable container that protects during carriage. Halfway between the two are dispenser packs that act as transport carriers and, when opened out, as self-service packs in the shops.

The *transport pack* invariably means the ubiquitous cardboard carton whether of single, double or tri-wall thickness. For a small requirement make friends with your local supermarket manager. Depending on the fragility of the contents, further cushioning can be provided by polystyrene sheet or granules, foam plastic of varying densities, air-bubble packs, padded bags or polyurethane foam. Good old rolled newspaper is hard to beat as well.

Damage potential depends on where and how often your goods are off-loaded. If you want to be depressed, wander round the back of some of the large parcel depots at a busy time. Packages under 10 pounds invite being thrown; over 10 pounds and up to 50 is probably safer. Goods that can be palletised are probably least at risk. Modern mechanical handling equipment – fork-lifts, conveyors and tail lifts – is pretty gentle with weight.

There is a good theory that delicate goods should be left in *transparent* wrappings. There was a preserves manufacturer who shipped to Europe in card boxes and suffered around 5 per cent breakages. By changing to a tray and clear shrink wrappings he showed everyone that glass was involved and breakages dropped to 1 per cent. Small carriers often pick up door to door with only one driver involved. In these cases you don't need to over-protect. The man knows that you know he is directly responsible.

The *outer* container must identify the destination, mark 'This way up' and any special instructions — 'Do not stack more than three high' or 'Use no hooks'.

Like the rest of marketing, packaging should be considered from the outset and not tacked on the end as an afterthought. Good packing will minimise loss, enhance goodwill and produce more sales and profit. The nature of your product — it could be a powder, liquid, corrosive substance or in tablet form — will dictate the type of pack. Humidity, sunlight, temperature, vibrations, staining, or attraction to insects, mice or indeed people will determine the design. The *size* of your pack is often governed by regulation or accepted trade practice. Anyone producing a new non-standard size could confuse the storeman, retailer and customer. You could also miss out on existing display racks.

Shelf life is crucial. Slow-moving lines in village stores sometimes stay literally for years. With little control over how the stockist maintains your product the correct pack is vital to continued customer satisfaction.

The range of materials increases year by year. Blister packs are finding increasing favour as the customer can see the product which is yet protected from knocks and humidity. They also make a cheap product look better. Clear films come in a bewildering variety. Plastic coated card is taking over from the old waxed carton.

The good pack will be your 'silent salesman'. It should protect what it sells and sell what it protects. With the growth of consumerism more people like to know what they are buying. There is a legal requirement to list ingredients on food preparations and fibre content on textiles. Your local Trading Standards Officer will put you wise.

Care *labels* are also helpful for fabrics. There are specialist label printers who can produce thousands on a roll in a multitude of materials. Tie or swing tags are a good eye catcher. If you are making craft items tell the folksy tale about yourself and the product. And why not a Union Jack?

'When all else fails read the instructions.' If you're selling a product that needs explanation, put the instructions on the outside of the pack *and* on any inside container as well as on a leaflet perhaps. The pack tends to be thrown away. Use the leaflet to tell the customer about other helpful lines you can send them. Build up a brand image, a loyal following.

As with all instructional material, get the village idiot to try it. The instructions are crystal clear to you, but then you know what's coming next.

Pictograms can be very useful. You can do away with the written word completely, particularly if you sell abroad, or to ethnic minorities in the home market.

Machinability

When you progress beyond calling in the neighbours to help and get into volume production, you will come up against machinability and assembly. There are some very sophisticated filling and packing machines about. Your pack should take advantage of the economies of mass production. Alternatively, put it out to a contract packer.

Boxes

BOX MAKERS

Like printers, box makers tend to go for long runs — 10,000 or more. Dies have to be specially made. As the machines tend to be large and expensive, short runs are not really economic. If you are not yet in the big league, find a small box maker who looks after the lower end of the trade.

Instead of ordering a purpose-made box, go for a die he already has or tack on to the end of a run he is doing for someone else. As in other trades you will find specialists. Some will stick to solid board, and others corrugated. A few specialise in fancy boxes.

PRINTED BOXES

Few small box makers tackle printing to any extent. You will get a basic screening that will identify the contents but not much else. One solution is to go to a specialist label printer. Although most jobbing printers will *say* they do labels, a specialist will do a more efficient job. The normal printer will print flat sheets, rather like postage stamps. The specialist will run them through on the roll — much easier to peel off and usually better value.

It is usually cheaper to pick a standard box and stick a full colour label on it than have the actual box printed, certainly for small runs.

Labels come in a wide variety of materials: paper, vinyl and foils. Short runs are very suitable for silk screening, a process that has made great strides recently. It will not only give opacity but surprisingly small print as well.

Finally, don't neglect to carry forward to your packaging the same style of print and colour used for the rest of your advertising and promotional material.

TESTING

As packaging can involve a fair investment, put out dummy boxes for client reaction first. Show them to your wholesaler, agent or shopkeeper. How does the product travel? Does a gross or 100 fit in your packing case? Post it back, drop it.

Go and look at the outlets where your goods will be displayed and you may well find that the competition has fitted out the shops with display racks. Check the measurements and make sure your packs are no bigger. A simple thing like this can sometimes make or mar a product. If the shopkeeper has no convenient place to display your goods, he won't bother.

There are lots of checks you can make before ordering a long run.

A thought or two

Some years ago a firm designed a new pack for fragile goods and sent an egg through the post in it. I'm assured it wasn't hard boiled. The resultant publicity kept the phone ringing for weeks.

Which? conducted a test on ladies' cosmetics a while back and found that one well-known brand consisted largely of egg white. It was the irresistible pack that shifted the goods.

HEADER CARDS

One of the cheapest, yet still effective, methods of packaging is the polythene bag and printed header card stapled to it. Poly bags are amazingly cheap when you buy them by the thousand. Punch a hole in the card to hang it by and you're away.

Header cards

FINDING THE ROOM

Storage of packaging materials takes an inordinate amount of room. Renting a *dry* garage must be the cheapest solution.

Point of sale (POS)

POS promotion is aimed directly at influencing the customer at, literally, the point of sale: the very place and moment where the buying decision is made. The retailer or wholesaler at the trade counter is therefore looking for leaflet displays, racks, price-lists, coasters, drip mats, dispensers, posters, catalogues and every other imaginable give-away that creates a buying atmosphere. What he is *not* looking for is poorly designed cardboard showcards that are oversized, fall over or perform no useful function.

There is possibly more wastage in this one area than any other form of promotion. Have a look around the stock room of any grocery or hardware store and count the unpacked boxes of expensive POS material.

Before producing any material have a chat with your stockist and ask what he wants and whether he will display it if you supply it. There is little point in buying in wire racks or printing off posters if stockists have no room, nor the intention of displaying it.

POS material tends to be produced by specialists and a visit to them and the trade show SHOPEX will enlighten you. There is also a trade magazine (*Point of Sale & Screenprinting*).

203

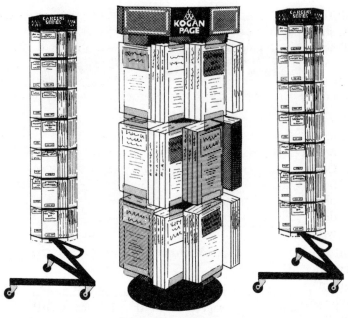

Point of sale spinners

Wall charts that form a standard reference for other items stand a good chance of being used. Trade catalogues are inexpensively bound either by the spiral plastic method or with hot melt glue.

On the fringe end of POS can be listed banners, balloons, carrier bags, mobiles down to the humble open/closed door sign.

Display

This is a vital ingredient in selling goods that aim to catch the eye. It is an art that can be learned although there will always be exponents of the spectacular. In this context I am only concerned with getting maximum effect from limited resources in small situations. Display has been described as 'a bringing together of ideas, colours, materials, and merchandise with thought given to its setting and lighting'.

A good display will attract attention, enhance certain features and encourage the right frame of mind to make a purchase. Many small firms ignore or have no conception of the basic demands.

The display in a shop window is frequently the first impact that you make on the customer. In the same way that adverts must catch the eye from a mass of competitors so too must good display lure the prospect. But not only for a shop window:

small firms need display for trade counters, exhibitions, country fairs, show cases anywhere your products are on view.

Window displays: starting with the most common need, your first constraint is the dimensions you have to play with. If you are working from a converted or older property the window may not be the ideal size for your display. If it is too large, you can:

1. Mask the top, bottom or sides by using covered fibre board panels or self-adhesive coloured plastic sheets.
2. Create a false floor to the window by placing 'island' boards on which your display is mounted, on a hidden plinth. You can have a succession of these across the window. This is one way of raising small items in a floor level window.

Small windows are, of course, more limiting. Rather than crowd everything in, it is perhaps better to change the display more frequently and, over the course of a month, show more merchandise. Opening the back of the window into the shop sometimes makes a small window seem more airy.

For a wide or tall window use blinds or drapes and treat it like a theatre proscenium.

LIGHTING

This is most important. Old-fashioned bulbs and tubes tend to give a very even tone with no highlights, shadows or pools of interest. Tracked spot lighting systems allow you to vary the depths and tones of colour, enhancing the main features and disguising a weak background. Beware of the increased heat that spots can produce in terms of fading and blistering, and its effects on food displays. Modern systems also allow projections of moving light in a variety of colours that can be eye catching if used with skill and discretion: probably of more use in large exhibition halls.

DISPLAY DESIGN

Good design is the subtle combination of abstract shapes (either individual pieces or groups) with the correct use of colour. It all starts with balancing the various items to form a pleasing visual harmony. It might seem easier to make the layout symmetrical, but generally more scope and interest are provided when the display is *asymmetrical*. This is achieved by placing the main feature off-centre and creating a balance by using variety, colour and lighting in a harmonious way.

COLOUR

In the fashion world colour is all-important. Some are 'in', others are history. It may help to paint large flat boards in single colours and place your merchandise in front. Try the effects of different lighting on them to catch the texture, shape and detail.

Some colours have associations with motives and reactions, including:

Turquoise: one of the luxury colours imparting a feel of deep pile carpets, walnut fascias and expensive jewellery. *Black* with *gold* has the same effect.

The browns: rustic, country crafts, wooden solidity, homespun honesty.

Yellow: the colour to catch the eye. Tests have shown that bright yellow is more noticeable even than red.

Red: for daring, danger, excitement.

Blue: the light blues for calm reflectiveness, peace, contemplation, 'blue for a boy'.

Green: a natural colour, of Wimbledon, cream teas and the countryside.

White: for cleanliness, purity, long-limbed girls, freshly ironed linen. If overdone it could mean hospitals or the corporation convenience.

PROPS

Rarely can your display rely on using merchandise alone. It is usually more eye catching, and creative, to use outside accessories that break up an otherwise monotonous or limited display. It can be a simple branch of the right shape, cork tiles, basketry or greenery of any description. Other equipment used with your product can be brought in. For example, gloves and scarves can be shown with ski equipment, glass and crockery with food or wine. Don't let the accessories become the focal point, however; they should simply lend interest, not dominate the layout.

PRICE TICKETS

Nothing can lower the overall image quicker than poor graphics. All lettering and prices on showcards and tickets must be of a high and uniform standard. Match the size to the item, in proportion, and the viewing distance. Stand back where the customer is and see if they are still legible. You can use proprietary brands like Letraset or develop a good freehand script.

Chapter 10
Exhibitions

Trade shows are an expensive exercise — demanding in money and time for preparation as well as at the show. Someone also has to cover you and your staff back at the works. Used sensibly they are a valuable marketing aid for many firms to try out new lines, generate fresh contacts, meet old buyers and hopefully, pick up sales.

Selection

There are around 3000 trade fairs held each year in the UK alone ranging from motor cars to fur and feather. The major venues are the National Exhibition Centre in Birmingham and Earls Court and Olympia in West London. Others, such as the Wembley Conference Centre and the Barbican, are gaining in popularity.

Many other regional exhibition centres are springing up often based on a large hotel. They are all listed in *Exhibition Bulletin* (see page 46). With so many to choose from care must be taken to pick the right one. Fair promoters are keen to push the merits of their own efforts and are fond of launching new concepts to fill alleged fresh gaps in the market. In general, stick to tried and proven shows. Ask for last year's catalogue and if possible visit the actual show before becoming a paying exhibitor. You can quickly form an idea of the merits of the show by picking out the brand leaders in your trade. Show organisers will also send you a list of exhibitors who have actually booked space in advance. The better shows will provide a visitor breakdown of last year's attendance — how many plant managers or specifiers etc. The figures should be audited.

General shows have vague titles — Spring Fair — while the more specialised shows will only attract visitors of that interest. Organisers are expected to put 'International' in the title only if more than 20 per cent of the space is taken by overseas exhibitors.

Exhibitions fall broadly into two distinct categories: trade only shows, where the visitors are all commercial buyers, and consumer shows for the general public. Some consumer shows have the first day reserved for trade visitors only. You will obviously bear this distinction in mind when deciding which show to attend. Although in sheer *attendance* figures the well-known Motor Show and Ideal Home Exhibition dwarf many trade shows, in volume there are far more specialist shows for trade buyers.

The more popular shows will be booked up perhaps six months ahead with preference on position given to previous exhibitors. Some literally have a waiting list from one year to the next. When you get the floor plan avoid booking a distant corner, down a cul-de-sac aisle, or even in a third-floor bedroom as some hotel shows tend to be. Good sites are near the bar and the loos. This is where your knowledge of the hall comes in.

Objectives

As with all promotional work you must have objectives. You must have a reason for attending and a strategy. Is it to test consumer reaction with a new product, expand sales in a specific direction, change the whole image of the firm, find agents to sell your goods, launch a franchise operation or simply, as so many seem to think, 'to wave the flag'?

There are five major points to bear in mind.

1. COST

Remember that whether 20 or 200 square metres are rented the fair organiser can only provide the same audience. You won't get any more people through the turnstile by having an enormous stand.

Space rental is just that: whatever is placed on that space is at additional cost. A *shell stand* provided by the organiser is usually three plain white walls, a fascia board with your name, common lighting, and sometimes floor covering and a front desk. Extras you *may* need are power points (sometimes amazingly expensive), spotlights, chairs (you will want to rest occasionally) coat rack, reception desk, leaflet and display racks, a better floor covering, muslin ceiling to hide all the cables and beams, and a waste-paper basket. You may well want to improve the lighting by extra spots and bring colour to the walls by drapes, tiles or display stands.

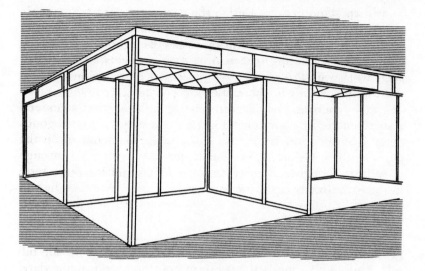

Exhibition shell stand

A phone on the stand can be a very expensive luxury. Think hard what use you will put it to before ordering as the organisers will always relay messages from base and you can dial out from public call boxes. If you do have your own phone make sure you use a telephone dial lock for after hours.

You can also hire models (both sorts). The more interesting variety speaks three languages, will smile sweetly all day, mop your fevered brow but may not have a clue about your product.

Whether you offer 'hospitality' is up to you. The hard stuff tends to be easing out though you do get the big spenders at any show. They are picked out by the hearty laughter, flushed faces and complete lack of interest in the customer.

Your stand design will be governed by restrictions on height and often weight, and how far you can intrude on the gangway. Unusual exhibits must be cleared with the organiser first. They are all careful about flame retardant materials. Heavy or bulky exhibits must be moved in early during the setting-up phase.

Although the show organisers often specify approved stand contractors this *doesn't* preclude your bringing in your own designs. They usually specify prior submission. Everything to do with exhibitions tends to be expensive. If you happen to be a joiner or in display, or have other practical skills, build your own stand fittings. Design them so you can use them again — and again. But, and it's a big one, be wary of doing any part of the erection on site. Entire shows have been stopped by exhibitors hammering in a nail or even changing a bulb, when such work was the prerogative of one or more unions. This is usually spelled out in the exhibition contract. Tempers tend to be frayed before a show and getting hold of the organiser's tradesmen to fit your stand together is a very frustrating business. I haven't yet been to a show where someone isn't still painting the walls on the first open day.

A final thought on cost: use carpet tiles and lay them back in the office ready again for next year.

2. STAND DESIGN

You have three choices: to take the exhibitors' shell stand provided, go to a professional exhibition designer or do it yourself. The middle one is the preferred option if your budget will stand it. There is quite a lot that a professional can do even with the basic shell stand by using good colour schemes. However, as I am mainly writing for the newcomer I shall assume that funds are tight.

Virtually every display fitting can be hired from the many exhibition contractors around. Watch the prices. Some knock the hire price off if you later purchase the equipment.

Growing in popularity and versatility are fold-away display panels that can have several other uses — on the road selling, reception or shop window displays, at seminars or anything else you may get involved in.

These are useful if you are renting space only, not even a shell stand. Make a cardboard model of the stand and move bits around to get an idea of size and impact. Get sample fabrics and see how they will look under the right lighting. Remember that the deeper colours — black, purple, dark greens — impart a feeling of luxury.

Create action on your stand

Try and get movement, light or sound on to the stand. As with all advertising, your priority is to get people to stop and look at your stand. What you do next is the easy part.

You may be competing with a thousand or two other exhibitors all trying to woo buyers on to their pitch.

Turntables large and small on which you can place any

product from a car to a matchbox can be hired at a reasonable price. Water, springs, runways and a whole host of contrivances can be engineered to impart a bit of life into your exhibit. Audio visual displays telling your story can be effective if the screen is big enough. Run a competition, raffle a bottle of whisky, give trials of model driving, anything to get people to *stop and allow you to influence them.*

One of the best draws I have seen was to photograph two pretty girls arm in arm with the prospect. The camera was a polaroid. The queue was enormous. Another employed a fruit machine but no money needed to be dropped in. No passer by could resist trying it.

One of the easiest methods to attract must be simply to leave a television set tuned to whatever sporting event is on at the moment. If you happen to hit Wimbledon you're made.

Avoid a step in your stand design at all costs. People have great reluctance actually to *step* on to a stand. They feel committed. If you can match your carpet with the one in the gangway, a psychological barrier will be removed.

If there is room on your stand, have a hidey hole where you can relax, have a smoke, make a cup of tea and loosen your tie. You'll also need somewhere to store your bag, reserve leaflets and samples.

3. PREPARATION

Don't leave the planning to the last minute. Draw up a list of all the things you need to buy or hire, not forgetting print, insurance and staff holidays. The organisers will certainly have asked you for advertising copy for the show catalogue and possibly the trade press will be doing a special feature. Make sure they are well supplied with good pictures and editorial. Be a little wary of how much you spend on advertising for this.

Don't leave leaflet printing to the last minute. Look at your price-lists. Do you need new ones? Have you distinguished between trade and retail, and — if it's overseas — a landed price (CIF) in that country? Translation? If you're going to a major public show it's worth running off a cheap handout for the masses and reserving your colour job for the discerning buyer. There can be few more depressing sights than your own precious leaflets blowing around the car park at the end of the day. Beware the kids. I'm sure they have a bet on how many leaflets they can collect.

Most organisers send you invitation cards that you mail out

(with your stand number) to your main buyers and customers. Use letter stickers and any opportunity to publicise your presence at the show.

Overseas shows demand more preparation. If you are going with a British Overseas Trade Board (BOTB) sponsored mission (see Chapter 11) there will be a pre-briefing with all the UK exhibitors. You will probably all chip into a common pool for publicity. The Central Office of Information (COI) will handle this very well. Be ready with a translated brochure if it is for a non-English country, even though many Europeans are quite happy in our tongue. Don't miss the shipping dates, which are often well in advance of the exhibition. Send as much as you can in advance of the exhibition, using the designated shippers to ensure receipt in good time. You don't really want to heave boxes of leaflets through airport lounges.

4. PRODUCT DISPLAY

The exhibits you show, with rare exceptions, must be spot on. No prototypes or sticky tape or scratches must mar your professional presentation. Ensure they match your literature. There is nothing more calculated to deter a buyer than to say, 'Of course, this is only the prototype. The final item will be much better.'

I would accept prototypes if they were from an R&D consultancy — that is the nature of their business.

Another exception? Ex Monte Carlo cars at motor shows, straight from the rally with the obligatory gash down the roof and mud over the doors.

Don't put your most interesting exhibit at the back of the stand. Place it where people can see it from the gangway.

Lighting as every shopkeeper knows is an art in itself. The judicious use of spots highlighting key items can be very effective. If you are using moving items make sure they don't trap visitors or get dislodged.

Tie down small and valuable items or put them in a locked display case. Arrange your display so that a glance will disclose a missing item. Leave free passage for visitors: 60 per cent of the stand can be taken up by this.

Signs and labels must *always* be properly printed. Handwritten or even typed product labels look awful. Most printers will set and dry-mount text to give that professional finish.

Cut-out display letters can be bought in a variety of styles and materials from mirror glass to polystyrene. Paint the polystyrene in your house colour.

Don't arrange your leaflets in too precise or geometrical a style. Visitors will be afraid to disturb the artistic integrity.

5. STAFFING

Before the show ensure that whoever is manning the stand is fully versed in the product range. Your representative must be able to discuss all the technicalities and be aware of potential delivery times and the effect on production capability. If applicable, shipping, packing and import dues must be known.

Never attempt to do the show on your own. Exhibitions are surprisingly exhausting. You need a relief to let you sit down, relax, wander round the other exhibitors (the competition) to pick up what else is happening. Avoid doing more than two hours at one stretch.

All stand personnel must have lapel badges to identify themselves. Take plenty of business cards to hand out. The most cost-effective way to hand out literature, if we're talking about expensive full-colour brochures, is simply to post it on. Keep a typewriter on the stand and type self-adhesive labels from the buyers' cards as you go. That ensures that every brochure asked for will get to the right person and not dropped at the show. It's efficient for you and looks efficient to the visitor. Never hand out sales literature without an exchange of addresses. Don't forget it's names and contacts you are after all the time.

A *visitors' book* must be established to record all enquirers. Leave a column for further action required which could be quotes to be prepared, follow-up visits or simply literature to be sent.

Show selling techniques

Manning a stand is like being at the zoo — only this time you are the animals. You're there to be peered at, poked, and to provide the entertainment. You must never look bored, tired or drunk, but always welcoming without being effusive, knowledgeable and a good advertisement for your firm. Although you have a ready-made audience coming through the turnstiles you still have to entice them on to your stand. The most vital spot on your display is 3 feet in front of it. That is the *decision point*. Either the visitor carries on past or he is attracted in. It's rather like the garage man who throws tacks on the road outside his empty forecourt. 'That'll bring 'em in!' You need to station a body slap bang in the middle of the gangway doing something to divert visitors. He or she needs to be inviting participation in your raffle or demonstration, details of which will be on your stand. Simpler is just to ask 'Have you seen our latest . . .?'

Don't be too eager to buttonhole those who come on the stand of their own accord. Let them get their bearings and study whatever has attracted them. Don't hover at their shoulder or pounce when they are not prepared.

It is never good practice to open with, 'Can I help you?' There is an even chance that the answer will be 'No' and where do you go from there? It is more fruitful to start a discussion:

'What interests you in this range?'
'Have you used our product before?'
'Let me show you how this works.'

You should establish to whom you are talking early on. It could be a competitor or the son of the chairman of your biggest customer. If you are using several staff avoid going into a huddle at the back of the stand. It looks like a private party and visitors are loath to break in.

Keep your visitors' book under control. They've been known to disappear on the last day: a goldmine for the competition with all those leads and all your money thrown away.

Keep the stand clean and presentable at all times. Empty the ashtrays, hide the gin bottle and sweep up those newspapers.

When any of your staff leave the stand make sure you know where they're going and when they are due back. Rests should be worked on a rota basis and taken well away from the stand. Use the time to go round all the competition.

If you take a *new* product to the show make sure a large sticker says so. That's the most important word in the exhibitor's dictionary. As the show progresses put some 'Sold' stickers on your exhibits. It impresses the visitors and depresses the opposition.

Follow up

All enquiries must be efficiently followed up either with a quote, further information or a visit. Never sign up an agent at the show itself. By all means display a board inviting representation but give yourself time to make investigations afterwards.

Keep any fair press office handouts on attendance and breakdown.

Hold on to the show catalogue which will be useful for contacts and a mailing list.

It is unfair to judge results on the attendance of one year's show. You will undoubtedly learn and adapt from your first effort. The visiting buyers also are a little wary of brand new names but will renew acquaintance in succeeding years.

If you use agents it is an obvious place to gather and swop experiences.

What a good model can do for you

Models are a good exhibition aid. Both sorts. This page is about the manufactured variety. If you are promoting a product that is too large to heave around then a professionally made engineering model could save you hernias. It would certainly be an improvement on photographs. Apart from the obvious merit of portability, models can be cut away to highlight internal workings or show up some particular feature. Different sections can be coloured to show the flow of liquids, gas etc. Perspex windows can be let in to reveal chambers. Products that are only on the drawing board can be speedily created by the use of models. Advance publicity or orders can be obtained without the expense of tooling up for production runs. Engineering models are increasingly used for proving the drawings. Translation from two dimensions to three frequently throws up missed connections in pipework or symmetry.

When commissioning a model try and get your money's worth by thinking ahead for other uses. Models can be used by design draughtsmen, for prototype tooling, by training personnel as well as for PR and sales aids.

Don't forget a case for the model, or keep it out of harm's way at exhibitions if it is at all delicate.

CHOOSING A MODEL MAKER
Professional model makers are not cheap to employ when you consider that by definition the skill is hand-held and labour intensive. Few machines can be used (except for metal models). Try and give a full brief — drawings, artist's impressions or photographs, dimensions — and work from a British Standard colour chart. If your instructions are little more than the proverbial back of envelope notes then research takes a lot of time. Look at other examples of his work and be sure to specify the degree of *detail* and finish you require. It is the amount of

detailed modelling that takes the time (and money). Model makers today are clever at reproducing many of the architectural and engineering surfaces seen on finished products. A high degree of realism can be obtained. They tend to use plastic mouldings and card which make the models resistant to humidity changes and easy to keep clean.

Apart from exhibitions, models can be good salesmen's aids if they can fit in a sample case. A whole range of products can be shown.

Yellow Pages carry details of model makers. You can also look for them in *Design* magazine. Many tend to specialise in architectural developments, engineering pipework or even film special effects. For good examples of the model maker's art visit the Farnborough air show or a major oil show.

Chapter 11
Starting in Exports

Around 40 per cent of UK trade is concluded through buying houses or agents based in this country. You need never leave these shores as negotiations can be conducted in English through firms over here. Delivery is made to a nominated shipper and payment made in sterling. Most of these buying media are of long standing.

Direct exporting is *not* fun. For a new small firm it can be very demanding in time and money spent mastering all the fresh techniques of documentation, agencies, customs, shipping, payment and often the language confusion. Consider what is involved. You have to find and understand a new market with all the problems of packaging, legal requirements and translation. Dealing at a distance is never easy, while fluctuations in the pound can ruin a good deal. Trips abroad to back up your agents and investigate the market can prove very expensive. Unless you have very good contacts abroad, I would tend to say in the early days — forget it.

Why export anyway? There is no intrinsic merit in exporting — often quite the reverse. The golden rule must be to develop a strong home base first then move on to what can be gained abroad. Do not regard export as a means of disposing of your domestic surplus. There must be solid objectives in taking that route which could be one of the following:

1. To spread the risk of tying yourself to one domestic market. A recession here is not necessarily mirrored abroad.
2. More profit in selling abroad. Not so long ago we were equals in Europe in terms of living standards. Today, in a frighteningly short space of time, the UK is becoming the poor man of Europe. Some luxury goods may command a wider market in the EEC.
3. Our professional services — design, consultancy, engineering, finance, computer software etc — are in great demand throughout the world. The developing nations, both oil rich and impoverished, can make very good use of experts willing to travel.

4. Growth. As world standards rise the possible markets for your goods expand at an accelerating rate.
5. To improve the product. Many products, once exposed to the harsher conditions overseas, take on innovations that result in a better article.
6. Morale. I add this somewhat tentatively but I do believe that small firms feel uplifted when they tackle a difficult market and succeed in making inroads. Bright staff may be retained in a forward-thinking company prepared to have a go. There is always the chance of foreign travel.

Staying in this country

Let's look at my first option and chase export business in this country. As a component supplier you can sell to a large firm who happens to be in the export trade. There is no problem here as you will simply produce to a specification.

There are hundreds of confirming houses, export merchants and buying offices who to a greater or lesser extent act for overseas principals in selecting and procuring goods for export. Most of them are based in London, many around Tottenham Court Road and Regent Street. Look in the *Directory of Export Buyers* (Trade Research Publications, Berkhampstead; copies in the bigger reference libraries) for a detailed breakdown of who deals in what. Among them you will see members of the *British Export Houses Association* (69 Cannon Street, London EC4N 5AB; 01-248 4444) who tend to be buyers for department|stores in the USA, Canada, Japan, South Africa and the Commonwealth. They often act simply as agents and will select samples to await the annual (or biannual) visit of the overseas buyer. Do the rounds. Dealing with export houses can be a lengthy business with sometimes endless requests for samples. Persevere: when the orders do come they can be worth while. Payment is invariably in sterling and delivery to a named shipper. Paperwork is minimal.

Direct exporting

Your first call should be to your nearest office of the British Overseas Trade Board. Most information by far is held at 1.Victoria Street, London SW1H 0ET; 01-215 7877, but there are some 10 regional offices. The BOTB is the government's main department for helping our exporters and they are able to help in a number of ways.

1. The *Export Intelligence Service* feeds back sales enquiries via our consulates all round the world. It is inevitably computerised and classified into much detail. Before you do anything else ask them to pull out the enquiries they have had over a previous set period to gauge where the leads are coming from. It is important to code in exactly what your interest is, otherwise you will get out a lot of garbage of no relevance. To receive new enquiries you pay around £50 for 150 notices. If you push them they may give you a free run.

2. *Scatter missions* are organised subsidised trips of groups of businessmen to specific countries. Brief the consulate abroad on your interests and they will try and line up appointments and a suggested itinerary for you. The groups are usually members of a Chamber of Commerce or trade association. They can be a very useful way of learning from other, perhaps more experienced, members of the business community.

3. The *Fairs and Promotions* branch mount a British presence at over 300 shows overseas. They usually rent a large block space and partition it out to UK exhibitors. There is great advantage in a small firm being part of a large national stand. Buyers come to visit the well-known large firms and must pass their smaller brethren. There is usually a common colour scheme and layout which pulls it all together. There is a subsidy on stand space, transport of exhibits and travel, depending on the venue. Much of the hassle is removed by being part of a well organised operation of this sort. Little things like a common pool for publicity and advertising can help a lot in getting over the message. Demand is keen for the major shows and early booking is essential. This must be the most painless way of gaining custom overseas.

4. The *Market Advisory Service* will attempt to investigate the particular sector for your product using the local knowledge of the commercial consuls in the countries concerned. A report can be given on the competition, price, pattern of demand and methods of selling. The section also suggests local agents who may be worth approaching to represent you. Full status reports can be obtained.

5. The *Statistics and Market Intelligence Library* (SMIL) at 1 Victoria Street, London SW1H 0ET will keep you busy for several days. There are volumes of statistics, directories

and fair catalogues. The problem as always is sifting out what you want from the mass of detail. Their country by country series *Hints to Exporters* give a useful outline of individual problems and cultures. There are several sponsored schemes to help you carry out in-depth market research.

OTHER SOURCES OF INFORMATION

You should join your nearest large *Chamber of Commerce*. Most towns have chambers of trade but they tend to be composed of retailers and have no expertise in exporting. The biggest are London and Birmingham but all the conurbations have chambers to help you. The more efficient will be able to offer regular sponsored group selling, or fact finding, trips abroad, group telex arrangements, documentation advice, carnets, certificates of origin and all the new impedimenta to smooth your sales efforts. The more progressive hold regular meetings to enable firms to discuss common problems.

Most chambers hold seminars on export practice and documentation and it would be helpful to send along the staff most likely to be involved. The more you can steep yourself in the strange new jargon and get a feel for the likely problem areas, the more you will be prepared.

Export clubs are another informal way of meeting fellow marketing men and learning about the pitfalls of selling abroad. They tend to be *ad hoc* groups of small business people perhaps sponsored by local councils and trade associations.

There are a variety of overseas Chambers of Commerce, embassy libraries (the US embassy in Grosvenor Square in particular) and joint trade bodies to foster links with overseas countries. Not all are too keen to help with exports as many are more geared to selling *you* something, but the sources of information are invariably there in great detail.

LITERATURE

All the major banks offer free literature and guidance. You will inevitably be using them a great deal for arranging payment, perhaps for obtaining status reports via their agents abroad, exchange control and currency. Try and get one of their staff from the overseas branch to visit. The smaller branches will probably not have many dealings with export documentation and it may pay you to move your account if much export is contemplated.

Exporting can sweeten the bank's relationship with you as priority has always been given on lending to those so engaged.

British Business is the weekly magazine produced by the Department of Trade and Industry that keeps you up to date on tariff changes, trade fairs and opportunities. Most libraries stock copies.

Export Times and *Export Direction* are two widely available specialist magazines.

Croner's Reference Book for Exporters (Croner Publications, 173 Kingston Road, New Malden, Surrey KT3 3SS; 01-942 8966) is one in their large series of loose-leaf, handy reference books on specialist subjects, loose leaf because you get a regular up-date as part of your annual subscription.

Freight forwarders

Another source of guidance is the freight forwarder. These are the people who will ship your valued goods all over the world to the port of destination. The paperwork probably causes more headaches to small firms than anything else. Every country seems to require different forms and there are changes every week. Unless you are engaged in a very stable part of the world and regularly ship items of the same character, I would urge you to pass all the paperwork over to a friendly freight forwarder. Certainly, he will charge you for the privilege, and small consignments may bear an uneconomic charge, but he is dealing with it every day. In general, don't look to your bank or the BOTB for matters of detail such as commercial invoices or certificates of origin. I have found a good freight forwarder far more practical and knowledgeable.

This is really the nub of the small firm's problems: where to get accurate advice on the practical day-to-day problems of exporting. Because exporting is a *practical* discipline with constantly changing demands and procedures, a slip up in the paperwork and your goods could be languishing in the customs shed or worse, on an open dockside, for months. I have also known goods that should have been paid for on collection delayed for 120 days due to an error in the draft.

What to export

Selling abroad is no different from the domestic market. You must find out what is needed and fulfil the demand. A study of the Export Intelligence Service, requests for UK goods published in your trade press, chamber bulletins and export magazines should be a lead. Although the multinationals are doing their best to make the world buy standard products, most countries still obstinately cling to their own peculiar likes and dislikes. If you stick to the English-speaking world you won't have to translate your packaging or instructions.

There are few restrictions on what can be *exported* from this country – mainly defence equipment to 'unfriendly' nations, and livestock. If in doubt ring the Export Licensing Branch, Department of Trade, Millbank Tower, Millbank, London SW1P 4QU; 01-211 6611. Livestock and agricultural products are subject to controls if exported outside the EEC – contact the Intervention Board for Agricultural Produce, Golden Cross House, Duncannon Street, London WC2N 4JF; 01-217 3433.

What other countries allow *in* is another matter. Naturally enough, developing nations try to protect their embryo industries, and protectionism seems to be rising not decreasing as the world recession continues. The restrictions can be effected by quota (import licence), customs tariffs or complicated technical standards. Electrical goods exported to Germany may have to pass six certification boards, making it a costly and time-consuming exercise. Probably the biggest deterrent is the likelihood of not getting paid. There are many countries where it is better not to venture unless you are prepared to accept the local crop as barter.

Whatever you export must obviously be suited to local conditions and customs. The material used must withstand the changed climate and be rugged enough to travel over perhaps corrugated roads. The instructions and packaging must be relevant, while the colour and general outward appearance may need redesigning for the overseas market.

Advice on the technical standards required can be found from a branch of the British Standards Institution, Technical Help to Exporters at Linford Wood, Milton Keynes MK14 6LE; 0908 320033. They have information on the requirements of over 160 countries. English translations are made of many of the important overseas codes of practice.

Where to export

You will probably find it simpler to export to English-speaking countries first – the old Commonwealth and north America.

Many retain our customs and style of life. Financial links are still strong with many British banks having subsidiaries and agents in those countries. As we are continually being exhorted to regard Europe as our back yard and not 'abroad' the EEC should come a close second. Travel costs in money and time are reduced and their standards of living are equal (or ahead) of ours. There are few restrictions on trade and no customs barriers, in theory! It is, of course, a highly devleoped, sophisticated and competitive market where quality, premium products will always sell if correctly presented.

The Third World, or developing nations, pose special problems. Payment is rarely simple and finding the right channel of distribution difficult. You are probably better dealing with a government or United Nations agency already working in the field where you look to them for the specification and payment.

COMMITMENT

It is a sad fact that in most countries now our share of the market is decreasing. Former strongholds of British produce have been allowed to wither to the Japanese, Germans or French. They seem to have put more effort into tackling the market. Close study of each individual market has been undertaken, modifications made to take account of the local conditions, languages learnt and perhaps most important, hard investment made with distributors in that country. It is this constant back-up to the selling operation that has paid dividends. Japanese businessmen travel abroad 20 times more often than ours. Unless you take a long-term view, are prepared to make frequent trips to see what is happening on the ground and support the local man with promotion and exhibitions, then direct exporting is not for you. Getting established abroad is a long, costly exercise and requires a great commitment to see it through.

Getting paid

One of the main attractions of dealing with export houses or buying agents in this country is the certainty of getting paid reasonably promptly and in sterling. Extended credit is not usually a sales requirement. Once you start dealing direct you come against two problems: how to ensure getting payment and avoiding exchange risks.

OPEN ACCOUNT

A surprising amount of trade is carried on open account, ie invoices are raised, the goods delivered and payment made by bank transfer. A large element of trust has built up. There is really no difference here between home and export business.

BILLS OF EXCHANGE

This is a simple document which enables an exporter to extend a period of credit to the other party to allow time for the goods to be shipped, collected and possibly sold. It is drawn on the importer and is presented for acceptance and payment through his bank. If it is a *sight draft* the importer must, as the term implies, pay the amount on first presentation whereupon he will be given the documents of title to the goods. If it is a *term draft*, ie due so many days (usually multiples of 30) after sight, then the client will sign his acceptance of the bill and it will be returned to the exporter. He can then discount (cash) the bill with his bank if need be, who will present it on the due date. Naturally, there is a finance charge for this service.

DOCUMENTARY LETTERS OF CREDIT

An irrevocable letter of credit is the safest way of transacting business abroad. The importer instructs his bank to open a credit in favour of the exporter setting out very precise conditions for the supporting documents, methods of despatch and details of the goods. Each bank confirms the agreement and, provided the paperwork is exact, you will get paid. Everything seems to be required in copious numbers of copies — commercial invoices, certificates of origin, shipping notes, customs declarations, bills of lading etc. You must obey the instructions to the letter otherwise inevitable delays or rejection will occur. Make sure that it is *confirmed* by a London bank.

FACTORING

An increasingly used method of extracting payment is to deal with an international factoring company who will handle all your collections, credit you in sterling, provide bad debt cover and often allow you to draw against invoices. The factoring companies tend to be owned by the major banks with international ramifications who, with their extensive networks, can find out a great deal about your prospective buyer. They can relieve you of a great deal of worry about paperwork and finance your export trade. Ask your bank who their factoring

SPECIMEN BILL OF EXCHANGE (Clients' names are fictitious)

£8,240

Keighley
11th August, 1982

AT SIGHT OF THIS SOLA OF EXCHANGE PAY TO OUR ORDER THE SUM OF STERLING

POUNDS EIGHT THOUSAND TWO HUNDRED AND FORTY ONLY FOR VALUE RECEIVED

Drawn under Irrevocable Credit of Barclays Bank International PLC Pennine House,

45, Well Street, Bradford No. FDC/2/6789 dated 20th July, 1982

To: Barclays Bank International PLC
       Pennine House,
       45, Well Street,
       Bradford

For and on behalf of
QUALITY WOOLLENS LTD

f. Arkwright
Director

The legal definition of a bill of exchange is:

1. an unconditional order in writing
2. addressed by one person (the drawer)
3. to another (the drawee)
4. signed by the person giving it (the drawer)
5. requiring the person to whom it is addressed (the drawee, who when he signs becomes the acceptor)
6. to pay
7. on demand or at a fixed or determinable future time
8. a sum certain in money
9. to, or to the order of, a specified person or to bearer (the payee).

The phrases are numbered to correspond to the various parts of the bill of exchange shown above. All the information above must be shown on every bill of exchange.

The specimen bill of exchange is a 'sight' bill which requires immediate payment by the drawee. If it called for payment after the date of the bill it would be a 'tenor' bill. Unless the documentary letter of credit stipulates that bills of exchange are required in duplicate, a single (sola) bill of exchange is acceptable.

Specimen bill of exchange
(Courtesy: Bank Education Service)

SPECIMEN DOCUMENTARY CREDIT (Clients' names are fictitious)

BARCLAYS International Pennine House, 45 Well Street, Bradford, W. Yorks.

Date 20th July, 1982
IRREVOCABLE CREDIT No. FDC/2/6789
To be quoted on all drafts and correspondence.

Beneficiary(ies)	Advised through
Quality Woollens Limited, Farthing Lane, Keighley, West Yorks.	

Accreditor	To be completed only if applicable
Harper-Simon Incorporated, Fifth Avenue, New York, U.S.A.	Our cable of
	Advised through refers

Dear Sir(s),
In accordance with instructions received from The State Banking Co.
we hereby issue in your favour a Documentary Credit for £8240
(say) Eight thousand, two hundred and forty pounds sterling   available by
your drafts drawn on us
at sight
for the 100% c.i.f.   invoice value, accompanied by the following documents:

1. Invoice in triplicate, signed and marked Licence No.
   LHDL 22 1982
2. Certificate of origin issued by a Chamber of Commerce
3. Full set of clean on board Shipping Company's Bills of Lading made out
   to order and blank endorsed, marked "Freight Paid" and
   'Notify Harper-Simon Inc. Fifth Avenue, New York"
4. Insurance Policy or Certificate in duplicate, covering Marine and
   War Risks up to buyer's warehouse, for invoice value of the goods plus 10%

Covering the following goods:
   100 Sheepskin Coats
To be shipped from Liverpool   to New York c.i.f.
not later than 10th August, 1982
Partshipment not permitted   Transhipment not permitted
This credit is available for presentation to us   until 31st August, 1982
Documents to be presented within 21 days of shipment but within
credit validity.
Drafts drawn hereunder must be marked "Drawn under Barclays Bank International PLC
Pennine House, 45, Well Street, Bradford   branch,
Credit number FDC/2/6789   "
We undertake that drafts and documents drawn under and in strict conformity with
the terms of this credit will be honoured upon presentation.
       Yours faithfully,

Co-signed (Signature No.   )   Signed (Signature No.   )

Specimen documentary credit
(Courtesy: Bank Education Service)

company is or write to the Association of British Factors, Moor House, London Wall, London EC2Y 5HE.

EXPORT INSURANCE

Allegedly the envy of the world is our Export Credits Guarantee Department (ECGD) which will insure your trade against non-payment by the buyer in a number of eventualities, including insolvency, failure to take up the goods, political interference of the buyer's country, war risks and cancellation of a UK export licence.

There are a number of policies, too complex to go into here, but it would be surprising if there were not cover for you. Services can be covered as well as goods. With the benefit of ECGD cover you are more able to offer attractive, and competitive, credit terms to your buyer. Of major import is that once ECGD are involved guarantees can be given to your bank enabling a most attractive interest rate to be enjoyed. They normally insure *all* your export turnover, and the rate charged is commensurate with the country and type of goods shipped. As a guide, a six-month insurance to a stable country will cost about 75p per £100.

Agents or distributors?

Agents overseas bring much the same problems and opportunities as discussed earlier in the domestic market (page 148). It is rarely sufficient to appoint agents, sit back and expect orders to flow in unless you pay regular visits, and back them up with trade shows and personal visits to clients.

Distributors or wholesalers will physically hold stocks purchased from you and sell on through their own local network of salesmen. Because they have tied up funds there is more incentive to get out and recover their investment, but there will naturally be a bigger margin for them. As a generality, the latter tend to be of more substance, longer established and will provide more continuity than agents.

The choice is often dictated by the nature of the goods. Where the items sold are of a large specialised nature and represent an infrequent purchase, agents may be the logical choice. If, however, stocks need to be held locally for regular replacement then a distributor may be more appropriate.

FINDING AN AGENT

You have a number of ways:

1. Put a notice 'Agents required' on your exhibition stand, here and abroad. Some domestic shows have a high overseas visitor attendance and you could well find your requirements here.
2. Study the trade press for your speciality. There are usually adverts for distributors seeking more goods. Your local Chamber of Commerce is also a good source.
3. The major clearing banks have extensive connections through their own overseas branches and agents. They can be very helpful as they will have hard information on the financial status of their contact.
4. The BOTB have an agency finding service that generally seeks to provide representation for you abroad by means of the overseas consulate's local knowledge. They are instructed to make a report containing the names of potential representatives with detailed information on their background and standing. The fee charged is £100 which is refunded if a visit to meet the agent is made within six months.

Transport and packing

Small packages (up to 20 kg) are best handled by the post office. The service is cheap and efficient. In recent years they have become more commercially aggressive and have several attractive schemes for contract clients and first-time users. See your local postal services representative (page 190).

When starting off you should engage the services of a good freight forwarder and get them to do all the documentation and transport procedures. It is a complex market with many pitfalls for the inexperienced.

The Research Association for the Paper and Board, Printing and Packaging Industries (PIRA) can advise on all aspects of suitable materials for transmission abroad taking account of climatic conditions. You can find them at Randalls Road, Leatherhead, Surrey KT22 7RU; 0372 376161.

Most of the world's trade is still shipped by sea, because it is easier to carry bulky items. The cost is far less than by air. The growth in this market has been in container loads enabling rapid transhipment from lorry to dock to ship without breaking bulk. Ideally, you wait till you can fill a container by yourself –

otherwise you have to share with other exporters. Your freight forwarder will know which lines regularly go to the nearest port of destination and with what frequency. Higher value, and smaller packs now increasingly go by air.

In Europe road transport has developed into a highly sophisticated service with major cities having daily deliveries. The last few years have also seen a rapid growth in personal courier services for emergency or high-value packages on a door-to-door basis.

Publicity

The *Central Office of Information (COI)* is the government's main propaganda agency for pushing out news items all round the world. It collects news items of British products, new inventions, large contracts etc and sends them out to our consulates abroad. They in turn feed their local press. Something like 50,000 stories and 20,000 photographs a year are sent out. If the story warrants it they will send their own photographer to your plant to get the best job. Many of the staff are ex-Fleet Street and in my experience provide a first class service. On occasions they will also produce film and video to slot into news programmes overseas. They will write scripts and do 'voice overs'.

It is particularly appropriate to use them if you are exhibiting abroad as they will be able to tie in the story with your presence.

I have left the best to last — it is all free.

The COI works closely with the BOTB and contact should be made through their regional offices or the headquarters at Hercules House, Westminster Bridge Road, London SE1 7DU; 01-928 2345.

The *BBC External Services* are also willing to broadcast British successes. Apart from the well-known BBC World Service in English, broadcasts are made in some 36 languages. Special programmes on farming, science, business and new ideas will give coverage to your efforts. Send for a leaflet on what they are looking for to the Export Liaison Unit, BBC, PO Box 76, Bush House, Strand, London WC2 4PH.

There are also a number of press agency services who will write a story, translate here and abroad with a native speaker, and send out to the appropriate journal overseas. It can be very effective if you have the right story and go to a top agency and is particularly good for engineering and technical products. The cost can be several hundred pounds for a story translated into, say, three languages. The skill lies in the expert translation as the wrong nuance can be devastating.

Some export terminology

The most casual reader will soon come against some jargon of the export trade. A few major terms are:

Bill of lading. The document given to you by the shipping line as a receipt and title (ownership) for the goods carried. A valuable document that tends to have several copies, some of which are sent to the importer and paying bank as evidence of compliance with your terms of trading.

Certificate of origin means what it says — an authenticated statement by the exporter backed by a Chamber of Commerce, and sometimes by an embassy, to state where the goods emanate from: particularly relevant to the Arab states and their long-running argument with Israel.

Commercial invoices are more detailed than domestic invoices. They usually contain a full description of the goods, packing marks, weights, insurance, and transport routes. Every country seems to require different methods of spelling out the same thing — some require consular and Chamber of Commerce authentication, some want declarations if not the whole invoice in their own language. They are also of major interest to the customs in both countries as a means of checking exports, imports and any duties to be levied.

FOB (free on board) is the usual method of quoting export prices. Added to your price will be the cost of transport to the specified port, dock charges etc up to placing on board ship (or aircraft). As the cost depends on which exit port is used it is best to add the name of the port as well — FOB Harwich, for example.

CIF (cost, insurance, freight) takes it one stage further. Added to the FOB price is the actual shipping charge to a named port and the cost of insurance on board.

Spot and *forward* rates of exchange. Spot rates are currency deals struck at once, while forward rates are those at which a bargain may be struck at some time in the future. There is a lot of speculation in exchange rates with dealers buying on behalf of genuine exporters and importers as well as pure speculators. Among all of them are central banks buying or selling to influence the country's exchange rate. You can protect the amount

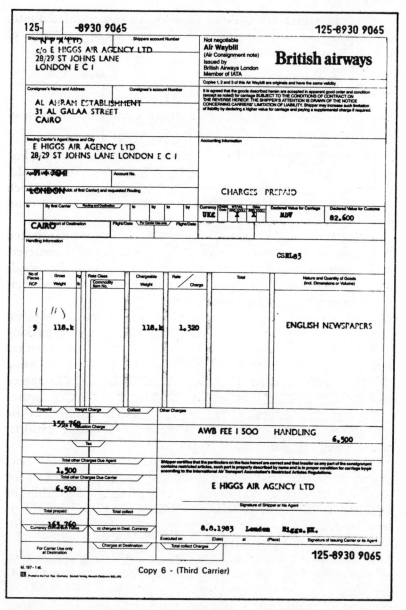

Air waybill
(Courtesy: British Airways)

SPECIMEN BILL OF LADING (Clients' names are fictitious)

Shipper QUALITY WOOLLENS LIMITED, FARTHING LANE, KEIGHLEY, WEST YORKSHIRE.	B/L No. 529 Shippers Ref. SW/4629 F/Agents Ref. S/291
Consignee (If 'Order' state Notify Party) ORDER	**Atlantic Shipping Co** ≋
Notify Party HARPER-SIMON INCORPORATED, FIFTH AVENUE, NEW YORK U.S.A.	Water Street Liverpool L47 2XX Tel: 051-626848 Telegraphs: Atlanco Liverpool Telex: 9978381

*Local Vessel	*From (Local port of loading)	Telegraphs: Atlanco Liverpool Telex: 9978381		
Ocean Vessel CONCORDIA	Port of Loading LIVERPOOL			
Port of Discharge NEW YORK	*Final Destination (If on-carriage)	Freight payable at BRADFORD	Number of original Bs/L THREE	
Marks and Numbers	Numbers and kind of packages: Description of goods		Gross Weight KILOS	Measurement M³
QW H-S INC. NEW YORK 1 TO 10	 10 CARTONS SHEEPSKIN COATS		 127	 0.510 cubic metres per carton
	FREIGHT PAID			

SHIPPED on board in apparent good order and condition the within mentioned Merchandise stated to be marked, numbered and described in this Bill of Lading (weight, measure, brand, contents, quality and value unknown) to be conveyed via any port or ports (for loading or discharging or for any other purpose), and as otherwise provided herein. In accepting this Bill of Lading the Shipper, Consignee, owner of the goods and the holder of the Bill of Lading expressly agree to all its terms, conditions and exceptions, whether written, printed, stamped or incorporated. Weights as shown in this Bill of Lading as declared by Shippers and the Master is unable to check same.

Number of Packages (in words) TEN	*A C Drake.*	Dated in Liverpool	1st August, 1982

Specimen bill of lading
(Courtesy: Bank Education Service)

of currency you are going to receive by contracting to sell at the time that your deal is made. You forgo any profit that may arise as a result of the rate moving in your favour, but for small exporters it is normally enough to worry about making a profit on the goods. Your bank's overseas department will advise.

SITPRO (Simplification of International Trade Procedures) is an attempt to reduce the complexities of export documentation. The basis of it is a master document from which, by using a copier and different overlays, the various other documents can be run off, avoiding constant retyping. Many freight forwarders and large companies are now using this scheme.

Chapter 12
Improving the Product Range: Innovation, Patents, Licensing and Design

This final chapter is concerned with innovation — the drive for new products. It should be apparent to all that the successful growth companies of this era are those who are continually bringing forward new products and services.

Clive Sinclair has become a household name with his new chip-related items fuelled by his inventive and far-seeing mind. In the service field Dyno-Rod are one example of marketing an unglamorous plumbing operation that has made profits for the innovator and franchisees.

Let's start with the *invention* and lead through all the processes to commercial exploitation. Many small businesses are based on one new idea but few realise initially how long it will take before sales can be made. To put it in perspective, the LP record took three years to reach the market from invention, the ballpoint pen six and the zip fastener 27! Never under-estimate the time taken.

Is it original?

There is little point in inventing a product that has already been developed. Your first task must be to research the 'prior art'. This can be done by following the procedures in Chapter 2 using the trade press and reference libraries, or by consulting a patent agent. Patent agents have a remarkably wide knowledge of inventions and industrial processes. Particularly useful are the indexes and information on the patents of 26 countries provided by Derwent Publications Ltd of 128 Theobalds Road, London WC1X 8RP; 01-242 6823. Patent abridgements are kept at the Science Reference Library, London and a few regional libraries. Searching can be difficult and professional searchers can be employed. A computer listing is now available from the Science Reference Library. Be careful what you disclose as this could invalidate your gaining protection later.

Is there a market?

An important early decision must be made — is there a wide enough market for the product? Try to evaluate objectively the existing lines. How do they perform? Reliably? Ergonomically? Aesthetically? Economically? Are the advantages of your product sufficient to sell it? Would a manufacturer change his production and re-tool for the new item? Is it fashionable, seasonal? To whom will it appeal?

Is the market sector for which you are aiming increasing or decreasing? Who is your target audience?

What protection does your idea merit?

If your market research reinforces the originality of the idea then protection by *patents* or other means should now be considered. A patent by itself will not make your fortune. Sometimes quite the reverse, as initially you may have to disburse a lot of money. Merely the filing of a UK patent application will cost a minimum of £500 (if you use a patent agent) and could well cost three times that amount. There is a school of thought that says you should get on with the development and exploitation of the invention rather than be concerned with patenting. If you neglect patent action at the start, you will inevitably lose all legal redress against copyists. To some extent patenting is bluff, as the costs of a *patent action* for infringement could be around £5000 a week. It sometimes develops into a battle to find who has the deepest purse. Those who file their own patents are really in no position to judge whether their efforts have been successful until an infringement action comes to court. That is when it is tested.

You do not have to incur the full cost of a formal application in the first instance. Most patent agents will advise on how to lodge an initial application yourself to avoid the worst pitfalls. This will give you up to 12 months in which you can further develop the idea to see whether it is likely to be worth seeking full patent protection and incurring the subsequent procedures up to grant of a patent.

Ideas by themselves are not patentable. An invention must be capable of industrial or agricultural application. Artistic works and computer programs are dealt with under copyright law; mathematical theories and business schemes are outside the realms of patent law.

Disclosure. Your own prior disclosure, or public knowledge, of your invention invalidates a patent. If it has been described, even in an obscure journal, your application could be overturned at a later date. The only exception is if the disclosure has been made in breach of a confidence imposed by you on the author, and this can be rather hard to prove.

The patent application

Patent applications fall into two parts. The first step involves filing a 'Request for the Grant of a Patent' (form 1/77) with the required fee (£10 at 1985 rates). You must include a specification in which the invention is fully described, together with any drawings sufficient for a 'suitably competent and knowledgeable person' to put into practice. The Patent Office will send a receipt establishing your *priority date*. But you are a long way from having a patent.

Within 12 months of this date you must file a request (form 9/77) for a preliminary search and examination (£75) including an abstract of the main points in no more than 150 words. The *claims* for the invention must be filed now if they have not been done before.

This 12-month period should be used to find whether there is any real market for the invention and to improve on prototypes. If you find amendments are necessary then a fresh application can be filed. If you do this within a year of first filing you can claim precedence over later publications of the same invention including your own disclosures except those made in strict confidence. However, this later application must be seen to relate strictly to the first one. The first application will then lapse.

THE SECOND STAGE

After the search report has been issued, your specification and claims will be published about 18 months after your priority date. This early publication still does *not* mean that you have a patent: what has previously been secret merely becomes public knowledge.

If you want to continue with prosecution of the patent then a request for substantive examination is necessary (form 10/77) with, you've guessed, a further fee (£90) within six months of publication.

The search report may reveal other near patents and you must decide what amendments may have to be made to your specification. The patent examiner and your agent now discuss amendments. This can lead to protracted correspondence and discussion.

When you've got your patent

Eventually, after about three and a half years from your first filing, grant of patent will be made. The maximum life of the patent will be 20 years providing the annual renewal fees are paid. At least, you don't have to start paying till the fifth year, but they then increase successively.

Finally, you should remember that a granted patent gives you no benefits other than the right, through the courts, to prevent anyone else making, using or selling the invention as long as the patent remains in being.

Foreign patents

Your UK patent will give protection to items produced in the UK only. Infringement will occur if any foreign-made replica is sold or used in this country. Various foreign treaties are now in force to gain world protection but it will not surprise you to learn that foreign patenting is much more complicated and expensive.

Other methods of protection

Protection from copying might be gained by registering the *design* under the Registered Designs Act 1949. Many products rely to a large extent for commercial prosperity on their exterior novelty and recognition. Examples in the consumer field are the Coca Cola bottle and Marmite jar. Design registration covers the *exterior appearance* only and not the mechanical ingenuity. The Act covers mass-produced items of 50 or more. Design registration tends to be applied to textiles, wallpaper, jewellery and domestic products. It must be said that the number of patents lodged far exceed design registrations.

It has never been a popular method of protection although the costs are far less.

A word about the Design Copyright Act 1968 which amended the 1956 Copyright Act: copyright automatically gives protection for works of *artistic merit*. As it has been held that an engineering drawing can retain copyright, any translation of a three-dimensional object from the drawing could be in breach of copyright.

There has been little case law to settle the point but it won't do any harm to retain a signed and dated drawing in a safe place. To prove it was made at the time post a copy back to yourself retaining the sealed envelope and receipt (recorded delivery). Keep it in a safe place. Another method is to get your bank manager or solicitor to date, rubber stamp and sign a copy.

Finally, *trade marks* can be a valuable method of promoting a good product. The rights to use Kodak and Hoover are worth millions. Fortunately registration is simple and cheap. The mark can be maintained indefinitely.

Developing the idea

There is invariably a delay in producing a new product. Most manufactured items have to go through various stages from initial idea to final product. The design will normally have to be tested in prototype form, which could well be a model made of simple materials and using simple techniques, but the tests must reproduce working conditions.

The prototype tests may reveal the need for redesign. The best method of manufacture must also be decided. Will it be stamped, machined or moulded? If of plastic, which type?

A short pilot run may have to be undertaken. As any buyer of a new car knows, the first part of the model run invariably gives most trouble. Transition from pilot to full production frequently throws up more problems.

Few inventors combine ingenuity, financial muscle and the management ability to produce a complete manufactured product. The successful ideas take off because of a marriage between the innovator and a manufacturer with enough vision, courage, patience and money to pursue the idea. A good recent example is the 'Workmate' and Black and Decker.

Unless you already have the production facilities, in 99 cases out of a hundred it would be pointless to set up manufacture yourself. There are many capable firms with plenty of engineering know-how looking for work. Naturally, if a joint venture is proposed, they will want convincing that there is a market for the product.

Launching your invention is analogous to getting your first book published. In theory there are plenty of publishers but in practice many have to be canvassed and rejection slips absorbed before (if ever) success is achieved.

Approaches should be made to manufacturers of similar products. These names can be readily found in trade year-books, associations' or industrial directories like *Kompass* (see Chapter 2).

It has to be said that most large companies delegate a smooth operator who is adept at handling what they regard as 'cranks' to deal with lone inventors. The more professional your approach by way of information and presentation the greater your chance of success.

KEEPING IT CONFIDENTIAL

Approaches must be 'in confidence' and inevitably, no company will entertain 'ideas' as such. A patent application must be filed and requests should be made to discuss possible manufacture under licence.

Confidentiality can be a very difficult hurdle. Some companies may reply that they cannot accept inventions submitted in confidence. If their own R&D department is working on the same idea, they would not wish to disclose that fact yet, at the same time, if their product is launched then accusations of piracy could be made. Fortunately, in this country the major manufacturers enjoy a good ethical standard and piracy is uncommon.

It is also tempting to look for signs of encouragement. Few businesses will say outright that your invention is of no use. Instead their replies will say that 'the factory is committed at present' or use flattering words — 'fascinating', 'ingenious', etc. Don't waste time, move on to your next contact.

Licensing

If your invention has commercial potential then you as patent-holder can license the rights to a manufacturer. It is a recent phenomenon that world-wide growth in licensing technology has sprung increasingly, not just from patent rights, but from the rights to know-how, copyright and trade marks.

Depending on your negotiating skills and cash requirements, you can either sell outright for a once and for all payment or argue for a down payment with successive royalties on sales expressed in a variety of ways. If you enter into an exclusive licence for a given territory make sure that you write in a get-out clause if nothing is developed.

Inventors often have an inflated idea of the commercial value of their invention. In the final analysis, the cost of producing a new product could break down to 95 per cent costs of prototype development, tooling up, research and marketing and just 5 per cent for the original concept. Don't expect a great deal more than a 5 per cent royalty on gross sales.

INWARD LICENSING

Licensing can fill the gap in a product range, enable a business to catch up with new technology, save expensive and perhaps fruitless R&D expenditure and the recruitment of highly qualified staff.

In the UK alone there has been a fourfold increase in licence royalties received as a result of exporting technology. It is interesting to note that Japan's post-war rise was largely built on inward licensing up to about the mid-sixties when the pattern has since been quite reversed. They are now very active in setting up licence deals all round the world.

Licensing allows a firm with limited resources and an imperfect R&D structure to buy in and compete with its larger brethren. Where the pace of technological change is rapid it may be the only way that less innovative businesses can remain in competition.

HOW TO FIND LICENCE OPPORTUNITIES

The sources are much the same as the other recognised channels of information: specialist magazines, trade journals, computer databases, trade fairs, embassies and consultants in technology transfer — the in-name for this activity. One well-known magazine is *International Licensing* published from 92 Cannon Lane, Pinner, Middlesex. *Technology Transfer International* available from 15, Selvage Lane, Mill Hill, London NW7 3SS is another. Overseas journals include the US General Electric *New Products and New Business Digest* and the *CATECH* publications from France. 1984 saw the first specific UK *exhibitions* devoted to new technology and licence opportunities while the huge Hanover Fair in West Germany has a hall devoted solely to these opportunities.

Probably the most well-known computer *database* for licensing is the American Dworkovitz Databank with on-line access in the UK.

Other sources include the *Commercial Newsletter* from the US embassy in London and information put out by the major

Chambers of Commerce and some of the overseas branches of the clearing banks.

All these information sources will tend to sketch in the merest outline what appears to be on offer. You still have to ferret around for more details, make the right contacts and start negotiating on the subject you think suitable. A more effective way may be to approach a specialist consultant, either an individual member of the Institute of International Licensing Practitioners (29-30 Warwick Street, London W1R 5RD; 01-584 5749) or the Licensing Executives Society (registered office only at 33-4 Chancery Lane, London WC2A 1EW). It is the professional body that coordinates the activities of the 300 members, some of whom are patent agents. There are also established technology consultancies with international offices who are developing this market of communicating information.

EVALUATING THE LICENCE

Possibly the hardest part of the exercise is trying to evaluate what is on offer. The key is quickly to establish a good relationship between seller and buyer. You have to satisfy yourself that what is on offer is indeed pertinent to your perceived market needs, and that there is not something better available. Keep the evaluation as near production conditions as possible and look for improvements that you can add from your own experience. Ask the licensor what back-up he is prepared to give. As you will probably be dealing with a larger concern, their resources could be vital to the success. There may be a component or vital raw material that he can supply more cheaply than you can purchase locally. Marketing expertise and resources may be available.

WHAT WILL IT COST?

There is no golden rule. The fees are normally termed a royalty payment and can be levied on the turnover as a fixed percentage, a sliding scale increasing as time goes on, a lump sum payment up front, a fee per item sold, index linked and so on. There is usually a minimum sum to be paid regardless of sales. What you have to weigh up are the commercial and marketing advantages of buying in the new technology in terms of a gain in lead time for research, increase in competitiveness, access to new markets or broadening the capabilities of the firm.

It is a complex decision and one that needs time to arrive at the correct conclusion.

WHAT CAN BE LICENSED

You must first take the elementary step of checking whether a valid patent is in force for this country. The licence would give you no protection if competition could start up with impunity. You must also satisfy yourself who is going to pay the annual renewals and find the money if infringement action is required. Check that the licence gives you what you are looking for — the right to sell as well as manufacture.

A *know-how* agreement is more difficult in that it deals with intangibles. Again you must be clear and define exactly what support you will be getting — a secret formula, process, drawings or expert training perhaps for some time. At the root of the agreement must be a secrecy clause to prevent disclosure to others except in confidence. The agreement is normally terminated if unwitting disclosure is made by the licensor or a parallel discovery is made by another party.

The right to use a specific *trade mark* can be very valuable as, unlike patents, they can go on for ever. As the mark is in effect a guarantee of identical quality the right to use a well-known mark is a worthwhile marketing tool. One of the problems today is the wholesale counterfeiting of branded goods — everything from Levi jeans and spark plugs to perfume and brake pads.

Alternatives to licensing: contract R&D

The alternative route to licensing a proven process is to commission research from an outside body. This can be another specialist consultant or small firm, or perhaps what more readily springs to mind, a university or polytechnic. With the frontiers of knowledge being pushed back ever more rapidly it is becoming increasingly difficult for firms to maintain comprehensive expertise in their field. We have become a world of specialists. The cost of keeping up to date with research and development, to say nothing of the staff required, has largely surpassed the resources of small firms.

The logical alternative is to buy in that specific requirement, to parcel out one specific problem area for solution by those with facilities, both in hardware and mental ability.

THE SOURCES TO TAP

These fall broadly into three categories:

1. Government research or other technical appraisal institu-

tions such as Harwell, the National Engineering Laboratory, the National Physical Laboratory, the Transport and Road Research Laboratory etc. A good source is the free book by the Department of Trade and Industry *Technical Services to Industry*.
2. The universities and institutes of technology having strong research links with industry: Salford, Bath, Cranfield, Imperial College, Edinburgh, Queen Mary's College etc.
3. Commercial organisations: PAT Centre, Cambridge Consultants, Logica, Pendar, Battelle etc, sometimes more generally known as design consultants.

There is a great wealth of expertise within all these organisations but the problem is identifying who does what and deciding who is best suited to take on the work. The government laboratories probably have closer definitions of what they can tackle and tend to be booked up on programmes for some time ahead. On the other hand, it is easier to pick out what falls within their field. The universities are the great conundrum. Within their hallowed halls lie some of the best brains in the country allied to some of the most sophisticated equipment, but most seem bent on their own academic pure research disciplines. Industry complains that they can rarely unlock the talent to commercial use, while the professors say that they are funded to pursue research and are geared to the needs of their students and the academic year. However, the climate is changing, quite fast in some quarters. The impetus has come from the education cuts, in that industry-funded research projects may keep departments going. The two sides are from necessity drawing closer together. Your search for contract R&D should start with the well-known commercially minded universities. As I write there are moves to set up a database to list all the expertise available within the campuses — a massive task but a necessary and logical step. HM Government have introduced five funded schemes to help both sides benefit from research. Details are available from the Science and Engineering Research Council (SERC) at Polaris House, North Star Avenue, Swindon, Wiltshire.

DESIGN CONSULTANTS
There are over 3000 of these consultancies in the UK offering a wealth of expertise in designing and innovating new products. They are not only concerned with high tech, chips, lasers and robots but also with more familiar materials that are used in

consumer products every day. An industrial designer should have a wide working knowledge of today's mechanical and production processes embracing the demands of aesthetics, ergonomics and market needs. They will be able to improve cosmetically the visual appeal of an old and proven product or design a completely fresh one. But design goes deeper than the outward skin. A large consultancy will have highly talented engineers from many disciplines to call upon. They will cover process systems, electronics, mechanical, electrical, production and graphic design.

Designing is not a cheap exercise but the government is able to help to the extent of funding a limited number of man days of consultancy time, providing you have 30 or more employees. It is known as the Design Advisory Service Funded Consultancy Scheme and details are available from the Design Council, 28 Haymarket, London SW1Y 4SU; 01-839 8000. If a microprocessor is involved in your new product you should apply for grant aid to employ a consultant under the MAPCON scheme. Details from the Department of Trade and Industry, MAP Information Centre, 29 Bressenden Place, London SW1E 5DT; 01-213 3932. The whole range of government aid to industry is obtainable (in outline) from the quarterly supplement to *British Business* called 'Guide to Industrial Support'.

The importance of good design

Style, elegance, ergonomics are all part of good design. Apart from the 'fitness for purpose' and mechanical ingenuity, the visual appeal is what distinguishes the humdrum from the thoroughbred. Its importance in a book on marketing lies in the fact that good design undoubtedly *sells*. A recent study has shown that an estimated 90 per cent of Britain's top companies have no commitment or appreciation of design as a means of improving sales. The paradox is that we have some of the world's top industrial designers, who derive most of their income from commissions obtained abroad. British industry has been painfully slow to realise that there is more to making a product than assembling a kit of parts.

Habitat are usually held up as one design-conscious company that bucks the trend to mediocrity. At the core of the organisation are not accountants but a group design team who have imposed a strong corporate identity on everything that Conran stores produce: not just the merchandise but the decor and appearance of all the stores, catalogues and advertising.

Design Centre label for approved products
(Courtesy: The Design Council)

We can all recognise good design when we see it: the problem is deciding how to achieve it. If you realise the need in your own firm the following courses of action are open to you:

1. As a first step take out a subscription to *Design* magazine, the monthly shop window on all that is best in design matters. It may open your eyes to what can be done with totally boring products let alone high tech marvels. It is published by the Design Council, 28 Haymarket, London SW1Y 4SU, who can also supply on subscription a bi-monthly consumer magazine, *Design Selection*.

2. At the same address is the Design Centre, a permanent but changing exhibition of the best designed UK products. Based here is the *Index*, a register of approved products that are eligible to display the well-known Design Centre label.

   This is an obvious marketing attribute. Buyers can consult the Index and some samples are on display. There is also an excellent bookshop stocking a wide range of design publications. A similar, smaller centre is at 72 St Vincent Street, Glasgow G2 5TN; also one in Cardiff.

3. Study the prestigious *design awards* made annually, usually by Prince Philip, for outstanding products in

245

different categories from cars to giftware. There is often a lot of publicity attached to these presentations.

4. The Design Council can advise on commissioning an industrial designer experienced in your field. They have several field officers who can visit you at your premises. If you have over 30 on the payroll then you should be eligible for a limited number of days' free consultancy (see page 244). It also brings together specialist manufacturers through its close working knowledge of industry.

5. The Society of Industrial Artists and Designers (SIAD) is the trade association of the industry and can advise on selecting the right person. Their address is 12 Carlton Terrace, London SW1Y 5AH.

6. For relatively simple jobs you could use your nearest college that runs a design degree course. Final year students have uncluttered minds and can often come up with novel solutions. What you will be unlikely to hit upon is the sophisticated knowledge of today's manufacturing processes. They should be glad of the chance to work on a real commercial product that may reach the market-place.

Finally, let's leave the last word with Sir Terence Conran, designer and marketeer extraordinary, whose firm was once small. Today he not only runs Habitat, but Mothercare, Richard Shops and Heal's, is one of the UK's top 100 companies and has been quoted recently on his formula for success: 'Make sure you have something unique to offer, something which the competition cannot easily emulate. Try and create a business that has some qualities which are your copyright. I do not mean necessarily in the legal sense. This is the reason we have been able to expand Habitat abroad successfully. We have something which is unique, not simply another furniture business.'

Further contacts

British Technology Group. Formerly known as the National Enterprise Board (NEB) and National Research Development Corporation (NRDC). At the time of writing their role has been greatly reduced and reorganisation has been taking place. Contact them at 101 Newington Causeway, London SE1 6BU; 01-403 6666. They are able to take up inventions and assist with the costs of development and patenting. They usually take a royalty on sales. A free leaflet is available on their help to inventors.

Institute of Patentees and Inventors. The institute helps its 2000 members by providing advice on the exploitation of worthwhile inventions, circulating lists of inventions to potential manufacturers, running seminars and publishing a journal. Further information from the Institute at Staple Inn Buildings South, 335 High Holborn, London WC1V 7PX; 01-242 7812.

The Patent Office. Patents in this country are handled by the Patent Office, 25 Southampton Buildings, London WC2A 1AY; 01-405 8721, and various publications are available free on request: 'Applying for a Patent', 'Applying for a Trade Mark', 'Protection of Industrial Designs'. These are obtained by direct application to London or by post from Sales Branch, the Patent Office, Orpington, Kent BR5 3RD.

Bibliography

The London Business School lists over 3000 books and journals on 'small firms'. My choice listed throughout this book is purely personal on what has come my way and I feel will be helpful to you. The accent generally has been on books that are readable and written with a light touch.

General

BBC Small Business Guide, Colin Barrow (BBC Publications). A fact book on sources not just marketing, but like any book of this nature, out of date as soon as it is printed. Nevertheless a good starting point.

How to double your profits within the year, John Fenton (Pan). Although most of the examples are geared to large firms there are many pertinent points for the smaller business. Entertaining reading. Go and see one of his road shows if you get the chance.

Tourism Marketing for the Small Business, ed Malcolm Wood (English Tourist Board). Although specifically intended for the hotel, guest house and craft businesses there are many good practical ideas here on systematic marketing on modest budgets.

Advertising

The Craft of Copywriting, Alastair Crompton (Business Books). Explores the mystique of how to write compelling ads.

My Life in Advertising and Scientific Advertising, Claude Hopkins (Bell Publishing, New York). The original genius of advertising. The man who brought you Pepsodent and 'Shot from a gun'. Written many years ago, still amazingly readable and relevant today because he counsels studying human nature and testing before all else.

Ogilvy on Advertising, David Ogilvy (Pan Books). Probably the most well-known advertising man today, he crossed the Atlantic and founded Ogilvy and Mather, now the fourth largest agency in the world. Profusely illustrated. Buy it.

PR

Be Your Own PR Man, Michael Bland (Kogan Page). Funny, easy to follow and stuffed full of adaptable ideas for the small firm. Get your own copy.

Doing it in style, Leslie Sellers (Pergamon Press). Written for sub-editors by an ex-Fleet Street editor. The best I've seen on how to write clear interesting English for the press. Write as he says and all your press releases will be printed. Now, alas, out of print, but get it through your library.

Using the Media, Denis MacShane (Pluto Press). Very left wing, punchy, practical and direct.

Selling

Better than any book are the excellent *Video Arts* training films featuring John Cleese and friends. They have won numerous awards for their pithy, accurate examples of how to sell, run exhibitions, handle complaints etc. If you can't wangle your way into a private showing (the films are for hire) ask when their next exhibition filming will be. Write to them at 68 Oxford Street, London W1.

Handbook for the Manufacturer's Agent, CP Stephenson (British Agents Register, page 149). Explains simply the role of commission agents and their principals. Essential reading if you are taking some on.

Direct response

Commonsense Direct Marketing, Drayton Bird (The Printed Shop). Quite the best book on direct marketing with many golden nuggets. Tends to concentrate on the mass consumer market but worth reading for the wit.

The Post Office Direct Mail Handbook, ed Les Andrews, (Exley Publications, 16 Chalk Hill, Watford WD1 4BN). Solid, comprehensive coverage of the direct mail field, written by several experts in their field.

Exports

Export for the Small Business, Henry Deschampsneufs (Kogan Page). A good introduction aimed more at the well established business who can afford sales trips overseas.

Export Handbook, BOTB publication. The guide to what the BOTB offers, with plenty of source contacts to follow up.

New products

The Design of Design, Gordon L Glegg (Cambridge University Press). Lucidly explains how to break down a seemingly insoluble problem into its component parts. Quite hilarious when describing his failures. Eminently practical.

Eureka, the very good monthly magazine for innovative engineering.

How to Invent, Thring and Laithwaite (Macmillan). A joint effort by two of our more brilliant inventors. Claims that anyone can invent if they know how.

Industrial Design in Engineering, ed C H Flurscheim (The Design Council). A very detailed survey of all the requirements of designing new products — ergonomics, style, form, materials, colour etc. Though aimed at the professional designer it will be illuminating to the relative layman.

SUCCESSFUL MARKETING FOR THE SMALL BUSINESS

The Inventor's Information Guide, Tamara Eisenschitz and Jeremy Phillips (Fernsway Publications, 3 Crane Grove, London N7). You will have to get this 88-page paperback direct (£2.95). Very good coverage on sources, patents and publications.

Patents, Trade Marks, Copyright and Industrial Design, Blanco White and others (Sweet and Maxwell). Layman's brief guide to the essentials.

The Protection of Industrial Design, George Myrants (McGraw-Hill). Covers this little-known area very thoroughly.

Others

The Corporate Personality, Wally Olins (Design Council). Delves into the whole mystique of corporate identity but purely from the large company viewpoint. Worth reading for an insight into all the nuances of image.

Display, an aid to selling, Alan Wheeler (Heinemann). A helpful guide to effective display using available materials.

Do it Yourself Graphic Design, John Laing (Ebury Press). While I can't go all the way with the author in claiming that anyone can produce professional graphics, it will give you a healthy respect for all the printing skills demanded today. Very well illustrated.

A Guide to Franchising, Martin Mendelsohn (Pergamon Press). The standard work. Takes you through all the steps from both sides of the operation with several research case studies and interviews with franchisees.

The Manual of Sales Promotion, John Williams (Innovation). Covers the whole field with emphasis on coupon redemption. Probably more useful to you are the sections on codes of practice. Of more depth is Peter Spillard's *Sales Promotion* (Business Books).

Marketing and *Management Today* are probably two of the better magazines worth reading regularly.

Your Business caters more for the small businessman.

Further reading from Kogan Page

Consumer Law for the Small Business, Patricia Clayton
Direct Mail: Principles and Practice, Robin Fairlie
Financial Management for the Small Business, Colin Barrow
Getting Sales: A Practical Guide to Getting More Sales for Your Business, Richard D Smith and Ginger Dick
The Industrial Market Research Handbook, Paul Hague
Law for the Small Business, Patricia Clayton.
Raising Finance: The Guardian Guide for the Small Business, Clive Woodcock
Running Your Own Antiques Business, Noël Riley and Godfrey Golzen
Running Your Own Boarding Kennels, Sheila Zabawa
Running Your Own Catering Business, Ursula Garner and Judy Ridgway
Running Your Own Driving School, Nigel Stacey
Running Your Own Pub, Elven Money
Running Your Own Small Hotel, Joy Lennick
Successful Expansion for the Small Business, M J Morris
Taking up a Franchise, Godfrey Golzen, Colin Barrow and Jackie Severn

Index

And now you can help us

No book on marketing would be complete without an attempt to find out more about its readers. Book publishing is an uncertain business. Although there has been a well documented rise in the numbers of small firms it is less easy to discover what they do and how they improve their management skills.

Kogan Page is always trying to cater for new demands and provide what the readership wants. We recognise that reading books is probably not very high on the priority list of growing businesses, but nevertheless would appreciate hearing what you thought of this book.

Kindly return the pre-paid slip below, or if you do not wish to spoil your copy, please use a separate sheet of paper.

Thank you.

To the Marketing Department, Kogan Page Ltd,
FREEPOST, 120 Pentonville Road, London N1 9JN.

My business has been going . . . . . . years.

The business is . . . .

I borrowed this book from the library. . . . . . .

I bought it because:

    I saw it in a bookshop . . . . . .
    I read a review . . . . . .
       (If so, which publication?) . . . .
    I read an advertisement . . . . . .
       (If so, which publication?). . . . .
    I received details through the post . . . . . .
    A friend recommended it . . . . . .

Have you found the book helpful? . . . . . .

Which aspects? . . . . . .

If not, please suggest improvements for any future editions

. . . .

What first attracted you to the book? . . . .

. . . .

Your name . . . .(No salesman will call!)

Position . . . .

Organisation . . . .

Address . . . .

. . . .

. . . .